Walks

through Britain's

History

Produced by AA Publishing
Reprinted October 2001, 2003 (twice)

Published by AA Publishing (a trading name of Automobile Association Development
Limited, whose registered office is Millstream, Maidenhead Road, Windsor, Berkshire
SL4 5GD; registered number 1878835)

ISBN 0 7495 3153 3

A01970

A CIP catalogue record for this book is available from the British Library.

With thanks to The Estate Office, Sandringham, for their permission to use mapping data,
belonging to The Estate Office, Sandringham, to compile walk map 84.

Map Illustrations: Raymond Turvey
Illustrations: Ann Winterbotham

Visit the AA Publishing website at www.theAA.com

Colour reproduction Chromagraphics, Singapore
Printed and bound in Italy by Amilcare Pizzi Spa

AA

Walks
through Britain's
History

Walk Locations

Contents

Walk Locator Map
Introduction

AGE OF MYSTERY
Early Britain 4500 BC–AD 43

1 The flint mines at Cissbury Ring
2 Castlerigg's ancient stone circle
3 A prehistoric puzzle in the Preseli Hills
4 Avebury's ancient monuments
5 *Feature Walk: Bronze Age life on Dartmoor*
6 The galloping white horse at Uffington
7 The Iron Age farmers of Pilsdon Pen
8 Old Oswestry
9 The mysterious Iron Age brochs of Glenelg

IMPERIAL OUTPOST
Roman AD 43–410

10 The Roman gold mines at Dolaucothi
11 Silchester Roman town
12 The Exeter–Lincoln highway
13 The Roman campaign headquarters at Ardoch
14 *Feature Walk: The Antonine Wall*
15 Roman drama in the heart of Chester
16 Great Witcombe's grand Roman villa
17 The Roman fort at Hardknott
18 A slice of Roman life at Bignor

INVASIONS & SAINTS
Saxons and Vikings 410–1066

19 Tintagel's Celtic connection
20 The missionaries and myths of Iona
21 Valley of the kings
22 From 'sea to sea' along Offa's Dyke
23 *Feature Walk: Through Viking York*
24 The architects of Earls Barton
25 Llangorse – 'lake of the sunken island'
26 Up the River Itchen to Saxon Winchester
27 Burpham: Anglo-Saxon settlement

ERA OF CONQUEST
The Normans 1066–1300

28 The mighty prince-bishops, overlords of the North
29 Lewes – town of the conquerors
30 The New Forest: king among deer parks
31 Farming medieval-style in Laxton
32 *Feature Walk: Sarum's Cathedrals*
33 Holy orders and riches at Fountains Abbey
34 A simple life at Dundrennan Abbey
35 The rise and fall of Lostwithiel
36 In the shadow of the mighty Conwy Castle

PLAGUE & CONFLICT
Medieval 1300–1485

37 Robert the Bruce, ambitious patriot
38 Guerrilla warfare in the Scottish hills
39 Dunstanburgh Castle: a mighty fortress
40 The monastic complex at Abbotsbury
41 *Feature Walk: Warwick's medieval castle*
42 The tale of Canterbury
43 Plague and pestilence in the Yorkshire Wolds
44 Song of the 'Men of Harlech'
45 The seat of power in Ludlow

BUILDING A DYNASTY
The Tudors 1485–1603

46 Lavenham – a timbered treasure
47 Henry VIII's coastal fort of St Catherine's
48 Along a drovers' road to the cave of Twm
49 The Abbot of Furness
50 *Feature Walk: Shakespeare's Globe*
51 Kendal Castle
52 Sir Walter Raleigh
53 Favourite home of Mary, Queen of Scots
54 Bess of Hardwick

GUNPOWDER TO WIG POWDER
The Stuarts 1603–1714

55 The wide skies of a man-made landscape
56 The indomitable spirit of Lady Anne Clifford
57 The Royal Oak at Boscobel House
58 A mission of faith
59 *Feature Walk: Carisbrooke's royal prisoner*
60 London: churches and commerce
61 Church matters versus military men
62 Wells and the 'Pitchfork Rebellion'
63 Killiecrankie: the first of the Jacobite battles

BIRTH OF INDUSTRY
Georgian 1714–1837

64 Arkengarthdale's ancient lead-mining mining industry
65 Bonnie Prince Charlie's escape to Raasay
66 The unforgiving coastline of Hartland
67 On the Slave Trade Trail
68 *Feature Walk: The age of canals*
69 The social reformers who built New Lanark
70 Mow Cop and the birth of a new faith
71 The Highland Clearances at Strathnaver
72 Crossing the Menai Bridge

AGE OF OPTIMISM
Victorian 1837-1901

73 Telford's Caledonian Canal
74 Marsden: a West Yorkshire wool town
75 The tin mines of Cornwall
76 Tennyson's home in Somersby
77 *Feature Walk: The tracks of industry*
78 Evolution at Down House
79 Llandrindod Wells
80 Lake Vyrnwy: giving water to Liverpool
81 Medicinal waters at the seaside

A NEW CENTURY
Edwardian 1901-1918

82 The world of Beatrix Potter
83 Letchworth: new town
84 A very royal estate
85 Music in the Malverns
86 *Feature Walk: Port Sunlight: model village*
87 Craiglockhart House: a World War I hospital
88 Castle Drogo, a famous partnership
89 In the steps of the 'Welsh Wizard'
90 The poet of Steep

JAZZ INTO THE ATOMIC AGE
Depression and War 1918-1945

91 George Orwell on the road to Wigan
92 Aspects of light at St Ives
93 Along the White Cliffs of Dover
94 The Dambusters' of Derbyshire
95 *Feature Walk: Portmeirion: fantasy village*
96 Victory and tragedy at Slapton Sands
97 Eisenhower: Supreme Commander
98 Cannock Chase and the price of war
99 Home of Dylan Thomas

TO THE NEXT MILLENNIUM
Modern Britain 1945-present

100 The first National Park
101 The drowned village of Capel Celyn
102 Views of the Severn Estuary
103 Liverpool: city of the 'Fab Four'
104 *Feature Walk: A Scottish Millennium Forest*
105 Striking oil in the North Sea
106 Machynlleth's long history
107 Along the Cuckoo Trail
108 Eden: eighth wonder of the world

The Impact of History

Walking Through History

WALKS THROUGH BRITAIN'S HISTORY brings you the opportunity to combine two wonderful aspects of living on this lovely island. You can follow carefully planned routes through beautiful and varied countryside, changing in character from mellow farmland to sweeping panoramas, from wild moorland to dramatic seascapes, from small villages to historic cities – often within just a few miles of each other, and each aspect itself changing with the seasons. But these are not simply scenic walks through town and country – instead, they tread some of the lesser-known paths of Britain's long, rich and fascinating history, with each period layered upon the one before not only chronologically but, often, quite literally, as a new age buries evidence of the preceding era below ground. You will soon discover that wherever you go in Britain, something exciting and memorable happened, perhaps only a hundred years ago, perhaps over a thousand.

New Stone Age

During the period beginning with the New Stone Age (from about 4500 BC), much of the British landscape was recovering from the ravages of the last Ice Age, and the hunter–gatherer lifestyle was slowly giving way to a more settled existence. Evidence of this new way of life is found in the prehistoric monuments dating from this period, which, incredibly, are still visible today – stone circles, hill forts, burial mounds, and even the mysterious figures cut into chalk hills.

Romans

The Romans, whose arrival heralded a completely different civilisation, made use of some of the Iron Age hill forts, as well as establishing many settlements of their own. They brought with them new methods of building, engineering, administration and farming, new foods and wine, a new language and a new religion – Christianity. Although much of their building has long since disappeared below ground, Britain is rich in evidence of the Roman occupation – their characteristic long, straight roads; fragments of walls in cities; orderly military defences; excavated remains of sumptuous villas with their wonderful mosaic floors and sophisticated central heating systems; and the complex baths, in the city named 'Bath' after them.

The Romans' departure saw the disintegration of much of what they had established – cities fell into ruin, villas and temples were abandoned, and the country was overrun with pagan invaders. Gradually order was restored, and a new civilisation began. Christianity was re-established, via missionaries in the south and Celtic missionaries in the west and north. Christian churches and Benedictine monasteries were built, and the first magnificent illuminated manuscripts were created. Anglo-Saxon 'kingdoms' were formed and laws were established. The landscape was dotted about with Saxon villages consisting of dwellings of wood or wattle and daub, topped with thatched roofs. Forest was cleared and the land ploughed into long, narrow strips ('ridge and furrow') for cultivation. Remains excavated from Saxon burial sites, such as the burial ship Raedwald of East Anglia at Sutton Hoo, Suffolk, indicates the great wealth of the chiefs.

Vikings

The violent Viking invasions interrupted the Saxons' ordered lives; but eventually the Vikings, too, settled into an ordered existence, and the cultural similarities they shared with the Saxons enabled them to live relatively peacefully, side by side. The Saxons by now lived under a united kingdom; and it was a crack in the strength of the crown that allowed renewed Viking attacks towards the end of the 10th century, resulting in the reign of the Danish king, Canute. The line of succession became more complicated, and the death of King Edward 'the Confessor' in 1066 opened England up to invasion from a new quarter – Normandy, in northern France.

Normans

With the Norman Conquest, led by a triumphant William of Normandy, came a period of rapid change. One of William's first tasks was to make his presence felt by erecting numerous castles. These were often built on the sites of Roman defences, and the first castles were usually of the wooden 'motte and bailey' type, later replaced by much sturdier stone castles, the remains of which can be seen throughout the country. The other architectural legacy of the Norman period lies in the religious buildings – from small country churches to the great monastic foundations with their magnificent cathedrals. Although many of these were largely rebuilt throughout the medieval period, becoming ever more elaborate, the distinctive rounded arches and heavy decoration that typify Norman, or Romanesque, architecture are still visible in most cathedrals.

The French language was introduced; however, the sound Anglo-Saxon system of law and administration was not abolished, but retained and built upon. Medieval new towns were laid out to a geometric plan, and vast areas of forest were planted as hunting grounds. The age of chivalry was born, a time when brave knights fought each other with colourful ceremony while their fair ladies looked on, and huge feasts were consumed in great halls. Centres of learning were founded, including the universities of Oxford and Cambridge and some of the famous public schools. This was also a time of constant wars, and of terrible plagues that were mortal to rich and poor alike.

In Scotland began the bitter fight for independence which was to last many centuries, while Wales provided the first Tudor king, ending the Wars of the Roses and restoring peace to England.

The reign of the notorious Henry VIII saw the birth of the navy and building of defences around the southern coastline; as well as the founding of new colleges and schools. The King's desperate bid to provide a male heir to the throne, resulted in a break with the Church in Rome and the introduction of the English Protestant Church. The consequences were far reaching as the dissolution of the monasteries also meant the destruction of countless medieval treasures and to religious persecution.

Queen Elizabeth I

In spite of all Henry's efforts, it was a female heir who was to become the other great Tudor – Queen Elizabeth I. During the age of 'the Virgin Queen', exploration to far lands began in earnest, literature, painting and music flourished, and the distinctive black-and-white timbered buildings appeared. But there was no heir to carry on the Tudor name, and ironically it was the Stuart King of Scotland – son of Mary Queen of Scots, executed by Elizabeth – who succeeded her.

In the mid 17th century a new internal conflict erupted, as Crown and Parliament battled for political power, involving much of the population of Britain. For a short while, Parliament triumphed; but the death of the parliamentarian leader, Oliver Cromwell, led to the restoration of the monarchy. This century also saw yet another destructive plague, while the Great Fire of London enabled the architect Sir Christopher Wren to make his elegant mark in the rebuilding of the city.

Industrial Revolution

Everyday life had for many centuries revolved around farming the land, both for providing crops and for breeding sheep – the wool trade brought great prosperity, and many of the rich medieval towns were built by wealthy wool merchants. But a revolution was waiting in the wings that was to change the face of much of Britain – the industrial revolution. Great leaps in technological advance-ment during the Georgian and Victorian eras lured people into the towns, where huge factories provided employment. Towns developed rapidly with new homes to accommodate this labour, while some philanthropic factory owners built whole villages for the purpose.

Gradually, the whole of Britain was opened up with networks of new roads, bridges spanning rivers, shipping canals for transporting the produce of underground mines. Even the impenetrable highlands of Scotland could now be reached by road.

The introduction of train travel completed the new-found freedom. Ordinary working people, who had always stayed close to home, began to take trips to the seaside, or into the country. Towards the end of the 19th century, the wealthy could enjoy another revolutionary form of transport – the motor car.

World War

The early years of the 20th century – the Edwardian era – are portrayed as a golden age. Modern civilisation was in place, but life still proceeded at a relatively gentle pace. Then came the World War I, followed by a strange mix of shock and grief and an almost unnatural jollity in the 'Roaring Twenties'; then years of depression, and before the world could barely draw breath, came World War II.

Air-raids over England left gaping holes and smouldering rubble where once buildings had stood; families were separated as children were sent away to the country for safety, and in some cases were never reunited; women worked the land and assembled munitions in the factories while their menfolk were scattered around the world.

As the second millennium drew to close, among the chief causes for celebration were advances in technology, great social and economic improvement and a greater understanding of ecological priorities. But for many people it also brought a nostalgic longing to slow down and tread the paths of history, perhaps to get a taste of a different existence, or perhaps to understand thoroughly the centuries of change that have brought us to where we are today.

A WALK THROUGH HISTORY

The book is divided into the eras by which Britain's history is usually plotted. It begins towards the end of a period that lasted for many thousands of years, and is known loosely as 'prehistoric' and closes at the end of the 20th century with the millennium celebrations.

Setting the Scene

The walks included in the book represent a cross-section of historical events, although there are of course many more that have had to be left out. The places around which the walks are based have been put into the era in which they have a special significance, even though the cities in particular may have historical connections with several other eras. Both Winchester and Canterbury, for example, were originally Roman cities, but are respectively more well-known for being King Alfred's capital of Wessex, and a centre of pilgrimage following the martyrdom of St Thomas Becket and the tales of Geoffrey Chaucer, so they are placed in the 'Saxons and Vikings' and 'Medieval' sections.

How to Use the Book

*Each of the 12 sections contains eight mapped, circular walks, plus one unmapped feature walk —
for instance, life in an Iron Age settlement or a visit to a Viking city — many of these walks will
appeal to readers with children, as there is plenty to enjoy here even for reluctant young walkers.*

What to Wear

The walks are designed to be an informative ramble, not a physical
challenge, but even so there are some simple and sensible rules to
follow. The most important item for your comfort and safety is a good
pair of walking boots, as these will support your ankles, especially in
rough or hill country, and keep your feet warm and dry in all
conditions. The vagaries of the British climate also make warm and
waterproof clothing essential. A breathable waterproof jacket,
waterproof trousers or gaiters and a warm hat may prove unexpectedly
welcome whatever the season, and are a must for winter walking.

For the longer walks that may take a few hours, a rucksack is useful
for carrying extra clothing, some energy food and a drink (a handful of
dried fruit and a bottle of water is ideal), your map, and any other
items such as binoculars and a camera.

Emergencies

If anything should go wrong on your walk, send someone to alert the
emergency services (phone 999), armed with a careful note of your
exact location. If possible, someone should stay with an injured person,
keeping him or her warm and dry until help arrives. Mobile phones are
an invaluable tool for such emergencies.

Follow the Rules

The walks in this book follow only public rights of way or well-
established, legal paths. You have a right to clear any blockage you may
come across, although we recommend that, if possible, you report any
problems to the responsible authority (usually the county council or
the unitary authority highways department). If you stray from the right
of way onto private property, you will technically be trespassing,
although you cannot be prosecuted unless you do damage.

The main thing to remember is to be considerate and respect the
life of the people who live and work along the route you are taking,
whether it is in the town or in the country.

Dogs

Many of the walks in this book are suitable for dogs but, again,
observing your responsibility to other people is essential. Keep your
dog on a lead and under control at all times.

Maps

Each of the walk maps has been checked and can be used to guide you
around the walk. However, some detail is inevitably lost because of the
restrictions imposed by scale, and there is always a possibility that some
of the landmarks may change or disappear, if only with the seasons, in
both town and country. For this reason, we strongly recommend that
the walk maps are used in conjunction with a more detailed map , such
as those produced by the Ordnance Survey or Harvey Map Services.

Parking

All the walks are numbered starting from a suggested parking place.
Where there is not an authorised car park, the suggested parking places
have been chosen to minimise disruption to other road users. However,
this does not guarantee that you have a right to park there. When you
park your vehicle, please consider other traffic, and in the country, bear
in mind the need for agricultural access.

Refreshments

The places mentioned in the text as serving refreshments have
been suggested by field researchers because of their convenience
to the route. Listing does not imply that they are AA inspected
or recognised, although some may coincidentally carry an
AA classification.

Grading

The walks have been graded to give an indication of their difficulty.
Easier walks, such as those around towns, over shorter distances, or
with little total ascent, show one fleur-de-lys. The hardest walks – over
greater distances, or including a lot of ascent, perhaps in hilly or
otherwise difficult terrain – show three fleur-de-lys. Moderate walks
show two fleur-de-lys. These gradings are relative to each other, and are
for guidance only.

Access

All the walks are on rights of way, permissive paths or on routes where
de facto access for walkers is accepted. On routes in England and Wales
which are not on legal rights of way, but where access for walkers is
allowed by local agreements, no implication of a right of way is
intended.

Safety

Although each walk has been carefully researched with a view to
minimising risk to walkers, it is also good common sense to follow
these guidelines:

1. Be particularly careful on cliff paths and in hilly terrain, where
   the consequences of any slip can be very serious.
2. Remember to check tidal conditions before walking on the
   seashore.
3. Some sections of route are by busy roads, or cross them. Take
   great care here, and remember that traffic is a danger even on
   minor country lanes.
4. Be careful around farm machinery and livestock, especially if you
   have children with you.
5. Find out what the weather forecast is for the day of your walk, and
   make sure you are equipped for changes.

For hundreds of thousands of years before recorded history began, people were living in Britain and shaping its landscape. Their world remains, on the whole, a mystery – though its monuments can still be found, scattered across 3rd-millennium Britain.

4500 BC – AD 43

Age of Mystery

Life for Britain's inhabitants hardly changed over hundreds of centuries: the most dramatic upheavals were caused by the weather. During several successive Ice Ages, glaciers provided a land bridge with Europe; in between, when the ice melted, Britain was an island again. Meanwhile, people wandered back and forth, adapting to the world around them. The first humans to reach Britain – about 450,000 years ago – were nomads, hunters and gatherers, who made tools of flint, and shelters of animal-hide and wood. In about 25,000 BC another Ice Age hit, and settlement was interrupted. When it resumed, about 10,000 years later, the settlers were 'modern' humans, of a different kind: *Homo sapiens*. They lived in and decorated cave shelters; they wore furs and elaborate bone jewellery; they hunted with spears and knives, and they communicated with sophisticated language.

By the 3rd millennium BC, Britain's neolithic communities were felling the trees that covered most of the country, creating clearings for crops and grazing. They shifted materials across land on sledges, or along the coasts and rivers by boat – little hide-covered coracles, common among Stone Age fishermen, are still used in Wales and Ireland today. During this era plain pottery was produced; tomb chambers and monuments built for the dead; and by 2800 BC, work had begun on Stonehenge.

THE METAL AGE
An old way of life seemed to be changing from about 2750 BC – as well as old ways of death. Collective burial in chamber tombs gave way to cremation in henges or individual burial in round barrows. Here, skeletons were surrounded by decorated pottery beakers, tools, and ornaments

made of gold and the new alloy – bronze. Some of the grave goods suggest considerable wealth and status: a beautifully embossed, leather-lined gold cape, excavated in Wales, is one spectacular example.

The Bronze Age revolved around farming, but other industries flourished, too. Any reasonably sized settlement had its own weaver, potter, carpenter, leatherworker and, of course, metalworker. By 1000 BC these settlements were being fortified with circular walls and palisades and earth ramparts, as migrating groups from the north competed for resources and threatened the security of herds and flocks.

After 600 BC a new group of tribes from Central Europe began settling in Ireland and Britain. The Celts had enjoyed trading links with the British for many years, but now they were taking centre stage. Using bronze and iron, the Celts produced weaponry and ornaments embellished with brilliant, swirling designs – such as the exquisite Battersea Shield, dredged from the Thames. They also made ploughs, enabling the most difficult soils to be worked. In the hierarchical Celtic society, slaves were at the bottom; freemen paid rent and produce to the tribal leaders, and the upper echelons of society included spiky-haired painted warriors, and druids. Religion permeated every part of life: gods and spirits inhabited trees, rocks and pools; sorcery and magic, woven through songs and stories, were passed down verbally and recited at court or round the central hearths of their circular houses.

The Celts lost their predominance after the Roman invasion, but they have never really gone away. Their language survives in Gaelic and Welsh, and in English words and place-names; and their fantastic tales live on in folk legends.

HISTORIC SITES

Stonehenge, Wiltshire: developed in several stages over 1,700 years. Stones are aligned with the midsummer sunrise and midwinter sunset.

Grimes's Graves, Norfolk: network of flint mines worked between 2300 BC and 1600 BC.

Skara Brae, Orkney: well-preserved late neolithic village of eight single-room stone huts, complete with stone furniture.

Bryn-Celli-Ddu, Anglesey: passage grave built under a circular mound.

Maiden Castle, Dorset: earth ramparts of an Iron Age hill fort.

Rollright Stones, Oxfordshire: late neolithic stone circle.

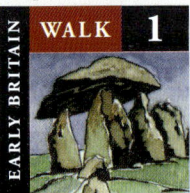

ABOUT • CISSBURY RING

This walk in the South Downs offers superb views and a feast of ancient sites. These include the flint mines at Cissbury Ring, a scheduled ancient monument, mined between 4500–2300 BC, and an Iron Age hill fort, home to a large community in about 350 BC.

West Sussex • SE ENGLAND

DISTANCE • 8 miles (13km)

TOTAL ASCENT • 700ft (213m)

PATHS • clearly waymarked and defined tracks; some muddy sections

TERRAIN • woodland and downland

GRADIENTS • some steep sections

REFRESHMENTS • none, but Cissbury Ring is a wonderful spot for picnics

PARK • Chanctonbury car park and picnic site (signed Chanctonbury Ring), off A283 west of Steyning and east of the junction with A24

OS MAP • Explorer 121 Arundel & Pulborough

The flint mines at Cissbury Ring

DIFFICULTY ✳✳

❶ Turn left out of the car park and continue to the end of the surfaced road. Keep forward on a bridleway by 'unsuitable for motors' sign. Follow the bridleway as it bends right along the bottom edge of the woodland until a blue waymarker points left, uphill; 70yds (64m) later fork right.

❷ Emerge into the open at the four-way junction of tracks at the top of the slope, with trees marking Chanctonbury Ring prominent away to your right. Turn left on the South Downs Way, and avoid side turnings.

❸ At a four-way crossing before a gate (with a stone memorial beyond), turn right to leave the South Downs Way on a cinder track signed 'public right of way' with a green waymarker.

❹ In ½ mile (800m), turn left at the bottom of a deep valley and take the path along the valley floor, following blue waymarkers, first between intermittent hedgerows, later alongside a fence on the right.

❺ At the end of the valley, turn right at a T-junction of tracks and, ignoring a left path just after barn on the left, continue to the car park at the end of the road.

❻ Detour left to Cissbury Ring by the National Trust sign; go through the gate and follow the yellow waymarker. Carry on to the next gate and take the steps up to the top. Turn right and walk around the ramparts, looking for the hummocky flint mine site. Return via the steps; take the track opposite through the car park.

❼ Keep forward at the next major junction of tracks, following a green waymarker, and fork right 40yds (37m) further on. (Left is private property and is fenced off.) At the fork of tracks with a grass triangle in middle, keep forward following the green waymarker and avoid the immediate next right fork. Follow the green waymarker straight ahead, ignoring the path to the left.

❽ After passing trees on your right, continue straight ahead following the green waymarker. Pass trees on your left, ignoring a left turning. Continue to a junction passed earlier on the walk. Before descending ahead through woods, detour left along the South Downs Way to visit Chanctonbury Ring. Return to the junction of paths and follow the blue waymarked route to return to the car park.

• DON'T MISS •

Chanctonbury Ring, the famous clump of beech trees, is a sad shadow of its former self since the devastation caused by the 1987 storm. But the site still offers commanding views over Sussex and the Iron Age ramparts enclose the site of a Romano-British temple.

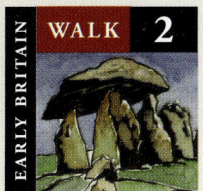
ABOUT • CASTLERIGG STONE CIRCLE

Castlerigg is one of Britain's earliest stone circles and is made up of 48 stones. Called the Druid's Circle, it was probably used as a type of ancient planting calendar. This is a challenging walk but the views on show have inspired poets and painters.

Cumbria • N ENGLAND

DISTANCE • 5½ miles (8.8km)

TOTAL ASCENT • 590ft (180m)

PATHS • some of the field paths to the circle can be muddy in winter

TERRAIN • woodland and pasture

GRADIENTS • short, steep climb from the car park, then easy gradients

REFRESHMENTS • none on the route. Many inns and cafés in nearby Keswick

PARK • Great Wood car park (NT), Borrowdale Road, by Derwent Water

OS MAP • Outdoor Leisure 4 The English Lakes – Northwestern Area

Castlerigg's ancient stone circle

1 From the back of the car park, go through a gate by a ticket machine and climb along the woodland path. Ignore the first left turn; at the next major junction of paths turn left to climb, steeply at first, beneath Walla Crag. Take the waymarked right fork, signed to the forest's edge, before following an enclosed path across fields.

2 Turn right on meeting a path by a stream. Cross the footbridge over the stream and climb to the lane north of Rakefoot Farm. Go left for a few yards, then right on a sunken path signed Castlerigg Stone Circle. Follow a wall on the left, across fields, before it swings left beyond a ladder stile.

3 Turn right along the A591 (ignore sign for Castlerigg Stone Circle). After 200yds (183m) turn left down the drive of The High Nest. A well-defined field path continues north across several fields.

4 Turn left on meeting a lane, then left again through the next gate to reach the stone circle. Beyond the stile at the top right-hand corner of the field, follow Castle Lane back to the A591 and Point **3** of the walk. Retrace the outward route to Point **2**. Now stay with the riverside path, bearing left at the junction of two paths, to enter Springs Wood, before descending further past Springs Farm.

5 Follow the road beyond the farm and turn left along the enclosed path to Castlehead Wood, signed Castlehead and Lake Road. Take the widest path ahead, then the second right fork by the field

boundary, to emerge on the Borrowdale Road. Turn left along the path across the road, then go right towards Cockshot Wood.

6 Once in the wood, turn left. Beyond a gate at the southern edge, the path cuts across a field

DIFFICULTY ✱✱✱

to Strandshag Bay, on the shore of Derwent Water.

7 Turn left along the path into the woods, then right along a stony lane passing Stable Hills (NT), back to the lake shore.

8 After following the shore past Broomhill Point to Calfclose Bay the path goes inland through the wood. Pass an NT collection box to reach Borrowdale Road opposite the pedestrian access to the Great Wood car park.

• DON'T MISS •

*Near Broomhill Point you'll pass close to the **Centenary Sculpture**. Known as the Hundred Year Stone, it was sculpted by Peter Randall Page from a split glacial Borrowdale boulder. The sculpture is dedicated to the first 100 years of the National Trust, from the early pioneers like Canon Hardwicke Rawnsley to the 20th-century trust members.*

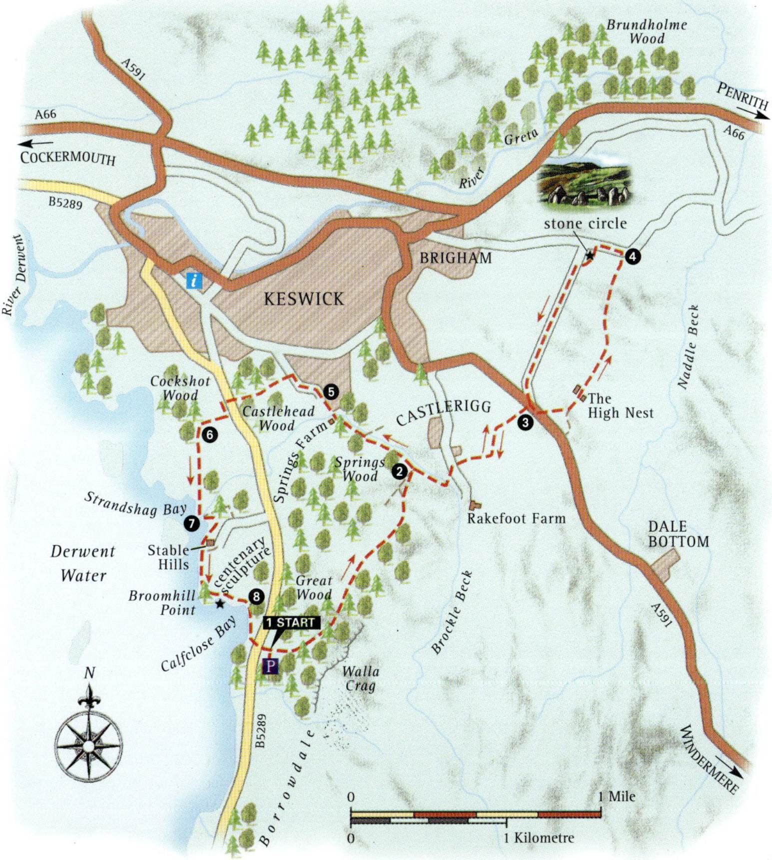

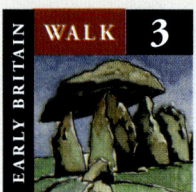
ABOUT • PRESELI HILLS

Hillwalkers know the delights of tramping this prehistoric highway. Dotted among the Bronze and Iron Age sites are blue rhyolite stones, relics of the Ice Age, believed to have been transported to and used to build Stonehenge, 150 miles (241km) away.

Pembrokeshire • WALES

DISTANCE • 10 miles (16km)	**GRADIENTS •** moderate
TOTAL ASCENT • 1,607ft (490m)	**REFRESHMENTS •** limited in Crymych
PATHS • some tracks; indistinct or pathless	**PARK •** in lay-by on the Mynachlog-ddu road, approximately 1 mile (1.6km) off the A478 at Crymych
TERRAIN • grassy; also rough (tussocky and boggy); occasionally rocky. **Note: this route is for experienced hillwalkers. It should not be attempted in poor weather conditions. Keep dogs on lead at all times on this walk**	**OS MAP •** Outdoor Leisure 35 North Pembrokeshire

A prehistoric puzzle in the Preseli Hills

❶ Take the track opposite the lay-by. When in open countryside, resist the temptation to climb the fine summit of Foel Trigarn; instead take a virtually level line, just above the boundary with the pasture below. Continue following the clear track ahead for 1 mile (1.6km).

❷ When the field boundary – a broad drystone wall topped with hedgerow – drops away to the right for the second time, you must follow it. (This avoids some extremely boggy ground designated a Site of Special Scientific Interest.)

❸ Follow the wall closely when it goes right then left. Descend gently, avoiding prickly gorse, to join a track from an untidy farmyard. Keep ahead on the main track, ignoring the fork to a farm on the right after 250yds (229m). Pass the elaborate post-box for Geulan Goch, and eventually reach a minor road and telephone box after ¾ mile (1.2km).

❹ Turn left, and left again within 100yds (91m); shortly take the left fork, which leads to Mirianog, a house; do not take the right-hand fork signed Tŷ Coch. Pass to the left of Mirianog, out into open country. (The hostile notice to dog owners echoes the difficulty of farming life here.)

❺ When the path forks take the left-hand option to visit the clustered slabs of Carn Alw. (Apart from its Stonehenge bluestones, this historic site was once a very small fort; aerial photographs reveal some evidence of field systems around it.)

❻ Aim right of another outcrop, Carn Breseb, on an indistinct path, eventually rejoining the path from Mirianog. On the ridge turn right, following this prehistoric highway, waymarked for some of its length by wooden posts, to the cairn and Bronze Age barrow atop Foel Feddau.

❼ (If time and energy permit, the Preseli's summit, Foel Cwmcerwyn, is a good mile/1.6km ahead and to the left.) Retrace your steps, then go further east along the ridge, over Carn Pica to Bwlch Ungwr.

❽ Veer right of the obvious path to visit the frost-shattered rocks of Carn Meini. Continue eastwards, picking up a farm track to the far end of a block of planted conifers.

❾ Turn left on a sinuous but clear path to Foel Trigarn. After viewing this impressive earthwork take a path which soon sweeps to the right, rejoining the outward route some distance before it enters the lane to return to the lay-by.

• DON'T MISS •

Pentre Ifan (off the A487, east of Newport) is a splendid burial chamber believed to be associated with Irish colonists, and dates from 3000 BC. The huge upright stones carry a massive, 17-ton capstone.

A487
EGLWYSWRW
FISHGUARD
CARDIGAN
B4332
Afon Nevern
Pentre Ifan ★
PONTYGLASIER
Afon Nevern
CROSSWELL
BRYNBERIAN
Afon Whitrook
Tŷ Coch ❹
PEN-Y-GROES
Mirianog
B4329
Afon Pennant
Carn Alw ❺
Geulan Goch farm
farm
❻
❸
Foel Trigarn
CRYMYCH
M y n y d d   P r e s e l i
Carn Breseb
Bwlch Ungwr
❶ START
★ lay-by
Foel Feddau
❽
Carn Pica
❾
Croes Fihangel
❼
Carn Meini
A478
Afon Tengyll
Foel Cwm-cerwyn 536
PENTREGALAR
MYNACHLOG-DDU
Afon Wern
Gors Fawr ★
Foel Drych 368
TENBY
N

DIFFICULTY ✱✱✱

0 ____ 1 Mile
0 ____ 1 Kilometre

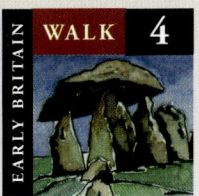
ABOUT • AVEBURY

Avebury is the largest stone circle in the British Isles and part of the village is located in this mysterious henge, built between 2600–2100 BC. Starting at the Alexander Keiller Museum, the walk takes you to the Sanctuary, West Kennet Long Barrow, and Silbury Hill.

Wiltshire • SW ENGLAND

DISTANCE • 6½ miles (10.4km)

TOTAL ASCENT • 250ft (76m)

PATHS • well-marked; low-lying sections (especially path between Silbury Hill and car park) may be muddy after prolonged rain; otherwise firm

TERRAIN • downland tracks, field paths, stiles, woods.

GRADIENTS • gradual climbs to the Ridgeway and to West Kennet Long Barrow

REFRESHMENTS • in village

PARK • designated car and coach park, well signed on north side of A4361

OS MAP • Explorer 157 Marlborough & Savernake Forest

Avebury's ancient monuments

DIFFICULTY ✲✲

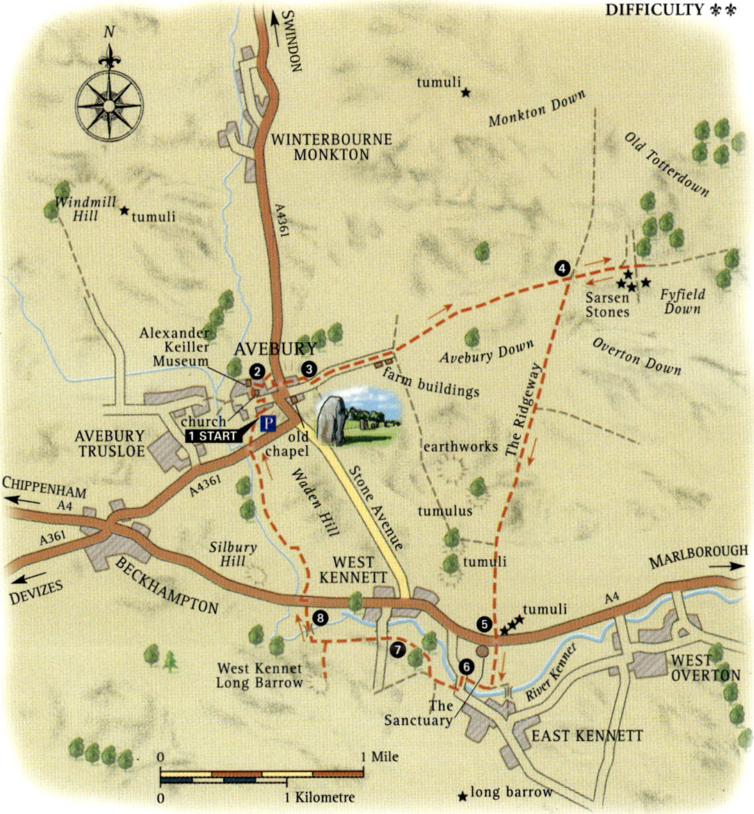

❶ With the entrance to the car park behind you, take the path in the right-hand corner, passing information boards. The bank, ditch and standing stones of the south-western corner of the henge are ahead of you. At the road (High Street), turn left and cross into the churchyard. Visit the museum beyond the church. Continue past the Great Barn and the National Trust tea-shop.

❷ Climb steps ahead, just beyond the National Trust shop, and enter the henge. Walk around the perimeter of the henge with the bank on your left. Turn right on to the fenced footpath beside the road, by one of the largest stones in Avebury – the Swindon Stone. Cross the road to see the two impressive stones of the Cove, then continue to the gap in the bank in the right-hand corner.

❸ Through a gate and turn left on to a track (Green Street). Passing farm buildings the track becomes wider and climbs gradually.

❹ Meet the Ridgeway. Before turning right along this track, detour ahead to see the 25,000 sarsen stones on Fyfield Down (some are visible from The Ridgeway). Return to the Ridgeway and continue south for 1¾ miles (2.8km) to meet the A4.

❺ Cross this fast, busy road with extreme care. Before continuing down the track opposite, visit the Sanctuary. The route continues down the right-hand edge of a field. In the bottom corner, turn right through a blue waymarked gate, along the edge of fields with the River Kennet on your left.

❻ Meet a road and turn left on to it, crossing a bridge. Turn right on to a signed byway on the the far side of a pumping station. When you reach a junction of paths, continue ahead following the footpath sign and almost immediately turn right (yellow waymark on tree) into a narrow tunnel of trees. Cross a stile and keep left round the edge of a field to meet a lane.

❼ Cross the lane and continue ahead. At the end of the second field, detour left to visit West Kennet Long Barrow. Return to the route and continue westwards and over the river to the A4.

❽ Cross the road, go through the gate almost opposite. Follow the sign for Avebury, passing close to Silbury Hill. Continue on the river bank to the A4361 and car park.

Map labels: N, SWINDON, tumuli, Monkton Down, WINTERBOURNE MONKTON, Old Totterdown, A4361, Windmill Hill, tumuli, Sarsen Stones, Fyfield Down, Alexander Keiller Museum, AVEBURY, Avebury Down, Overton Down, The Ridgeway, farm buildings, church, 1 START, old chapel, earthworks, AVEBURY TRUSLOE, CHIPPENHAM, A4, A4361, A361, Waden Hill, Stone Avenue, tumulus, DEVIZES, BECKHAMPTON, Silbury Hill, WEST KENNETT, tumuli, MARLBOROUGH, A4, tumuli, WEST OVERTON, West Kennet Long Barrow, The Sanctuary, River Kennet, EAST KENNETT, 0 1 Mile, 0 1 Kilometre, long barrow

Bronze Age Life on Dartmoor

This easy linear walk across the open moor to the Bronze Age settlement at Grimspound, in Devon, and a visit to the third-highest pub in England

The Ground

It is hard to imagine life on Dartmoor 3,500 years ago but you can get a glimpse of those times at the ancient settlement of Grimspound by the Grimslake stream on the gentle slopes above the Challacombe valley. The climate was more equable then, and much of the moor was forested. It is thought that neolithic peoples began to clear areas for pasturage and that process was intensified during the Bronze Age, when it is estimated that there could have been over 5,000 people living here in small, stone-built settlements, following a peaceful agricultural existence. Dartmoor is peppered with evidence of their presence in the form of stone circles and rows, cairns, standing stones, hut circles and pounds.

Legacy of a Community

One of the the moor's finest ancient monument, Grimspound is an impressive 4-acre (2ha) stone-walled enclosure, containing the remains of 24 hut circles, which housed up to 50 people and their livestock around 1300 BC. Situated in a dip between Hookney and Hameldown tors, Grimspound has a lovely, open aspect and its non-defensible position backs up the belief that those were peaceful

times, and that such walled enclosures on the moor – around 150 have been located – were simply to contain livestock.

The settlement was extensively examined and partly rebuilt by the Dartmoor Exploration Committee in 1894, when it was selected as its first site for archaeological investigation. The huts are characterised by their solid granite door frames and porches, and would have been thatched originally. The site has survived well on account of its granite construction; its remoteness has also protected it from later raiding of the stone for the building of walls and roads. At one time the enclosure wall (or possibly double wall) was around 6ft (2m) high and 10ft (3m) wide.

The route passes Warren House Inn, and from here you can see the Four Acres, four stone enclosures. Legend has it that Jan Reynolds made a deal with the devil to ensure him success for seven years. Jan made his fortune playing cards and forgot the agreement; when the devil caught up with him he cast the cards aside and the aces turned to stone. Interestingly the name 'Grimspound' also has demonic connotations: some think that the enclosure was named during Saxon times as 'Grim' (the devil's) pound' – the place where the devil kept his livestock.

WALK 5 — A WALK THROUGH PREHISTORY

❶ Go through the gate where you park and walk straight on, following the signs for a public bridlepath to a road near Firth Bridge. Follow the path slightly uphill; about 100yds (91m) after leaving the wall and wood on your right the broad, grassy path forks; keep left, then left again about 50yds (46m) later to gain the hilltop near the memorial stone (left), commemorating the crew of an RAF bomber that crashed here in March 1941.

❷ Keep straight on; the path drops down gradually to reach the north entrance to Grimspound, with wonderful views ahead. In the centre of the enclosure you pass a large, restored hut circle. Walk on and out of the south entrance, and

have a look at the ruins of the enclosure wall.

❸ Turn right and follow the restored walkway downhill to cross the Grimslake to meet the lane. Turn right again; after about 100yds (91m), just past a deep gully on the left, turn left and pick your way downhill to the footpath signpost to the right of Headland Warren farm. Go straight on (signed Warren House), keeping the wall left. Follow the path over the hill and down to meet a track leading through the old tin workings; bear right. Very soon the track meets a stream (left); turn left to cross this, then follow the track uphill to meet the road just east of the Warren House Inn.

❹ After your break, retrace your steps to the signpost by Headland Warren farm. For a variation on the route turn right (signed bridlepath for Challacombe farm) and walk through the gate and past the farmhouse. Stay on the farm drive to meet the lane, then turn left to reach the road just below Grimspound. Turn right and retrace your steps over the moor to Natsworthy Gate and your car.

Distance: 3¼ miles (5km)

Total ascent: 328ft (100m)

Paths: heathery moorland tracks and grassy paths

Terrain: open, rolling moorland

Gradients: one long steady climb from Natsworthy Gate, and a short steep ascent towards the Warren House

Refreshments: Warren House Inn on the B3212, the third-highest pub in England at 1,400ft (427m)

Park: by the lane at Natsworthy Gate; follow signs for Manaton and then Natsworthy (right at Heatree Cross) from the B3212 Moretonhampstead to Postbridge road, or signs for Natsworthy from the B3387 (from Bovey Tracey) just past the village green in the centre of Widecombe

OS Map: Outdoor Leisure 28 Dartmoor

Difficulty: ✱✱

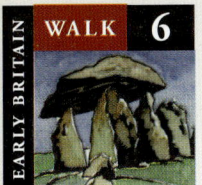
ABOUT • UFFINGTON WHITE HORSE

The White Horse was recorded in medieval records as 'a wonder', but its purpose remains a mystery. The walk also takes you to Wayland's Smithy, a 5000-year-old long barrow, along the Ridgeway, Britain's oldest road, and to Uffington Castle, an Iron Age hill fort.

Oxfordshire • SE ENGLAND

DISTANCE • 7 miles (11.3km)

TOTAL ASCENT • 415ft (126m)

PATHS • mixture of downland tracks, field paths and tarmac roads

TERRAIN • exposed downland and gentle farmland. Keep dogs on leads across the farmland of the Vale of the White Horse. Parts of the Ridgeway are suitable for dogs

GRADIENTS • one long, quite steep climb to the Ridgeway

REFRESHMENTS • The White Horse Inn at Woolstone

PARK • large free car park off B4507 signed Uffington White Horse & Waylands Smithy

OS MAP • Explorer 170 Abingdon, Wantage & Vale of White Horse

The galloping white horse at Uffington

① From the car park go through the gate and follow the outline of the grassy path along the lower slopes towards the hill. Make for a gate and cross the lane to join a bridleway. Keep left at the fork, by a bridleway waymark, and walk along to the head of Uffington White Horse.

② Descend steeply on the path to the tarmac access road, keeping the chalk figure of the White Horse on your immediate left, or, if you wish to avoid the steep, grassy down slope, retrace your steps to the lane. Bear right and continue down to the junction with the B4507.

③ Cross over and follow the road towards Uffington. Pass Sower Hill Farm and continue to a path on the left for Woolstone. Cross the stile and keep the hedge on your right. Make for two stiles in the field corner. Continue across the next field to a stile, cut through trees to the next stile. Keep ahead with the hedgerow on your left.

④ Cross the stile, turn left at the road and walk through the picturesque village of Woolstone. Bear left by The White Horse Inn and follow the road left to All Saints Church. As you approach it, veer right across the churchyard to a stile and a gate. Cross a paddock to a further gate and stile.

⑤ Turn left up the road and take the first right at the footpath sign. Follow the field edge, keeping the hedge on your left, to eventually reach a stile.

⑥ Turn right and walk through the trees to a footbridge. Cross it to a field, head diagonally left to a stile and turn right. Follow the field edge to a stile within sight of a thatched cottage. Cross and go ahead to a stile, the cottage is now level with you on the left.

⑦ Cross the road and follow the D'Arcy Dalton Way. Make for a stile, cross a paddock and head for the road by the village sign for Compton Beauchamp. Cross over and take the drive to the church, next to the manor. Retrace your steps to the sign and walk up to the junction with the B4507.

⑧ Cross over and climb quite steeply up to The Ridgeway. Turn right to visit Wayland's Smithy. Bear left to continue the walk. Follow the track to a crossroads signed Woolstone and continue on the Ridgeway uphill to reach the grassy ramparts of Uffington Castle on your left. Leave the track here, cut through the remains of the fort to the access road and return to the car park.

DIFFICULTY ✸✸

• DON'T MISS •

All Saints Church at Woolstone is a lovely small, chalk-built church. Inside you will find a Norman lead font and some striking 20th-century Stations of the Cross. During World War II a German bomb blew out all the windows. Close by is the tiny village of Compton Beauchamp, with its Tudor and Georgian manor house.

UFFINGTON

VALE OF WHITE HORSE

The White Horse Inn
WOOLSTONE
Sower Hill Farm
All Saints Church
COMPTON BEAUCHAMP
KNIGHTON
St Swithun's Church manor
Dragon Hill
B4507
WANTAGE
Uffington White Horse
1 START
Woolstone Hill
White Horse Hill
Uffington Castle
The Ridgeway
Uffington Down
Wayland's Smithy
The Ridgeway
B4000

N

0   1 Mile
0   1 Kilometre

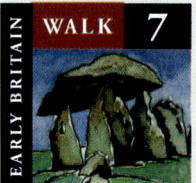
Pilsdon Pen, territory of the Durotriges tribe, commands a superb defensive position. By 600–400 BC the hill fort was a busy trading centre and the farmland you cross on this walk would have been familiar to generations of Iron Age farmers.

DISTANCE · 6 miles (9.6km)

TOTAL ASCENT · 450ft (137m)

PATHS · well-marked; tracks may be muddy and difficult after prolonged rain (boots essential); otherwise firm; some road walking

TERRAIN · grassland, fields, scrub, woodland

GRADIENTS · one short, steep climb and descent; otherwise gradual

REFRESHMENTS · pub at Birdsmoorgate

PARK · lay-by on south side of B3164 at junction with minor road to Pilsdon village, 2 miles (3.2km) west of Broadwindsor

OS MAP · Explorer 116 Lyme Regis & Bridport

The Iron Age farmers of Pilsdon Pen

1 Cross the road and climb for 437yds (400m) to the top of Pilsdon Pen. Take the path in the far right corner, through three ramparts. At the fence, turn right to the National Trust notice board.

2 Go through a gate, turn right with a plantation of young, broad-leaved trees on the left. Where the planting ends, turn downhill, diagonally right to a gateway. Follow the track to a lane. Cross and continue for ¼ mile (400m) to Lower Newnham Farm.

3 At the farm, turn right, then left between barns. Keep ahead on the permissive path around the edge of field (can be muddy) to a bridge in a gap in the hedge. Cross the bridge and follow the track uphill. Before the track ends turn right over a stile and go along the field edge for 273yds (250m). Cross stiles and head diagonally right up the field to go through a gate.

4 Turn right, down lane between high hedges. At a farm drive, keep ahead to the B3164. Turn left on to the road for 273yds (250m).

5 Leave the road at the sign for Wall Farm. Immediately turn left uphill on a narrow track between banks with trees on top. As you enter woodland, keep ahead on a ridge, to the right of waymarked tree. Continue close to the ridge following the line of low-spreading beech trees to right.

6 As the beech bank curves right before a clearing, walk straight ahead to the brow of the hill. Here, turn left on a crossing path and

head up to the line of trees on the horizon. Aim for the National Trust Lewesdon Hill sign, a third of the way along from the right.

7 Enter beech woods and follow a broad path. Over the rise, keep ahead on the grass, soon curving right, with steep beech hangers either side. At the end of the flat top, take the obvious, narrow path ahead, passing the NT sign. Beech trees crown the banks on either side. Keep near to the right bank and follow path into a gulley. Meet a track and turn right.

8 Go through a gate and turn right on to a lane. Pass Higher

Brimley Coombe Farm and Lower Brimley Coombe Cottages. Keep straight ahead on the track. Drop down round a wooded gulley, and climb to a gate. Don't go through the gate, but follow the track uphill to the right, along the side of the hill. Where the main track swings right, turn left on to a narrow path between hedges. Go through a gate, then follow the blue waymarker uphill. Meet the B3164 and turn left to return to your car.

DIFFICULTY ✤✤

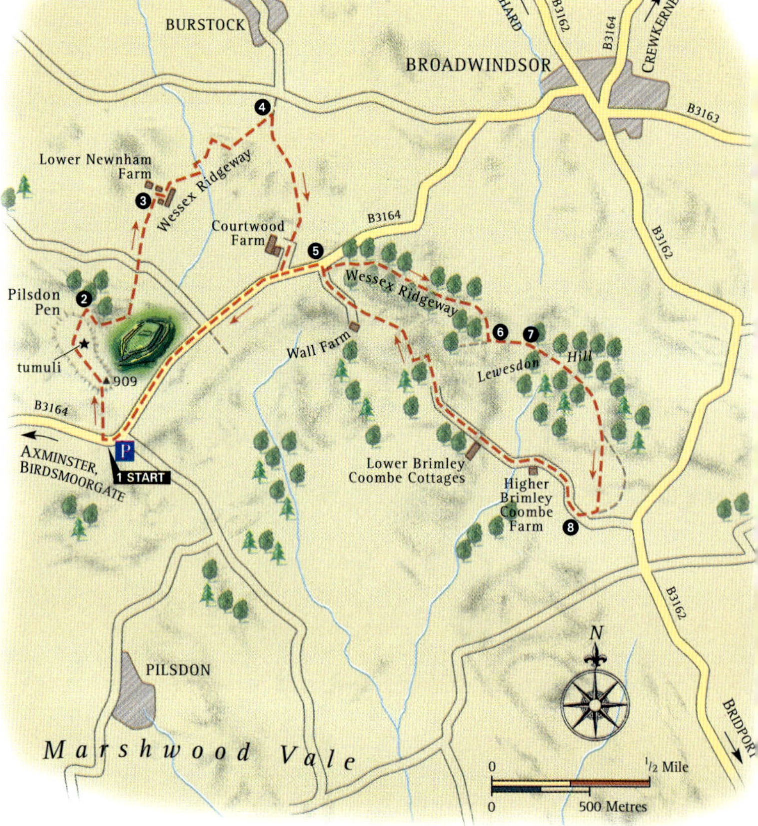

BURSTOCK

BROADWINDSOR

CHARD

CREWKERNE

B3162

B3164

B3163

Lower Newnham Farm

Wessex Ridgeway

Courtwood Farm

B3164

Wessex Ridgeway

Pilsdon Pen

Wall Farm

Lewesdon Hill

B3162

tumuli

▲909

B3164

AXMINSTER, BIRDSMOORGATE

1 START

P

Lower Brimley Coombe Cottages

Higher Brimley Coombe Farm

B3162

PILSDON

N

Marshwood Vale

BRIDPORT

0 ___ ½ Mile

0 ___ 500 Metres

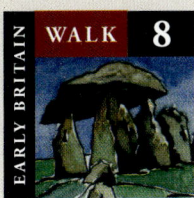
ABOUT • OLD OSWESTRY HILL FORT

Old Oswestry hill fort probably underwent at least three phases of building, starting around 600–400 BC. Once you get to the site, information boards offer a self-guided tour and it is a good place, on a fine day, to stop and enjoy the panoramic views.

Shropshire • C ENGLAND

DISTANCE • 7 miles (11km)

TOTAL ASCENT • 450ft (137m)

PATHS • good ; some sticky mud possible

TERRAIN • tracks, field paths, stiles, tarmac roads

GRADIENTS • gentle

REFRESHMENTS • near by in Oswestry

PARK • Gatacre recreation ground. Take the B4580 from the town centre. Where the B4579 forks right, turn sharp right into Oak Street, then first left into York Street, left into Gittin Street and right into Gatacre Avenue. The car park is at the top.

OS MAP • Explorer 240 Oswestry, Chirk, Ellesmere & Pant

Old Oswestry

❶ Go down Gatacre Road, passing to the right of some allotments. Turn right into Liverpool Road, which later becomes York Street. Turn right into Oak Street, left into Willow Street, then first right into Welsh Walls. At a sharp left-hand bend turn right into Brynhafod Road, later Brynhafod Lane.

❷ Take the hedged bridleway beside 'Everglades'. Follow this for ½ mile (800m), continuing straight ahead where the path crosses the road. At a gate, turn right over a stile (waymarked). After two fields cross a fence beside a tiny brook. Turn left. Within 55yds (50m), before a large oak, go left through a gate, then follow the fence on your right.

❸ Go across a very narrow field, keeping the cream cottage (High Fawr Cottage) and wooded strip one field to your right. Go diagonally left across the next field to the gate. Maintain this direction through several gates and across a track from High Fawr Farm, aiming for the white cottage with a red chimney (Oerley Cottage).

❹ In the corner of the field, by the cottage, turn sharp right to follow the plantation boundary. At the end of the trees, carry straight on across the field, crossing a fence by a big holly bush. Bear left to the far field corner; turn left through the gate and cross the field to another gate.

❺ Turn right on to the bridleway and continue for 400yds (366m). Cross the B4580. After 328yds (300m) take the Brogyntyn Estate driveway and continue for 1 mile (1.6km) to the gatehouse and the B4579. Cross diagonally left, on to a waymarked lane. Fork right of Pentre-Pant on a track. Waymarked fields, a hedged lane,

and several gates lead to Cross Lanes Farm. Go through the waymarked gate in the right-hand corner of the field and through the farmyard.

❻ Turn left on to the tarmac road. Soon turn right at a T-junction. Follow this winding lane (ignore Yew Tree Cottage driveway). At the first no through road sign turn

right, do not go ahead. Note Wat's Dyke on the left. Continue for 100yds (91m).

❼ At the second no through road sign keep straight ahead, not left. Shortly pass an enormous barn with traditional decorative brickwork. Go straight ahead to a waymarked stile, avoiding the farm.

❽ Follow a hedge aiming for Old Oswestry Hill Fort. At the fort turn right, and follow the boundary to reach a minor road. Turn left to the hill fort entrance. When you have finished exploring the site, go through the gate opposite and bear left across the field to the stile in the far corner and return to the car park.

DIFFICULTY ✷✷

[Map: Old Oswestry walk route — showing HENGOED, LLANGOLLEN, A5, B5069, Yew Tree Cottage, Cross Lanes Farm, Wat's Dyke, Pentre-Clawdd, Pentre-Pant, site of castle, Old Oswestry Hill Fort, SHREWSBURY, B4579, B4580, Brogyntyn, High Fawr Cottage, Oerley Cottage, Oerley Hall, High Fawr Farm, Everglades, 1 START, allotments, treatment works, OSWESTRY, B5069, Tourist Information Centre. Scale: 0–½ Mile, 0–500 Metres. N compass.]

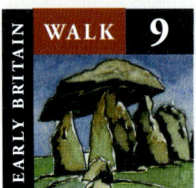

Brochs, built from 100 BC, are found only in Scotland. On this scenic and remote walk you'll see two, Dun Telve and Dun Troddan. Their builders and purpose are a mystery, but these bell-shaped, dry-stone towers remain as a testimony to the skills of the engineers.

Highland · SCOTLAND

DISTANCE · 8 miles (13km)

TOTAL ASCENT · 148ft (45m)

PATHS · mostly good, but can be muddy after heavy rain

TERRAIN · metalled and forest roads; beach

GRADIENTS · mainly flat, one section with a gentle gradient

REFRESHMENTS · none on route. Five Sisters Restaurant, Sheil Bridge, 9 miles (14.5km) from Glenelg

PARK · at the war memorial near the end of Glenelg village

OS MAP · Pathfinder 220 Shiel Bridge

The mysterious Iron Age brochs of Glenelg

❶ From the war memorial head south, following the signs for Glenelg Brochs. About a mile (1.6km) past the turning to Sandaig, the remains of a hill fort can be reached via a faint track leading up towards some rocky crags on the left.

❷ From the fort continue on the faint track to return to the road. Turn left and continue to the Dun Telve Broch on your right. Dun Troddan Broch is just a little further, on the left, a short distance up the hillside. Notice the proximity to good agricultural land which was essential to the Iron Age inhabitants and a notable feature of the location of many of the brochs in this part of Scotland.

Nearby you can visit **Sandaig**, *south of Glenelg, which featured as* Camusfearna *in* Ring of Bright Water *by naturalist Gavin Maxwell (1905–1962). The book became a best-seller and the subject of a film. Look for the memorial to his otter, Edal, which died in the fire that also destroyed his house in 1968. If you have some more time in the area it is worth travelling about 16 miles (25km) northeast of Glenelg Brochs to visit* **Eilean Donan Castle**, *an 18th-century Jacobite stronghold. It is one of the most picturesque castles in Scotland, built in the early 13th century by Alexander II of Scotland.*

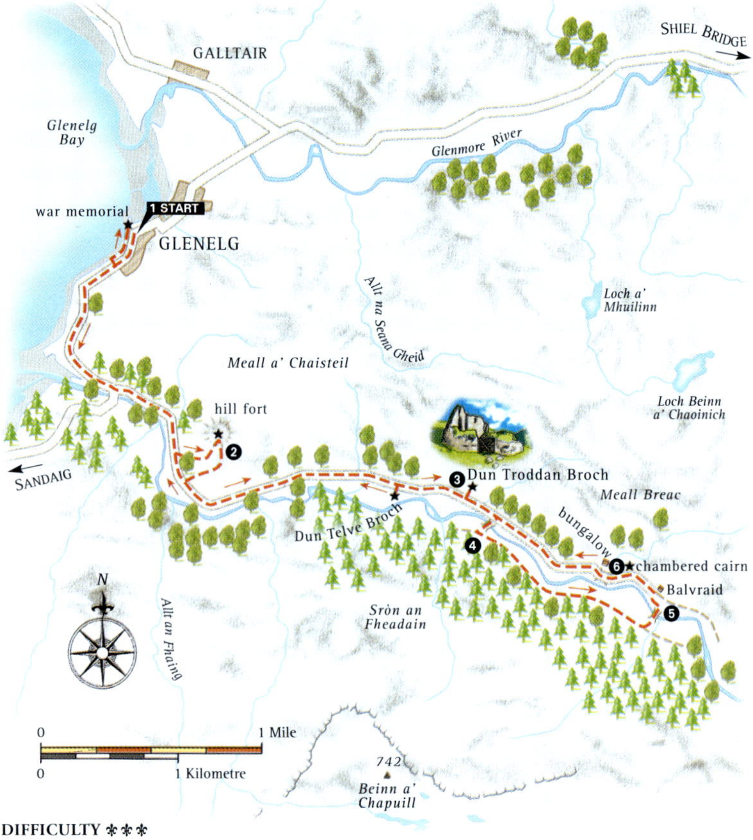

Access is via the kissing gate and a path.

❸ Visible from Dun Troddan is a wooden house with a turf roof. Just beyond it, and before some caravans, is a turning on the right

leading to a bridge over the river. Cross here and turn left on to a forest road.

❹ The road climbs gently from here, then forks. Go left, through a gate, then downhill towards a bridge over the river. Cross it, but take great care as it is in poor repair, then climb a gate on to a dirt track.

❺ Follow the track left, bear left where it joins the farm road and

continue past Balvraid farm. About 200yds (183m) past the farm look out for the chambered cairn on the right –a mound of stones covered in grass.

❻ From here continue on the road, cross a bridge by a modern bungalow and go left following this road for just over a mile (1.6km) back past the brochs to the outskirts of Glenelg. Leave the road here and walk along the beach back to the war memorial.

GALLTAIR

SHIEL BRIDGE

Glenelg Bay

Glenmore River

war memorial

1 START

GLENELG

Loch a' Mhuilinn

Meall a' Chaisteil

Allt na Seanna Gheid

hill fort

❷

Loch Beinn a' Chaoinich

SANDAIG

Dun Troddan Broch

❸

Meall Breac

Dun Telve Broch

bungalow

❹

❻ chambered cairn

Balvraid

❺

N

Allt an Fhraing

Sròn an Fheadain

742

Beinn a' Chapuill

0 _____ 1 Mile

0 _____ 1 Kilometre

DIFFICULTY ✱✱✱

*When the Emperor Claudius sent troops to invade
Britain in AD 43, he was tackling unfinished business.
Ninety years earlier, Julius Caesar had led
his warships on two raids against the 'barbarians' who
lived on the northern edge of the Roman Empire.*

ROMAN

AD 43–410

Imperial Outpost

Caesar's campaigns had yielded little more than a haul of prisoners and hostages and some good publicity in Rome; but they left us with the invaders' accounts of life among the Celtic tribes – and one particularly vivid glimpse of the druids of Anglesey, who faced their enemy across the Menai Strait, gesturing and praying, while wild-haired women waved flaming torches. The whole incident gave the Imperial legionnaires a severe fright!

A century later, Claudius, too, found that the British Celts were no walkover. Despite inter-tribal warfare and treachery, the Britons resisted the Romans for many years, notably under the determined leadership of Caractacus (Caradog), who, after his eventual capture, was rewarded for his valour with 'honourable exile' in Rome. Others kept up the struggle, even after they were deemed 'client kingdoms'. One such kingdom was the East Anglian Iceni people: in AD 60, their king's widow, Boudicca, took vengeance on the Romans for the rape of her daughters, massacring the citizens of *Camulodunum* (Colchester), London and *Verulamium* (St Albans). The Romans, in turn, slaughtered Boudicca's people and any others suspected of rebellion.

In the following years the Empire expanded its control of the new province, overrunning Wales, northern England and southern Scotland. Eventually troops were withdrawn to go and face other conflicts on the Danube – so northern Britain remained free of Roman rule, a division later marked by Emperor Hadrian's Wall, built from AD 122.

ROMAN LIFE

Britain was part of the Roman Empire for four centuries and, after the terrible bloodletting of the 1st century AD, lived largely in peace with its masters (even Hadrian's Wall was as much a customs barrier as a military border). In the period of diplomacy that followed, self-governing tribal authorities were established, called civitates: each elected its own magistrate, and was centred on a large town. Towns of varying size and importance soon flourished, with aqueducts, amphitheatres and temples. Thousands of miles of long, straight roads were built to speed communications, armies and goods across country – many still function today. Roman religion mingled with British beliefs – in *Aquae Sulis* (Bath), the sacred springs of the Celtic water goddess, Sulis, were simply rebranded, and Sulis merged with the Roman goddess Minerva. Roman fashions and tastes were adopted by wealthy Britons, who Romanised their names, spoke Latin and built increasingly elaborate villas. The luxurious palace of Fishbourne, in Sussex, provided a perfect model – with its mosaics, underfloor heating and enclosed garden, it was more suggestive of the Mediterranean than of the damp Chichester coast. The demand grew for imports such as olive oil, wine, silk and glass, mainly for an elite minority; the daily drudge of most Britons carried on much as it always had.

It all began to crumble in the 4th and 5th centuries AD. The Roman Empire, vast and overstretched, was under attack on several fronts. In AD 408–9 Saxons began raiding the British coasts, and two years later the Emperor Honorius, struggling to contain troubles elsewhere, told the province to defend itself, without the aid of Imperial muscle. Rome maintained a hold on the northern isles for a few years – but its grasp was weakening. As the 5th century AD progressed, Britain entered another new phase of its history.

HISTORIC SITES

Fishbourne Palace, near Chichester: Roman villa in the grand style.

Caerleon, Gwent: one of Europe's biggest Roman military sites.

Hadrian's Wall: the 73-mile (117km) border with the north.

St Albans: the walls of Roman Verulamium, and superb artefacts in the museum.

Bath: the Roman spa complex dedicated to Sulis Minerva.

Cirencester: everyday objects and mosaics in the Corinium Museum, and the Four Seasons mosaic at nearby Chedworth Roman Villa.

Welsh gold is still highly prized today and it's probable that the promise of rare metals such as lead and gold was a factor in the Roman invasion in AD 43. The mines are open from April to September and out of season there is a self-guided tour leaflet available.

DISTANCE • 4 miles (6.4km)

TOTAL ASCENT • 459ft (140m)

PATHS • good; slippery in places

TERRAIN • tracks, field paths, stiles and tarmac roads

GRADIENTS • some quite steep but not long

REFRESHMENTS • café at the gold mines, a pub in the village or take a picnic to have the trig point

PARK • National Trust Visitor Centre car park in Pumsaint village

OS MAP • Explorer 186 Llandeilo & Brechfa Forest, Llanybydder

The Roman gold mines at Dolaucothi

❶ Turn left on to the main road for 44yds (40m); then left into a beech avenue. Just beyond a right turn, signed Dolaucothi Farm B&B, climb a stile (red waymarker).

❷ Ascend diagonally on a grassy sunken lane to enter a well-established conifer plantation through a gate. Go uphill (pasture on your left), soon bearing slightly right, deeper into the forest. In about 328yds (300m), after a gate, turn half-right, staying within the forest. Walk a further 164–219yds (150–200m).

❸ Here the path turns downhill, into thick dark forest. Within 109yds (100m) reach a clear T-junction. Turn left, uphill, through further dense woodland. Soon emerge from the woods on to a lovely curving track to reach a modern gate.

❹ Turn sharp left on to a new farm track; immediately go through a second gate. Soon, after 27yds (25m), turn sharply up to the right (no track) to a ridge and a hedge inside a new double fence.

❺ Follow this for 44yds (40m) beyond the Pen Lan-dolau trig point. Cross the fence and turn left. Follow red marker post over a stile through a felled area (hazardous tree stumps). Turn left to re-enter standing forest ahead. Soon reach a gravel track.

❻ Turn left. After about 328yds (300m) turn abruptly right (marker post) for a sharp descent on a forestry track. As soon as you see a gate 109yds (100m) ahead and, beyond it, a footbridge, stop.

❼ Turn right (marker post), on a narrow path into, initially, felled forestry. Soon this path forms a dark dense corridor and joins an old, narrow-gauge railway track. One field before the Dolaucothi Farm buildings, reach a corner with two gateways.

❽ Turn through the gate on the left. In 44yds (40m) turn right, and proceed through stiles to the dilapidated walled garden. Turn left on to a track; after 329yds (300m) cross a stone bridge. Just after the shady picnic site turn right over a stile, on to a delightful elevated riverside path, to a T-junction.

❾ Turn left here to visit the gold mine. Otherwise, turn right, go down steps, cross a stile into a meadow and follow the riverside to the road bridge. Turn right, soon passing the beech avenue taken earlier, to return to the start.

DIFFICULTY ✱✱

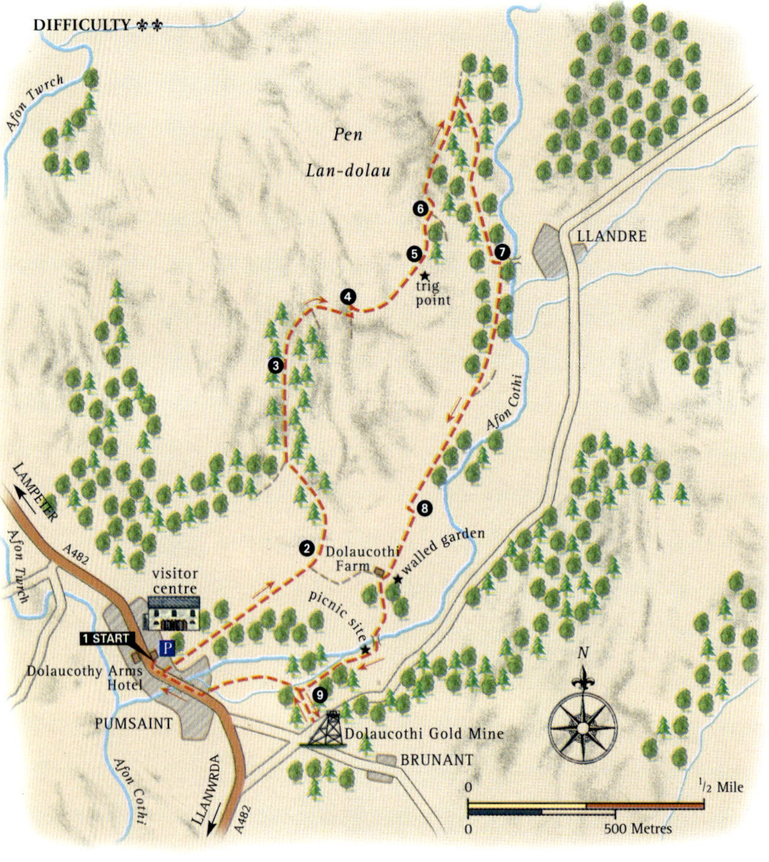

Map features: Afon Twrch, Pen Lan-dolau, LLANDRE, trig point, Afon Cothi, LAMPETER, A482, visitor centre, 1 START, P, Dolaucothi Arms Hotel, PUMSAINT, Afon Twrch, Afon Cothi, LLANWRDA, A482, Dolaucothi Farm, walled garden, picnic site, Dolaucothi Gold Mine, BRUNANT, N, 0 — 1/2 Mile, 0 — 500 Metres

• DON'T MISS •

The National Park visitor centre in Pumsaint is a 19th-century former coach house for visitors to the Dolaucothi Arms, and has a series of information panels on the village, the Dolaucothi Estate, and a Roman fort (no longer visible).

ABOUT • SILCHESTER

Calleva Atrebatum, or Silchester, was built shortly after AD 43. Once a bustling town complete with streets, temple and amphitheatre, it was inexplicably abandoned in AD 400–500. Uniquely, a complete circuit of walls remains at the site.

Hampshire • SE ENGLAND

DISTANCE • 5 miles (8km); optional circuit of walls, about 1 mile (1.6km)

TOTAL ASCENT • 98ft (30m)

PATHS • likely to be very muddy after rain

TERRAIN • fields, woodland, old lanes, some road walking

GRADIENTS • lots of stiles to negotiate, steep woodland paths

REFRESHMENTS • Calleva Arms pub, Silchester; Romans Hotel, Silchester

PARK • car park for Silchester Roman site on Wall Lane (free), on Mortimer side of modern Silchester

OS MAP • Explorer 159 Reading, Wokingham & Pangbourne

Silchester Roman town

❶ Leave the car park via its entrance, cross the road, and take the old lane (fingerpost) directly opposite. Where the path rises, turn right at the fingerpost down a green tunnel of rhododendrons and holly. Cross a stile, keep left round the edge of the field and cross another stile. Cross a farm track and the stile opposite. Keep to the edge of the field, with the fence left, and cross the stile at the end.

❷ Ignore the track straight ahead, turn left along the old path at the field edge. Look right to see an ancient earthwork on the horizon. At the end, cross a stile and keep straight ahead along a line of oak trees. Continue downhill through the flinty field, following the hollow of an old field boundary, to a stream at the bottom.

❸ Cross a stile, footbridge and another stile, and keep straight up the hill. Half-way up, turn left and cross a stile into the woods. Cross the footbridge and continue up through birches (larch plantation on the left). At the top go through the gate and keep right along the field edge, to pass behind houses. After the last cottage (Rose Cottage), turn right over the stile and walk up the driveway.

❹ At the lane turn right, passing stables and an old farmhouse, right. Keep ahead down the old lane to the bottom of the hill. Where the track forks, keep right. After the bridge, turn left and go straight across the field towards a stile at the edge of the woods.

❺ Cross the stile and go ahead into trees. Cross a track, and a stile over a wire fence. Emerge from the woods and continue straight across the field towards a gate. Cross the stile and follow the path diagonally down to the right.

❻ At the bottom of the hollow, cross the bridge and stile and head diagonally left up the field. Before you reach the top corner, go through the squeeze gate on left, and turn right on to the gravel lane. This becomes a road by the thatched cottage (The Mount), and leads to a junction with a post-box. Turn right and through the squeeze gate for the Roman amphitheatre.

❼ Return to the road (Wall Lane) and turn right. Follow this past Manor Farm, into Church Lane. Stone walls can be seen on the right, and St Mary's Church. Keep heading downhill, and follow the path up on to the top of the wall.

❽ (Optional route: follow walls round for a complete circuit.) Retrace your route to this crossing point and stay inside the walls on a path along a fence. Turn right and go through the churchyard. Keep left, through a gate and along the path, with

farm buildings on your right. Keep on this path, and bear left on to a track which runs for ½ mile (800m) across the Roman town. Pass excavation site (closed).

❾ At the opposite side, go left, then right through the gate. Follow the path for ¾ mile (1.2km) to the museum. (To reach modern village, cross the road and bear left, to take footpath through the trees.) Retract your steps to point ❾ and go left. Turn right just before the wooden gate to the car park.

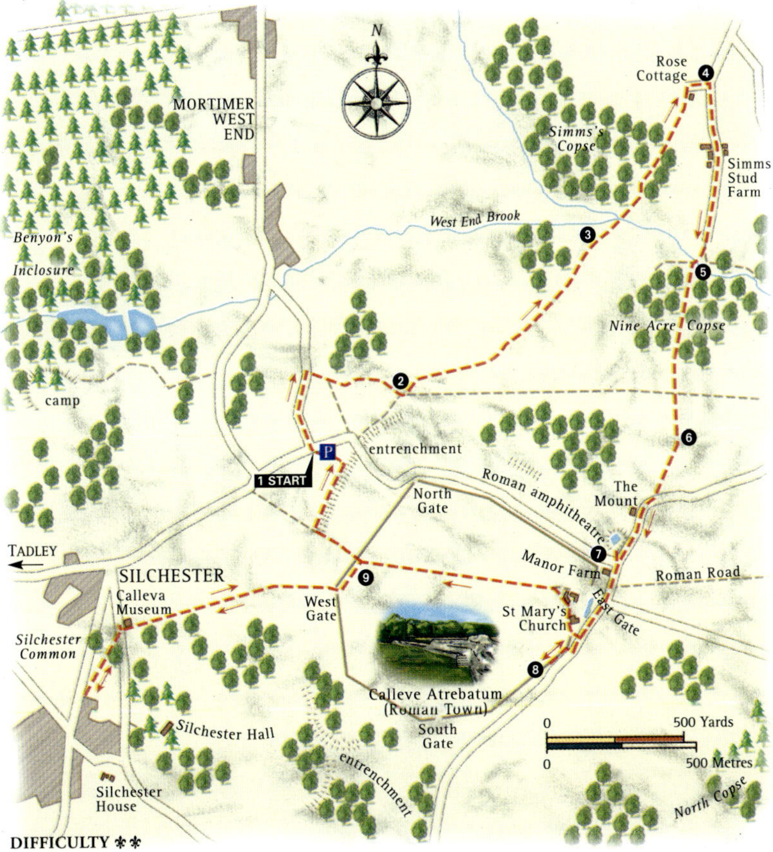

[Map of Silchester Roman town, showing the walking route with numbered waypoints. Locations marked include: Mortimer West End, Rose Cottage, Simms's Copse, Simms Stud Farm, West End Brook, Benyon's Inclosure, Nine Acre Copse, camp, entrenchment, P START, North Gate, Roman amphitheatre, The Mount, Manor Farm, Roman Road, Tadley, Silchester, Calleva Museum, West Gate, St Mary's Church, East Gate, Silchester Common, Calleve Atrebatum (Roman Town), South Gate, Silchester Hall, Silchester House, entrenchment, North Copse. Scale: 500 Yards / 500 Metres.]

DIFFICULTY ✳✳

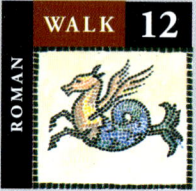

Shortly after the Roman invasion, military roads were laid across Britain to enable speedy movement of troops. As well as being straight, you can often identify them by the agger, the raised platform between ditches which makes for their distinctive profile.

DISTANCE • 5 miles (8km)

TOTAL ASCENT • 390ft (119m)

PATHS • field tracks, country lanes and a converted railway track bed

TERRAIN • pastureland and edge of town

GRADIENTS • steep ascent from Welton Hollow and Clandown Bottom

REFRESHMENTS • none on the route but several pubs in Radstock, Welton and Midsomer Norton

PARK • 100yds (91m) up Millards Hill or carefully down the lane towards Welton Manor Farm

OS MAP • Explorer 143 Shepton Mallet & Mendip Hills East

The Exeter–Lincoln highway

DIFFICULTY ✱✱

❶ Walk down the lane towards Welton Manor Farm, go through the left-hand gate and follow the right-hand field edge to a stile. Cross and continue for 300yds (274m) to another stile on the right. Walk diagonally across the field, heading for a railway bridge. Cross the stile and climb the steps to the Norton–Radstock Greenway. Turn left and follow the former railway for 500yds (457m) to some bollards across the track.

❷ Turn left and cross the stile into the field. Keep the hedge on your left and follow the rising path to a gate into an enclosed lane. Follow this section of Roman road (the Fosse Way) between hedges and up on to the top of the hill. Continue as it dips back down between hedgerows to Clandown Bottom. Cross a stream and turn left as you emerge in housing.

❸ Turn left at the T-junction along Springfield Place. Pass the old chapel (converted into housing) and go through an arch in the row of cottages ahead to a gate and field beyond. Follow the streamside path up the valley. At the end of the field cross the stile and continue on a better track with the stream on your left. Cross a stile by a gate and bear right to join a farm track coming down the hill. Turn immediately left and continue through a gate on to a road.

❹ Cross, go through the gate opposite and walk up the track with the stream on your left. Near the head of the valley, aim for the top left-hand corner by a pond. Cross the stream, go through a gate and follow the left-hand field edge up to a stile in the corner. Stay with the hedge to the next stile. Cross, turn half-right aiming for a stile diagonally opposite.

❺ Emerge on a road and take the lane directly opposite. After 100yds (91m), as the lane swings left, take the footpath on the right along the edge of a field. Cross a stile at the far corner and continue with the hedge on your right, then go across the opening to a side field. Turn left at the end on an enclosed lane; turn right. Cross the stile and turn left into a field. Follow the left-hand edge until it becomes an enclosed lane. Go through the gate and go down the hill to join a farm track. Turn left by Springfield Farm.

❻ Turn right at the junction. In 200 yds (183m) turn left through a stile, then turn right beyond a gap in the hedge. Follow the hedge through two fields and, 50yds (46m) into a third field, turn left to join a crossing path over a stile on the far eastern side.

❼ Follow the enclosed Binces Lodge Lane, past a white house on the left, until it becomes surfaced and joins a minor road on a bend. Go straight ahead to another junction on the right. Turn right past a row of houses. At the end of the road keep straight on down the snicket (narrow alley between houses) to emerge on the bend in Millards Hill, 100yds (91m) above the start.

ABOUT • ARDOCH ROMAN FORT

Unlike its more southerly neighbours, the hostile Scottish tribes proved no easy conquest for the Roman troops. Remains of the marching camps, forts and series of garrisons all point to Rome's might, 2000 years ago, and the strength of resistance they encountered.

Perth & Kinross • SCOTLAND

DISTANCE • 4 miles (6km)	**GRADIENTS •** minimal
TOTAL ASCENT • minimal	**REFRESHMENTS •** Braco Hotel
PATHS • firm, but there can be puddles after rain	**PARK •** on roadside in high street of Braco village
TERRAIN • woodland and fields	**OS MAP •** Explorer 369 Perth & Kinross

The Roman campaign headquarters at Ardoch

• DON'T MISS •

Ardoch Old Bridge, just upstream from the present crossing, was built in the early 18th century to carry a military road from Stirling up into the Highlands. It formed part of a system involving roads and garrisons, intended to suppress the northern clans whose distant ancestors may have possibly battled with Agricola in Roman times.

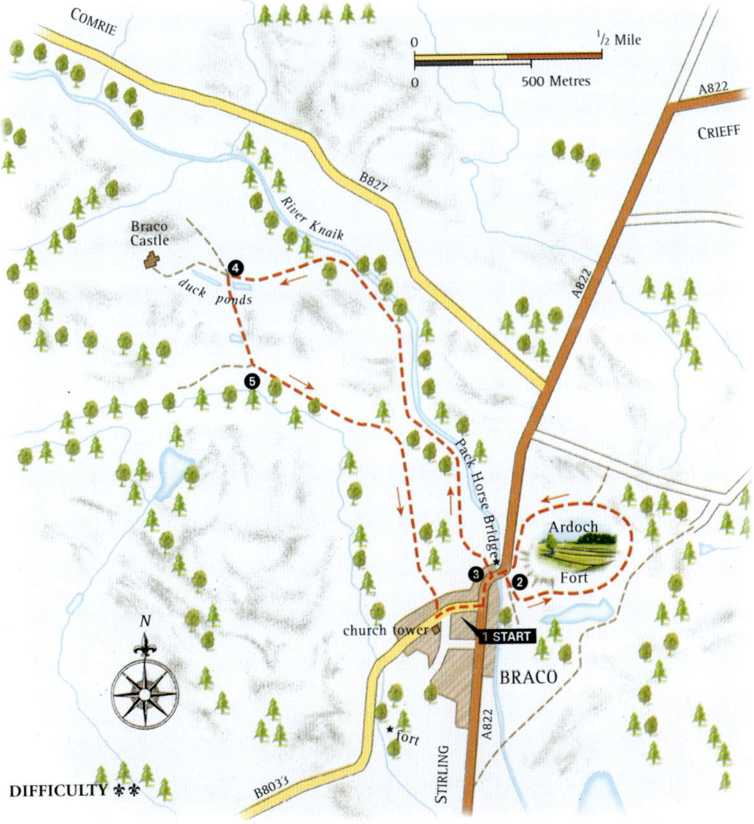

❶ Park in the high street and walk through the village on the A822 Crieff road. Cross a bridge over the River Knaik, a stream which, under various names, flows from the foothills of the Highlands to the Allan Water and the Firth of Forth.

❷ Immediately beyond the bridge, turn right and enter Ardoch Fort through a small wooden gate. Following the forts' massive inner rampart, you can appreciate the complexity and strength of its defences. Walk in an anti-clockwise direction around the perimeter fence. (The land on the other side of the fence belongs to the Ardoch Estate.) Within the fence are a large number of impressive angular ditches built as a series of defence mechanisms. The great marching camps extend for more than ½ mile (800m) to the north, but are best seen from beside the road to Comrie. Once you have explored the site, return to the entrance and go back across the bridge.

❸ On the village side of the bridge, turn right through the stone-piered entrance of a private road. Follow the track through attractive woodland above the river's waterfalls and rapids, before veering to the left to reach a crossroads.

❹ Turn left, continuing on the track between two duck ponds. The hills on the south-east horizon are the Ochil Hills, which include the summit of Ben Cleuch at 721m. Behind you, to the north, you can glimpse the bracken-covered foothills of the Highlands. The Romans realised that if they were to conquer Scotland, they first had

to control this broad and fertile valley through the hills now known as Strathallan.

❺ Turn left at a T-junction. Looking back across the fields from this point there is a good view of Braco Castle, an imposing mansion with medieval origins that, just like

a Roman villa would be, is the focus of a large, well-run estate. The track skirts cultivated fields, grazing lands and managed woodland. Turn left at the juction with the B8033, opposite the remains of the tower of Braco Free Church (1845), and return to Braco high street and your car.

DIFFICULTY ✱✱

(map of the walk route showing Comrie, B827, River Knaik, Braco Castle, duck ponds, Ardoch Fort, Pack Horse Bridge, church tower, BRACO, Crieff, Stirling, A822, B8033, with scale ½ Mile / 500 Metres and compass rose marked N)

The Antonine Wall

The boundary that once marked the Roman Empire's northern limit, between the Forth and the Clyde in Scotland

A Frontier for Brittania

Once the Romans had abandoned their ambition to include the whole of Britain in the empire, they had to decide on a northern frontier. In terms of controlling local tribes and protecting the rich province from invasion, they could rely on strategically positioned forts and military roads, but in times of peace a more formal frontier was required. There were taxes to be levied on imports; there were criminals and other undesirables whose movements needed to be checked. Most importantly, travellers should be suitably impressed when entering the greatest empire in the world.

The most substantial and long-lasting of these frontiers was the wall constructed on the orders of the Emperor Hadrian following his visit to Britain in AD 122. But within 15 years of completion a new emperor, Antoninus Pius, decided on a frontier 100 miles (160km) to the north, retaking lands in southern Scotland that the Romans had abandoned some 60 years before.

A Wall of Turf

The Antonine Wall spans Britain's narrowest land-crossing, running 40 miles (64km) from the Firth of Forth to the Clyde. Unlike its predecessor, it was built of turf, but was nonetheless substantial, and 16 forts were built at regular intervals along its length. There were also signal stations, a military road and complex secondary defences to deter attack by cavalry or chariots. Trees now cover some of the site but the turf ramparts over the stone foundations of the Roman fort are still clearly visible.

Manned, according to inscriptions, by auxiliaries from distant corners of the empire, the frontier served its purpose for some 20 years until about AD 158, when a further change in policy led to a withdrawal back south and the re-commissioning of Hadrian's Wall. One of the best-preserved sections of wall is at Rough Castle, near Bonnybridge, where its course may be followed to both west and east of the public car park.

WALK 14
A PATROL ALONG THE FRONTIER AT ROUGH CASTLE

❶ Having parked, return down the lane for about 300yds (274m) and turn right through a gate into a park-like field of trees and open grassland. The Roman frontier is still unmistakable: a deep, wide ditch, or vallum, overlooked by a substantial bank – all that remains of the turf wall.

❷ As you follow its course back to the car park and beyond, picture it when newly built. Set on stone foundations, it was a massive 15ft (4.5m) in width and stood at least 10ft (3m) high, with a timber palisade along the parapet. You may notice stones from the foundations half-buried in the turf, but your mind must recreate the watch-towers and beacon-platforms.

❸ Beyond a burn tumbling through a sheltered glen is Rough Castle fort: a four-square compound protected by ramparts. This was the base for a small garrison, together with administrative clerks and an officer elite. Enter through the west gate and imagine the barrack blocks and granaries on your route to the principia, or headquarters building.

❹ Turning left, exit through the north gate. Ahead of you is a serried grid of pits; each one contained a bunch of sharpened stakes, known as lilia, or lilies,

that could prove most effective in deterring an assault. Turning to the right and recrossing the frontier, you can explore the fort's 'annexe'. This contained the bath-house, potteries, blacksmiths and other workshops.

❺ Beyond the annexe, a stile leads on to a woodland path that follows the frontier for a further mile (1.6km) and, although the earthworks are overgrown, it is here that one can best imagine the landscape of 2,000 years ago. To the south lay an empire that stretched to Africa and Asia; to the north lay mountains and impenetrable forests haunted by barbarians. The wall was a boundary between two opposing worlds.

Distance: 2½ miles (4km)

Total ascent: 50ft (80m)

Paths: firm grass to west of Rough Castle; muddy stretches through woods to east of fort

Terrain: open grassland and woods

Gradients: easy

Refreshments: pubs and cafés in Bonnybridge and Falkirk

Park: car park at Rough Castle

OS Map: Explorer 349 Falkirk, Cumbernauld & Livingston

Difficulty: ✱✱

ABOUT • CHESTER

The 20th legion of the Roman army was garrisoned in Chester onwards from AD 88 and a large civilian town grew up next to the fort. Apart from the Roman-Medieval walls, the city has a number of interesting Roman remains including an ampitheatre.

Cheshire • C ENGLAND

DISTANCE • 4 miles (6.4km)

TOTAL ASCENT • 25ft (8m)

PATHS • pavements

TERRAIN • city streets

GRADIENTS • one climb to the city walls

REFRESHMENTS • many cafés and pubs in Chester

PARK • Little Roodee car park off Grosvenor Road; numerous other car parks; park-and-ride drops off in the city centre

OS MAP • Explorer 266 Wirral & Chester

Roman drama in the heart of Chester

❶ Begin at The Cross in the city centre and walk west for 328yds (300m) along Watergate Street until you reach the junction with City Walls Road. Go right slightly to gain access to the red sandstone city walls and turn left to walk in an anti-clockwise direction along the walls, soon passing the Roodee Racecourse on your right.

❷ Cross over the A483 Wrexham road and follow the walls around for 437yds (400m), passing the early Norman Chester Castle, rebuilt from its ruinous state in the 19th century, on the left and following the course of the River Dee on the right. In 109yds (100m) cross Bridgegate. In 164yds (150m) the walls turn north, away from the river; the Roman Gardens are below on the right.

❸ Come down from the walls at New Gate and turn right into the Roman Gardens. After exploring the gardens, leave where you came in, turn right to see the Roman Amphitheatre in 55yds (50m), and the Chester Visitor Centre, which offers an excellent introduction to the city, further along on the far side of the road.

❹ Return to New Gate and continue the circuit of the walls. After 328yds (300m) swing west to cross Northgate and then St Martins Gate, then turn south to reach Watergate where you first ascended the walls.

❺ Descend the walls and turn left along Watergate Street, back to The Cross. Turn right down Bridge Street, with access to the Roman bath and hypocaust through the

Spud-U-Like shop. (Not signed, but go in and down the stairs to the left of the counter.)

❻ Further down Bridge Street is the Chester Heritage Centre, well worth visiting before returning to The Cross. Here you turn right and immediately left up Northgate Street, until you reach Chester Cathedral which is set back slightly on your right.

❼ Spend some time exploring this fine 14th-century red sandstone cathedral with its fine Norman stonework and rich carvings. Once a Benedictine monastery until its dissolution in the 1540, unlike many Chester survived to become the cathedral for the Diocese of Chester just one year later. After visiting the cathedral, retrace your steps to The Cross to finish the walk.

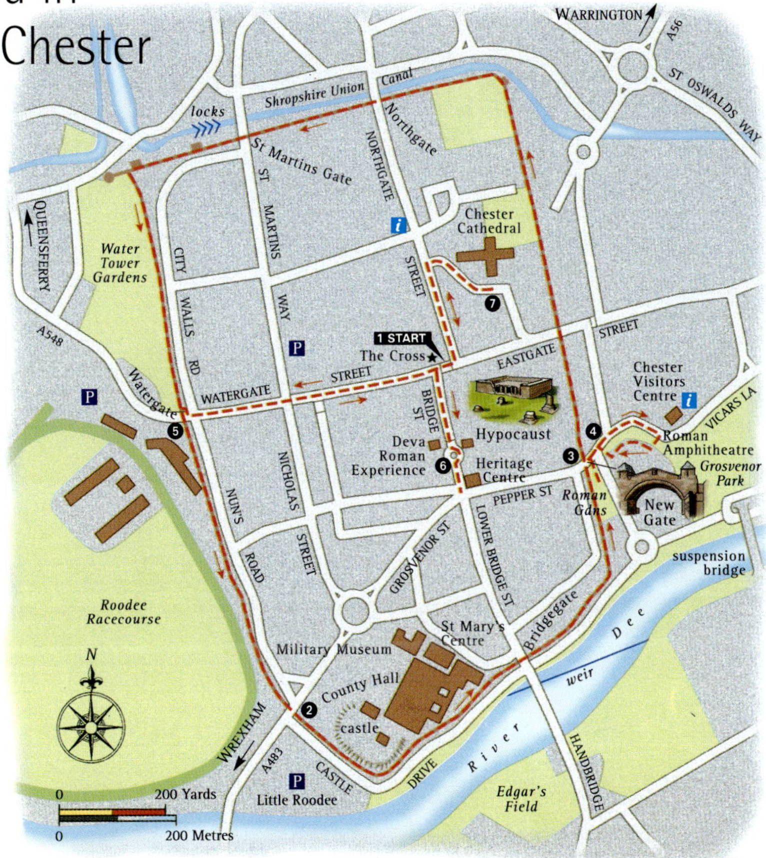

DIFFICULTY ✱

DON'T MISS

Chester Zoo, to the north of the city, is one of the finest zoological parks in Europe, a pioneer in showing animals in their natural surroundings. At 110 acres (44ha), it is the second-largest in Britain after London Zoo.

Map labels:

WARRINGTON

A56

ST OSWALDS WAY

Shropshire Union Canal

locks

St Martins Gate

NORTHGATE

Northgate

Chester Cathedral

QUEENSFERRY

Water Tower Gardens

CITY WALLS WAY

ST MARTINS

A548

A548

CITY WALLS RD

Watergate

WATERGATE

WATERGATE STREET

1 START
The Cross

EASTGATE

STREET

Chester Visitors Centre

VICARS LA

Hypocaust

Deva Roman Experience

Heritage Centre

BRIDGE ST

Roman Amphitheatre

Grosvenor Park

NUN'S ROAD

NICHOLAS STREET

PEPPER ST

Roman Gdns

New Gate

suspension bridge

GROSVENOR ST

LOWER BRIDGE ST

Roodee Racecourse

N

Military Museum

St Mary's Centre

County Hall

castle

Bridgegate

Dee

weir

River

HANDBRIDGE

WREXHAM

A483

CASTLE DRIVE

Little Roodee

Edgar's Field

0   200 Yards

0   200 Metres

ROMAN

WALK 16

ABOUT • GREAT WITCOMBE

The setting alone, reminiscent of a Mediterranean landscape, makes this walk worthwhile. The villa commands superb views across the valley and the remains, which show the original floor plan, leave you in no doubt that this was once a sumptuous country house.

Gloucestershire • SW ENGLAND

DISTANCE • 7½ miles (12km)

TOTAL ASCENT • 700ft (213m)

PATHS • good; slippery in places

TERRAIN • bridleways, tracks, field paths, stiles, tarmac roads

GRADIENTS • mostly gradual; climbs are steep but short

REFRESHMENTS • seasonal tea-shop near start; Air Balloon pub, Brockworth and Gloucester near by

PARK • Roman villa car park, 1½ miles (2.4km) from Brockworth turn-off A417

OS MAP • Explorer 179 Gloucester, Cheltenham & Stroud

Great Witcombe's grand Roman villa

❶ Take the path downhill from the car park for 33yds (30m). Follow waymarkers to a gate and the Cotswold Way; turn left. Soon pass The Haven Tea Garden on the left and continue to a big junction; here conifers have infiltrated the indigenous beeches. Turn left.

❷ Soon pass a dilapidated ornamental gateway. After 437yds (400m) turn right at a T-junction (left is a private drive). Continue for 328yds (300m), to a clear fork of tracks. Go right, slightly uphill, for 186yds (170m).

❸ Turn sharply right and back to leave the Cotswold Way and follow a bridleway signed Horse Trail to Brimpsfield, which goes uphill, then left to the B4070. Turn right and in 22yds (20m) cross the road and continue ahead signed Brimpsfield 1½ miles (2.4km). At a T-junction turn left. Keep the fence/wall on your right. The path, initially enclosed by tree-lined walls, opens on to a bend in the road. Continue ahead along the road to reach a T-junction of minor roads.

❹ Cross the road and continue ahead on a bridleway. Join a farm track and in 22yds (20m) turn left over a stile to Birdlip. Turn left at the road. Take a path beside a school; walk on cricket field side of a football pitch fence. Beyond a flagpole turn half-left. At a B-road turn right, then take the old road, left, to Barrow Rake Viewpoint plaque.

❺ Take the obvious path (Cotswold Way) on the escarpment. Later, in woodland, the track descends to a road. Go straight over and down through trees; soon turn right to rejoin the road. Just after a sharp bend take the public bridleway to the right.

❻ Continue straight ahead, keeping the fence on your left. Go to end of barns being converted. Cross a stile, turn partially left, downslope, to another stile then a gap in trees. Follow right-hand edge of a field down to a house. Follow the path beside the house and down a long drive. Take the second footpath on left (shortly after footpath beside green-surfaced tennis court), climb stile and diagonally cross two small fields to another road. Go straight across into fields.

❼ Take field paths, turning half-left across the third field towards houses. Follow a path between houses leading to a minor road. Turn left; in 44yds (40m) turn right (waymarked), and after 22yds (20m), at end of a garden, take the stile on the right to cross diagonally to the reservoir road. Cross the causeway.

❽ Skirt Witcombe Reservoir on a good track (ignore a footpath on the right, beside buildings) which later rises with a stream on the left (ignore left turn signed Private). The track later deteriorates. Keep straight ahead uphill (do not cross the stream) through pastures. To enter the Roman villa proceed uphill and around it through farmyard. The car park is 328yds (300m) ahead.

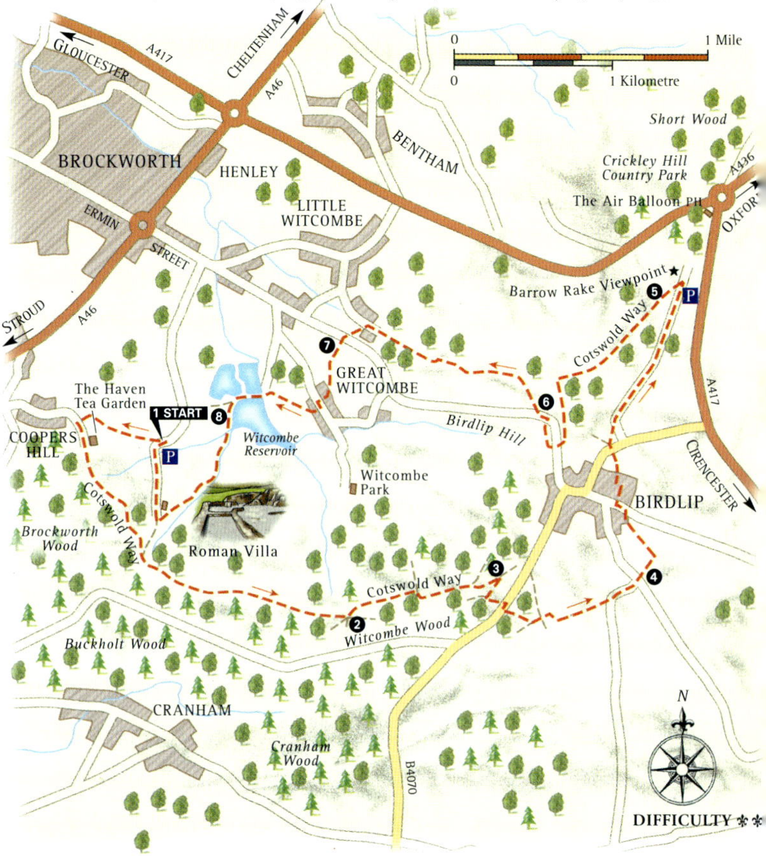

GLOUCESTER A417 CHELTENHAM A46

BROCKWORTH HENLEY BENTHAM

ERMIN LITTLE WITCOMBE

STREET

STROUD A46

The Haven Tea Garden

COOPERS HILL

Brockworth Wood

1 START ❽ Witcombe Reservoir

Roman Villa

Buckholt Wood

CRANHAM

Cranham Wood

Cotswold Way

GREAT WITCOMBE

❼

❻

Birdlip Hill

Witcombe Park

Cotswold Way ❸

❷ Witcombe Wood

Barrow Rake Viewpoint ★ ❺ P

Cotswold Way

BIRDLIP

❹

A417

CIRENCESTER

Short Wood

Crickley Hill Country Park

The Air Balloon P.H.

A436

OXFORD

B4070

0 .... 1 Mile

0 .... 1 Kilometre

N

DIFFICULTY ✱✱

ABOUT • HARDKNOTT FORT

From the Duddon Valley you see the fort as the high point of your journey. After rounding the craggy Harter Fell, you climb, in the invaders' footsteps, to reach the outer walls of the fort – against a backdrop of the mighty Cumbrian mountains.

Cumbria • N ENGLAND

DISTANCE • 6 miles (10km)

TOTAL ASCENT • 1,509ft (460m)

PATHS • mountain paths, can be muddy and indistinct in places. Compass advised

TERRAIN • forest and rugged fellside

GRADIENTS • two steady climbs

REFRESHMENTS • none on the route. Newfield Arms, Seathwaite; Bower House Hotel, near Eskdale Green

PARK • Birks Bridge car park, near Birks

OS MAP • Outdoor Leisure 7 The English Lakes – South Eastern Area

The Roman fort at Hardknott

❶ Cross the bridge over the River Duddon and immediately turn left along the waymarked bridleway which heads south before climbing through oak woods to Birks Farm. Once through the gate into the yard (caution – farm dogs), veer right on to a forestry road.

❷ Turn left at a T-junction of forestry roads, ignoring the bridleway signed to Harter Fell, the waymarked footpath to the right, and the two left forks. The track climbs steadily through the trees and rounds the southern flanks of Harter Fell before ending at a vehicle turning circle.

❸ Continue on a rocky bridleway traversing the west side of the fell for 500yds (457m) before leaving the forest through a gate. Stay close to Spothow Gill for ¹/₂ mile (800m) then swing right, cross a small gill and go through a gate to descend the bracken-clad slopes beneath Birker Fell's crags. Pass through another gate and cross Dodknott Gill to reach Jubilee Bridge, which spans Hardknott Gill.

❹ Climb out past a small car park to the Hardknott Pass road. Turn right here to climb paths that take short cuts between bends in the road. If you prefer, you can continue along the road but it can be very busy in summer.

❺ A footpath signpost (32in/81cm high) points the way left up the fellside to the fort at Hardknott. Continue on the faint path from the back of the fort towards the crags of Border End. Swing right short of the crags to emerge on the roadside just before the summit of Hardknott Pass.

❻ Climb the short stretch of road before turning right on the bridleway, signed to Birks. At the highest point, the summit of Hardknott Pass, ignore the right turn, and descend south-eastwards down peaty slopes, keeping the spruce trees of Dunnerdale Forest on your right.

❼ At the foot of the slope go through a gate into a small enclosure, turn left over a step stile in the wall and through another gate, then continue on a grassy track towards Black Hall Farm. On reaching the farm, go over a stile, then turn right on a track heading towards the River Duddon. The well-defined track traverses rough pasture between the river bank and the forest to reach the bridge at the back of the car park.

DIFFICULTY ✽✽✽

Map labels

Hard Knott 549

Hardknott Castle

Border End

Hardknott Pass

River Esk

Black Hall Farm

Roman road

AMBLESIDE

Hardknott Gill

lay-by

Jubilee Bridge

RAVENGLASS, ESKDALE GREEN

Castle How

Dunnerdale Forest

Spothow Gill

Harter Fell 652

Dow Crag

turning circle

Birker Fell

Kepple Crag

Brandy Crag

Birks Farm

River Duddon

Green Crag

Tarn Beck

N

SEATHWAITE

P 1 START

0 ——— 1 Mile
0 ——— 1 Kilometre

• DON'T MISS •

The Ravenglass and Eskdale steam-driven narrow-gauge railway, which runs from Ravenglass to Dalegarth, near Boot. Built as a 3ft (1m)-gauge line in 1875 to carry iron-ore, it was converted to the present 15in (38cm)-gauge in 1915, when the mine closed.

ROMAN

WALK 18

ABOUT • BIGNOR ROMAN VILLA

A stroll along a section of Roman road and the breezy South Downs leads you to Bignor Roman villa. The excavated remains at Bignor date from about the 4th century AD but suggest that the inhabitants enjoyed a lifestyle not so different from our own.

West Sussex • SE ENGLAND

DISTANCE • 8 miles (13km). Short walk omitting Stane Street 5½ miles (8.8km)

TOTAL ASCENT • 262ft (80m)

PATHS • clearly waymarked, defined tracks, quiet country lanes; some muddy sections

TERRAIN • woodland and downland

GRADIENTS • gentle to moderate, with one steady climb

REFRESHMENTS • White Horse pub, Sutton; tea room at Bignor Roman Villa. Picnic benches along Stane Street at Point 5 (in the woods) and Point 6 (in the open)

PARK • roadside parking near the White Horse pub, Sutton

OS MAP • Explorer 121 Arundel & Pulborough

A slice of Roman life at Bignor

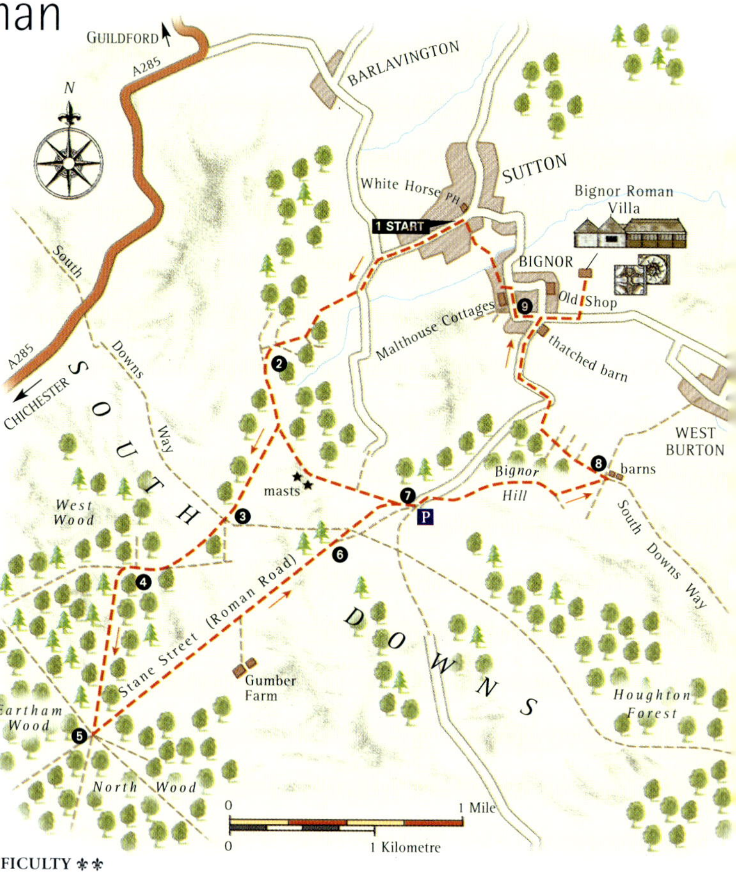

GUILDFORD
A285
N
BARLAVINGTON
SUTTON
White Horse PH
1 START
Bignor Roman Villa
BIGNOR
Old Shop
Malthouse Cottages
thatched barn
South Downs Way
A285
CHICHESTER
SOUTH DOWNS
West Wood
masts
Bignor Hill
barns
WEST BURTON
P
Stane Street (Roman Road)
Gumber Farm
Eartham Wood
North Wood
Houghton Forest
0
1 Mile
0
1 Kilometre

DIFFICULTY ✱✱

1 Take the road left of the White Horse, signed Barlavington and Duncton. Beyond the edge of the village, bear left on to the road signed as a dead end, ignoring the right turn to Barlavington. After 250yds (229m), where the road bends left, bear right on to a bridleway. Continue and climb steadily up a wooded escarpment, ignoring a signed footpath, left.

2 At staggered track junction at the top, continue ahead for 30yds (27m) then bear left following a blue waymark arrow up the hill and beyond the treeline towards two masts. At Bignor Hill NT sign fork left and in 50yds (46m) turn right. (For a shorter walk continue ahead, avoiding right turns, to the car park at Point 7.)

3 At a five-way junction (NT Slindon Estate sign, left), ignore South Downs Way (which crosses your path) and take next right turn on to a lesser path (fence on right, woodland on left). At next junction turn right towards forest.

4 Soon after entering the forest, follow a blue waymark arrow left, downhill. The track is bordered on the left by an old boundary dyke. Follow the blue arrows.

5 At the bottom, at a seven-way junction by a bench, turn left, signed Bignor, along the ridge of Stane Street. Avoid side turns. Continue through a gate, across open land.

6 By a bench, ½ mile (800m) after a NT sign on the right for Gumber Farm, avoid the gate ahead and take a stile up on your left behind a bench, cross the track and continue along Stane Street. Keep forward at the junction on the South Downs Way (which joins from the left), turning right at the next signpost where the view opens out.

7 At the car park (by a signpost with Roman names – *Londinium* etc), continue along the South Downs Way, which forks right on a track heading over the summit of Bignor Hill. Continue on the South Downs Way, bearing left where signed.

8 At a junction by barns, turn left on to a bridleway, heading slightly uphill through woods. Ignore side turns. The track levels, then descends. Turn right at a road T-junction, downhill. At T-junction by a thatched barn, turn left (go right for Bignor Roman Villa).

9 After a right bend, take the second signed path on the left, just after Malthouse Cottages. Pass through the garden below the house, then alongside a stream on the left. Ignore the first footbridge. The path soon crosses footbridges and comes out into an open field. Continue up the field to a stile left of the nearest telegraph post. Cross the next field via an uncultivated strip to Sutton.

The post-Roman era has been called the Dark Ages – though it was no intellectual desert. If there was a dark time, it was in the years of invasion, turbulence and change. The invaders themselves left no written records, but monks such as Gildas, Bede and Nennius chronicled the events of the period.

SAXONS AND VIKINGS
410–1066

Invasions & Saints

New masters replaced the Romans from 449, when German mercenaries – Saxons, Angles and Jutes – arrived at the invitation of a British leader, Vortigern. Their job was to help fend off foreign incursions, but instead they took the opportunity to establish their own rule in the south. Within 150 years much of the ex-Roman province was known as the Angles' Land – England. Meanwhile, the Britons continued to resist their invaders – commanded, according to legend, by King Arthur, who faced them in battle around the turn of the 6th century, culminating in the 12th and final battle on Mount Badon.

Religion was also about to undergo a profound change. In 565 a Celtic missionary monk, Columba, travelled to the Pictish lands in the north, and converted first their king, Bride, and then his people to Christianity. Pope Gregory, 30 years later, sent a missionary party to do the same for the English, and, under the protection of King Ethelbert, his man Augustine became the first Archbishop of Canterbury. In the 7th century churches sprang up across the country; landowners eager to secure their place in the afterlife provided land and funds for monasteries that soon accumulated huge wealth and influence. This was 'the age of saints'.

By now Britain was a patchwork of kingdoms, one of which, Mercia, set about swallowing up its neighbours by force and politics – particularly under its 8th-century king, Offa. His campaigns against the Welsh left an enduring legacy in Offa's Dyke, which still more or less marks the English Welsh boundary.

Then, in 789, a lightning raid on the Dorset coast signalled the arrival of a new threat – the Vikings.

THE NORSE CODE

For years the Vikings, or Norsemen, made sorties from Scandinavia to plunder the British coasts and their treasure-filled churches. After enduring several assaults, the monks on the Holy Island of Lindisfarne finally fled in 875, taking with them their beautifully illustrated Gospels. Gradually the Norsemen gained ground and established settlements – first in the north of Scotland, on Shetland and the Orkneys. But it didn't all go their way. Britain's inhabitants fought back, sometimes successfully – Viking leader Ragnor Lodbrook was captured and thrown into a snake-pit. His son, Ivar the Boneless, took his revenge by slaughtering the Northumbrians at York, and establishing Danish ascendancy in northern England.

Alfred, King of Wessex (the West Saxons), rallied his own people several times against the Danes. When not fighting the Danes, he bought their peace with gold – 'Danegeld'. In 886 Alfred's truce with the Danes divided England between Wessex, Mercia and the Danelaw – but this wasn't the end of the matter. Sporadic war continued between the Scandinavians and the Wessex kings, supported by the Welsh princes. Danish attacks on the Picts wiped out their kingdom of Fortriu. In its place emerged Alba, kingdom of the Scots: their king, Constantine II, turned back the tide and held the Danes at bay for 50 years. Life in Britain was unpredictable and sometimes violent. But that wasn't the whole picture. Scholarship, art and poetry flourished. New towns developed, law and administration regulated life, while the Saxons marked out an efficient system of shires and courts. Trade flourished and Britain was becoming affluent enough to attract the ambitious William of Normandy.

HISTORIC SITES

Glastonbury, Somerset: 8th-century abbey and legendary resting-place of King Arthur.

Wimborne Minster, Dorset: founded in 705, looted by Vikings and refounded by Edward the Confessor in 1043.

Burnsall, Yorkshire Dales: Viking gravestones in St Wilfrid's churchyard.

Ripon, North Yorkshire: 7th-century cathedral crypt (England's oldest).

Whitby Abbey, North Yorkshire: setting of the Synod of Whitby in 664.

St Laurence, Bradford-upon-Avon, Wiltshire: rare intact Saxon church.

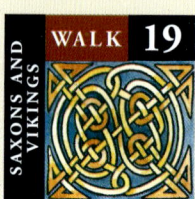

ABOUT • TINTAGEL

Steeped in Arthurian legend and lore, it's not surprising that Tintagel remains so popular. But this walk offers a different perpective on this famous landmark as it explores 'Din Tagell', part of the Dumnonia kingdom, the stronghold of a Celtic king.

Cornwall • SW ENGLAND

DISTANCE • 4 miles (6.4km)

TOTAL ASCENT • 262ft (80m)

PATHS • undulating, sometimes rocky coast path; quiet lanes and fields, some muddy after wet weather

TERRAIN • rugged cliffs, coastal farmland

GRADIENTS • some steep ascents and descents on coast path

REFRESHMENTS • Castle Beach Café at the entrance to Tintagel (April to end October); pubs and cafés in Tintagel

PARK • lay-by on the right at the bottom of the hill on the B3263 Tintagel to Boscastle road, just past Willapark Manor Hotel

OS MAP • Explorer 111 Bude, Boscastle & Tintagel

Tintagel's Celtic connection

❶ Cross the road and follow the sign to the coast path, which leads down a tarmac drive to pass Trout Leap restaurant and right over the stream on a railed footbridge. Follow the rocky path through the ruins of Trewethet Mill (Celtic Trust) and cross the stream to enter Rocky Valley (NT). By the next bridge keep straight on to join the coast path.

❷ The path veers left and continues up a long flight of steps to cross Bossiney Common above Benoath Cove, then drops steeply down concrete steps to a gritty track by Bossiney Haven.

❸ Walk straight on up concrete steps and over a stile, then down steps to cross the stream via a stile/wooden-railed footbridge and on to Willapark (NT). Follow the path up steps and through a wooden gate; keep straight ahead (herringbone wall, left) to reach the top. Turn right and walk to the end of the headland to enjoy the views ahead. Retrace your steps to the coast path.

❹ Continue right as the path undulates along Smith's Cliff, and through a kissing gate above Gullastem. The path leads on to Barras Nose (NT) via a stile and gate; follow the path to descend over craggy terrain to Tintagel Haven and the castle entrance via a footbridge over the stream.

❺ Turn left and walk inland past the English Heritage shop.

❻ Just past the toilets follow the coast path signs steeply right and uphill to pass another entrance to the castle, then left along Glebe

DIFFICULTY ✱✱

Cliff to reach St Materiana's Church. Turn left and follow the lane inland to Tintagel village.

❼ Turn left; follow the road to a sharp left bend, with Pendryn Guest House on the right. Go straight ahead on the track, signed to the coast path. Cross the stone stile and the next field, then cross a wooden stile and go straight on, keeping the wall on your right. Go

through the gate/stile and follow the wall round to the right to rejoin the coast path on Smith's Cliff. Retrace your steps to meet the gritty track by Bossiney Haven (Point 3).

❽ Turn right and walk inland to the edge of Bossiney via a kissing gate; toilets on the right. Cross the B3263; turn left and follow the pavement back to your car.

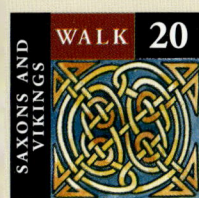
ABOUT · IONA

Iona is still considered a sacred island and has long been associated with the spread of Christianity in Britain. In 563 St Columba landed on the island and founded a monastery. The monks deserted in 825 when the monastery suffered a series of savage Norse raids.

Strathclyde · SCOTLAND

DISTANCE • 6 miles (9.6km)

TOTAL ASCENT • 140ft (43m)

PATHS • mostly good, even in bad weather

TERRAIN • made-up roads, farm tracks, hill paths, grass and beach

GRADIENTS • flat to moderate

REFRESHMENTS • in summer, restaurant and tea rooms in village

PARK • car park at the jetty on Fionnphort; ferry to Iona

OS MAP • Pathfinder 341 Iona & Bunessan

The missionaries and myths of Iona

❶ After leaving the ferry, walk straight ahead, passing the Spar shop and the entrance to the nunnery. At the end of the road turn left, go through a gate and continue along a rough road until it reaches a collection of farm buildings.

❷ Turn left and follow a straight road until you reach a crossroads. Turn right and head west, along another straight road, towards the coast. Go through a metal gate, fork left and cross the machair (low lying land formed from sand and shell fragments) to the beach.

❸ Turn left and walk along the beach of a double bay then turn left and head across the machair until you reach a stony path. Turn right on to this and continue up hill until you reach a lochan.

❹ Take the left-hand path round the lochan. Follow it across a heather moor, past a series of mounds and downhill to the beach at St Columba's Bay, where Columba first landed in AD 563.

❺ Return by the same route but at the end of the stony path keep

DIFFICULTY ✳✳

Map labels: Caolas Annraidh; STAFFA ferry; Carraig an Daimh; Dun I ▲ 100; Auchabhaich; IONA; abbey; ❼ graveyard; Maclean's Cross; ★ BAILE MÓR; St Ronan's Bay; 1 START; ferry; Sound of Iona; Camas Cuil an t-Saimh; ❻; ❷; nunnery; FIONNPHORT; Cnoc Druidean; Lochan Staoineig ❹; Druim an Aoineidh ▲ 74; ❺; St Columba's Bay; N; 0 1 Mile; 0 1 Kilometre; Sound

· DON'T MISS ·

The neighbouring island of **Staffa** *can be reached on a boat trip from Iona. From the landing spot you can walk along the top of the natural hexagonal basalt columns and enter Fingal's Cave, where the sound of the sea in the cave inspired Felix Mendelssohn to write* Hebrides Overture.

straight along the line of a fence and when it ends follow the faint track and a series of stone markers back to the road and the gate.

❻ Turn right through the gate and head east along the road. At the coast follow the road left to the village. Turn left at the jetty and right into the nunnery, exit by the far gate and follow the road to the

abbey. The abbey and nunnery, founded in 1203 by monks of the Benedictine order were only restored in the early twentieth century and the cell where St Columba slept excavated.

❼ Turn right through the gate into the graveyard. Note that only three of the tall crosses built here remain: the 9th-century St John's

Cross, 10th-century St Martin's Cross and 15th-century Maclean's Cross mark the remains of the eight Norwegian and many Scottish kings that were buried here, Follow the path anti-clockwise and exit by the far gate. Turn right into the abbey grounds. From here return to the road, turn left and follow it back to the village.

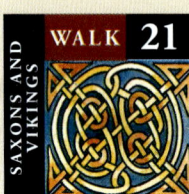

WALK 21

SAXONS AND VIKINGS

ABOUT • LYVENNET VALLEY

This walk visits a series of sites including Ewe Close and Ewe Locks, part of the ancient kingdom of Urien, warrior king of Rheged. The Rheged Visitor Centre, on the edge of Penrith, celebrates the time of this old British kingdom and is well worth a visit.

Cumbria • N ENGLAND

DISTANCE • 6½ miles (10.4km)

TOTAL ASCENT • 720ft (219m)

PATHS • some unclear. Can be extremely muddy

TERRAIN • pastureland and open fell

GRADIENTS • some steep grassy slopes

REFRESHMENTS • The Butchers' Arms, Crosby Ravensworth

PARK • by the village hall in Crosby Ravensworth

OS MAP • Outdoor Leisure 19 Howgill Fells & Upper Eden Valley

Valley of the kings

DIFFICULTY ✳✳✳

❶ Cross the bridge opposite village hall, turn right down left bank of beck. Turn left, signed Wickerslack, bear left between sheds, join track zigzagging up field beyond. At the top go ahead through a gate, cross field between telegraph poles. Over crown of the hill, aim for field corner nearest buildings. Cross stile and immediately another, walk diagonally across to a stile behind Crake Trees farm.

❷ Behind farm, turn left to a gate and a zigzag track up a field. The path is indistinct by remains of a stone enclosure. Follow its left-hand edge to a post and a thorn bush to your left. Cross ditch by the thorn and follow it to a wall. Turn right, wall on left, through two gates to a junction of tracks.

❸ Left through gate then right up road. In 100yds (91m) go left, pass a farm and down a lane, signed Haber. At the end, go through gate, bear right to a track. At the end, go through a gate into a field. Go half-left to bottom left-hand corner. Take right-hand gate, continue down the field; cut the corner at the bottom to go right, through gate. Bear left to Haber farm and go left of buildings. Turn left below cow sheds, go right through a gap in field boundary. Cross field and through a gap in wall. Turn left on to a muddy track, continue to the bottom.

❹ Turn right. Pass High Dalebanks. On grassy track follow signs to Oddendale (wall left). When track is enclosed by boulders, turn left to a bridge. Cross bridge and a stile, climb bank, bear right, between two humps. Walk to Slacks ruin. In farmyard bear right, through gate. Turn left to Lane Head. At top of farmyard (ruin) go through gate to open fell. Turn left, follow grassy

track. In 100yds (91m) go right, to corner of wall on left. In 30yds (27m) beyond fence in field on left, the Roman road crosses your track. Beyond is Ewe Close.

❺ As track descends, carry on across fell (no footpath) for 200yds (183m) to Ewe Locks. Turn left downhill for ¾ mile (1.2km) on to track, Slack Randy. Turn right, by a boulder on to a good track.

❻ Right again through metal gate; double back across fellside. Follow path down to gate in left corner of field. Fence on right, pass through another gate. At crossroads of paths go left, to Lyvennet Beck.

❼ Ford beck (footbridge 200yds/ 183m upstream). Go through gate, turn left over a bridge to another gate. Ascend track to a gate. Turn left across field to a stile next to a

gate, continue through three fields to Holme Bridge.

❽ Left over bridge then right over a footbridge into a field. At the far side, cross a stile and continue with beck on your right. Follow the path along the bottom of a steep bank, cross a stile and turn right over a ladder stile by a bridge. Turn left through a gate on to a lane, at the end turn left to village hall.

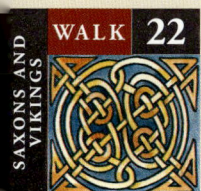
ABOUT • OFFA'S DYKE

In the 8th century Offa, King of Mercia ordered the construction of a dyke. It was to be both a physical border and emblematic of the division between Mercia and Welsh lands. This walk starts in Llanymynech, located in England and Wales.

Shropshire • C ENGLAND

DISTANCE • 6 miles (9.6km)

TOTAL ASCENT • 450ft (137m)

PATHS • clear paths, short section of road

TERRAIN • woodland, heathland, canal towpath

GRADIENTS • one steep ascent

REFRESHMENTS • tea rooms and pubs in Llanymynech

PARK • car park off B4398, behind Dolphin Inn and post office

OS MAP • Explorer 240 Oswestry, Chirk, Ellesmere & Pant

From 'sea to sea' along Offa's Dyke

DIFFICULTY ✲✲

❶ At the far end of the car park, take the towpath east for 55yds (50m). Pass under the bridge, ascend steps to the A483, cross the road and walk north for 164yds (150m). Take the lane ahead signed Offa's Dyke Path (don't bear right).

❷ Just past The Coach House, take the right fork; 11yds (10m) beyond Peny Foel Cottages take the right fork. Go to the end of the tarmac (ignore Footpath 26 sign). Cross the stile that leads behind the end house, and in 109yds (100m) ascend steeply, left, signed Offa's Dyke Path. At the top turn left and cross the stile.

❸ At the quarry turn left and follow the Offa's Dyke Path signs carefully for 656yds (600m) round the foot of the rocks, until you reach a gate to the golf course. Follow the path to the left round the edge of the green.

❹ Follow Offa's Dyke Path in and out of the woods along the fourteenth hole. Beyond the green, at a waymarker, bear left and leave the golf course, without losing height, passing through scrub and woodland. In 437yds (400m) cross a stile into a coniferous plantation; 109yds (100m) beyond this, reach a redundant stile in a small gully. Do not follow Offa's Dyke Path left, but keep straight on ahead on a ridge to a stile beside a vegetable garden.

❺ Do not turn right to tarmac, but go straight ahead (waymarker in undergrowth), through woods. In 55yds (50m) keep left, hugging the escarpment edge. In 219yds (200m) take the kissing gate into

pasture. Continue, keeping the field bounday on your left, and ignore the second gate on the left in 11yds (10m).

❻ In 164yds (150m) pass through a bigger gate and go straight ahead along a track (fence rejoins in 98yds/90m). Go through another gate in 77yds (70m) and continue along a narrow muddy path, ignoring the left fork. In 273yds

(250m) reach a gravel track (building 33yds/30m ahead) and turn right.

❼ In 197yds (180m), where the track bends left to pass a dilapidated corrugated shed ahead, keep straight on up a muddy bridleway to a cream-painted stone-built cottage. Follow its access track for about 547yds (500m) to a T-junction at Green

Corner. Turn left and continue down the lane that becomes a road through a new estate, to the main road.

❽ Turn right on to the main road for about 200yds (183m); just after the 40mph sign turn left down Rhiw Revel Lane. Across the bridge turn left and left again on to the towpath. Follow the towpath back to Llanymynech.

Map labels

Llynclys Hill Nature Reserve

OSWESTRY

A495

PORTH-Y-WAEN

cottage

Offa's Dyke Path

Crickheath Hill

Green Corner

A483

Offa's Dyke

PANT

golf course

River Tanat

Offa's Dyke Path

Llanymynech Hill

Offa's Dyke

quarry

A483

sewage farm

N

The Coach House

heritage area

LLANYMYNECH

Shropshire Union Canal

P
1 START

WELSHPOOL

The Lion Hotel

B4398

B4398

A483

0 .... 1/2 Mile

0 .... 500 Metres

Through Viking York

The Jorvik Viking Centre, located on the site of the Coppergate excavations in York, vividly recreates a 9th-century settlement whose winding streets are still walked today.

From Ivar the Boneless to Eric Bloodaxe

In 866 Danish invaders, led by Ivar the Boneless, sailed up the River Ouse and captured York. Since the Roman Legions had left in around 410, the city had been captured by the Anglians in 525, and become Christian when King Edwin was baptised in a new wooden church in 627. By the 9th century, York was a prominent centre of trade and learning – a rich prize for the Viking invaders. York became the capital of a Viking kingdom, with new streets, many more buildings – some several storeys high – and a thriving merchant class. Some of York's churches were founded, and the Minster rebuilt. The Viking reign was brief, however. The last Viking king, Eric Bloodaxe, died at the Battle of Stainmore in 954, and was succeeded by the English King Athelstan.

In Viking footsteps

The Romans built a long, straight road from the south-west into the heart of York. Typically, the Vikings ignored it, forming their own, twisting path down to the river bank – Micklegate, the 'great street'. Irregular, diagonal routes served them best, linking their churches – such as Holy Trinity in Micklegate and St Mary Bishophill, both probably founded in late Viking times – and running alongside the River Ouse. It was the river that provided them with access to the sea, and along its banks and those of its

tributary, the Foss, fish were landed, craftsmen made their wares and merchants set up up their stalls.

The Coppergate excavations revealed the complex life of the densely packed Viking city. Nearby, the Danish kings had their palace; their quay beside Ouse Bridge, built out from the treacherous, muddy banks of the river, is still known as King's Staith. The bridge itself was originally a Viking structure of wood, and, except for ferries, was the only river crossing in the city for a thousand years. Street names reflect their Viking origins: many end in 'gate' – *gata* is still the Scandinavian word for a street. Goodramgate was the street of Guthrum, one of the Viking kings, and Coney Street was the King's Street.

York's greatest church, the Minster, is near the site of the first wooden church. There was a 9th-century cemetery under the present south transept. A little way beyond the city walls, originally Roman and repaired and strengthened through the centuries, the northern Earls, who came to power at the end of the Viking period, built themselves a stronghold. Known as Earlsborough, it occupied a site between Bootham and Marygate. Linking Earlsborough to the heart of the city, the winding street, now successively Lendal, Coney Street and Spurriergate, brought the Viking inhabitants back to their wooden bridge and the foot of their new 'great street', Micklegate.

WALK 23   VIKING WAYS AND THE VITAL RIVER

❶ From the car park, turn right, then right again at the traffic-lights. Go through Micklegate Bar. Take the next right (Priory Street). At the end, turn left, pass the church, then turn right along Bishophill Senior. Opposite the Golden Ball pub, turn left down Carr's Lane. At the bottom, turn right along Skeldergate, keeping left at the fork. Go under Skeldergate Bridge. Continue along the river bank and cross the Millennium Bridge.

❷ Go by the white gate and walk up Maple Grove to Fulford Road. Turn left towards the city centre. Walk up Piccadilly between the Travelodge and

medieval tower (Fishergate Postern). After the mini-roundabout, turn left along a glazed passage signed Castle Area, Jorvik Viking Centre. Go right, through glass doors, and out into St Mary's Square. The Viking Centre is diagonally right.

❸ After your visit, continue from the square up the slope between the Viking Centre and Boots store. At the top of the slope, turn right. At the traffic-lights, go straight on, and after the Marks and Spencer store turn left up the Shambles. At the top, turn right. Go half-right across King's Square into Goodramgate. Where the road bends right, turn left

and follow the road, passing between York Minster and St Michael-le-Belfrey Church. Continue up High Petergate and through Bootham Bar.

❹ Cross at the lights and go up Bootham. Turn left down Marygate by the circular tower. Just beyond the church, go left through the archway. Continue ahead to leave the gardens by the lodge. Cross and keep ahead down Lendal, and straight on to the traffic-lights by St Michael's Church. Turn right, cross Ouse Bridge, go through two more sets of traffic-lights and up Micklegate. Pass through Micklegate Bar. Turn left back to

the car park.

Distance: 5¼ miles (8.4km)

Total ascent: 75ft (23m)

Paths: city pavements

Terrain: historic city centre and riverside

Gradients: one climb, up Micklegate

Refreshments: very wide selection in York city centre

Park: in pay-and-display car park in Nunnery Lane, off A1036

OS Map: Explorer 290 York, Selby & Tadcaster

Difficulty: ✷

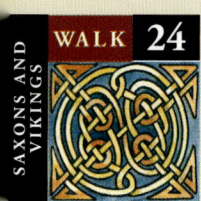

ABOUT • EARLS BARTON

Earls Barton is one of the finest examples of Saxon architecture and building. Extensive church building in the 9th century marked the rise of Christianity in Britain and Earls Barton stands as testimony to the endurance of the church.

Northamptonshire • C ENGLAND

DISTANCE • 7½ miles (12km)

TOTAL ASCENT • 75m (246ft)

PATHS • outside the village the route follows good field paths (can be muddy) and well-surfaced tracks. Patches of nettles by the river

TERRAIN • open farmland

REFRESHMENTS • café in the village square, near the church

PARK • car park east of the village centre and street parking

OS MAP • Explorer 224 Corby, Kettering & Wellingborough

The architects of Earls Barton

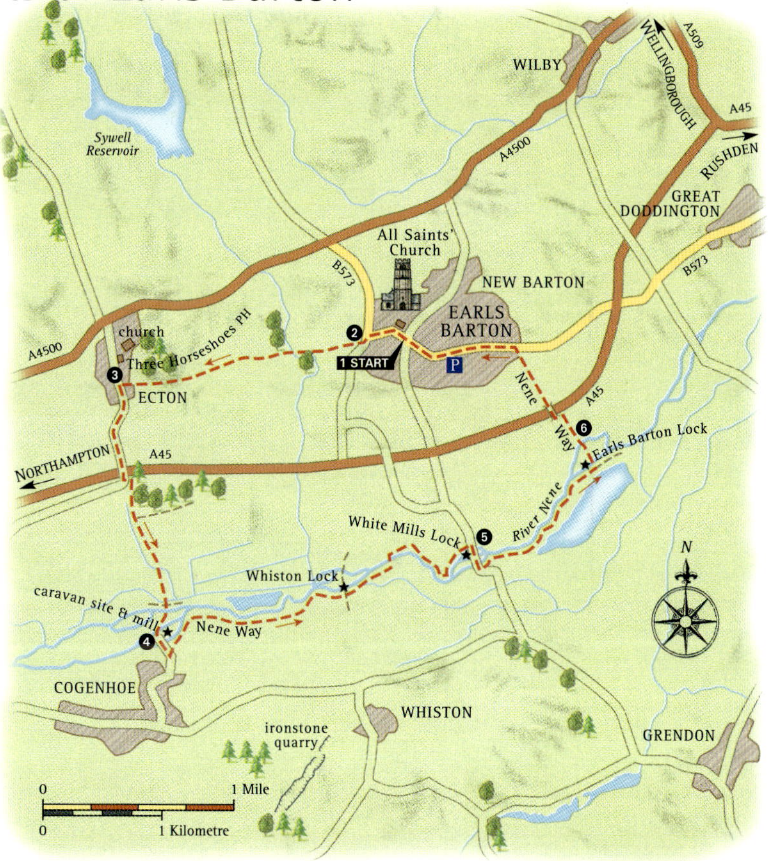

❶ Leave the churchyard by the western gate and walk out of the village along West Street to a main road. Turn left, continue for 100yds (91m) and pass through a kissing gate on the right.

❷ Walk down the field, passing a power line post to a stile at the bottom. Continue along the edge of the next field, leaving over a stream. Keep the same direction up the next field to a gap in the top hedge, and carry on along a path across two fields towards Ecton, which can eventually be seen ahead. In pasture, cross to a gate in the far right-hand corner and walk out on to the main street.

❸ Turn left, continue for ½ mile (800m) beyond Ecton and cross a road bridge. Immediately after, go left on to a track descending beside the main road and turn right on to a farm track across the fields. At the far end, continue ahead (on the right fork) along a fenced path. Ignore the crossing track ahead and continue over a branch of the Nene by a packhorse bridge into a flood meadow beyond. Another bridge by a sluice lock leads into a caravan site at Cogenhoe Mill.

❹ Carry on across more arteries of the river to pass the mill and then immediately turn left through a gate into a field, signed The Nene Way. A riverside path leads downstream, past Whiston Lock to a bridge, ¼ mile (400m) beyond. Cross the river and continue down to White Mills Lock, where the path emerges on to a lane.

❺ Walk right, cross the river by three bridges, then turn left into a picnic area. Follow a riverside track past a gravel works and then

DIFFICULTY ✳✳

on beside a lake to reach Earls Barton Lock. Cross the river.

❻ Over the river, continue through a meadow, leaving by a stile by a mill cottage. From here a track climbs back up the hill and over the main road. Turn left at the top on to Doddington Road and return to Earls Barton.

• DON'T MISS •

Ecton's church is another church worth a visit (keyholders are listed in the porch). As you walk through the village towards the church, note the lovely mellow ironstone houses and the 18th-century village poor school, provided by John Palmer. Long before the Nene was improved by the installation of weirs and locks in the mid-18th century, it was an important transport route. Saxon builders brought the faced stone blocks for the tower of Earls Barton's church along it from quarries at Barnack located near Peterborough.

Map labels: WILBY, WELLINGBOROUGH, A509, A45, RUSHDEN, Sywell Reservoir, A4500, GREAT DODDINGTON, B573, All Saints' Church, NEW BARTON, EARLS BARTON, church, Three Horseshoes PH, A4500, ECTON, 1 START, Nene Way, A45, Earls Barton Lock, NORTHAMPTON, A45, White Mills Lock, River Nene, caravan site & mill, Whiston Lock, Nene Way, COGENHOE, WHISTON, GRENDON, ironstone quarry, N, 0 1 Mile, 0 1 Kilometre

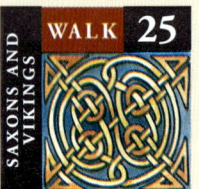
ABOUT • LLANGORSE LAKE

The crannog (artificial island) in Llangorse Lake is thought to be the ancient seat of the kings of the kingdom of Brycheiniog. This walk circumnavigates the lake before an ascent offers striking views of the lake and the Brecon Beacons.

Powys • WALES

DISTANCE • 8 miles (13km)

TOTAL ASCENT • 900ft (274m)

PATHS • good; slippery in places. Lakeside paths may be underwater after prolonged heavy rain in winter months

TERRAIN • tracks, field paths, stiles, tarmac roads; roots in forest

GRADIENTS • some steep sections

REFRESHMENTS • caravan park shop at start; pubs and a shop/post office in Llangorse village.

PARK • car park beside public lavatories, between caravan park and sailing club

OS MAP • Outdoor Leisure 13 Brecon Beacons – Eastern Area

Llangorse – 'lake of the sunken island'

❶ Aim for a concrete footbridge, left of the caravan park on Llangorse Common. Go diagonally left, soon observe the crannog, cross more fields, circumnavigating the lake (partly fringed with woodland), to reach St Gastyn Church at Llangasty-Tal-y-llyn.

❷ Turn right. After Llan (a house) take a waymarked footpath, left. Soon walk with the hedge on your right. Turn right, cross two fields diagonally, to a sunken lane, left of a farm. Turn right to a minor road.

❸ Go left. Take the first left turn, signed Cathedine half a mile. Turn right, beside Rectory Cottage. Take stiles through three fields; cross the fourth field diagonally to the B4560 (fast road). Turn right for 55yds (50m). Take a rough track to the right of farm buildings.

❹ Take a less distinct track (blue waymarker) before the ford, ascending along the left side of a lightly wooded stream. In an eroded gully find a gate up to the left. Follow this sunken lane until it peters out.

❺ Turn left, above a fence and broken wall, then soon go through an old gate (blue waymarker) to pass a farmhouse ruin. Continue on a path, now through bracken, until 55yds (50m) before the track descends to a gate.

❻ Turn sharp right, uphill, on a zigzagging green path. Turn left at a fence, then left again at fence corner. Descend to a converted barn. Continue to find a sheep track along field's left edge, go down to a gate among larches, beside overgrown, broken wall.

❼ Walk through the forest, back into bracken. About 100yds (91m) beyond a stream crossing, descend beside a farm track. At the next gate cross the farm track, taking the line of greatest slope down the field to the riding and climbing centre below.

❽ Turn right, then right again towards Cae-cottrel (farm). Take a stile on the left. Skirt this field to the left. Pass into the next field by a gap in the hedgerow (tiny stream), skirting left again, to farm buildings and a track.

❾ Turn right, following the lanes to Llangorse village. At a blind corner, immediately before St Paulinus's churchyard, take a narrow signed footpath beside a house. Cross fields to return to the start of the walk.

• DON'T MISS •

St Gastyn Church at Llangasty-Tal-y-llyn is impressive for the simple beauty of its location and architecture (inside and out). The Brecknock Museum in Brecon is also worth a visit, as is Y Gaer (also called Brecon Gaer), about a mile (1.6km) from Brecon – a Roman fort, dated c. AD 80, and occupied well into the 4th century.

LLANFIHANGEL TAL-Y-LLYN

N

caravan park

Llangorse Common

1 START

outdoor activity centre

sailing club

crannog

Llangorse Lake

TALGARTH

B4560

St Paulinus

LLANGORSE

❾ farm

Cae-cottrel

❽

Cwm

Mynydd Llangorse

❷ St Gastyn Church

LLANGASTY-TAL-Y-LLYN

Llan

❼

PENNORTH

CATHEDINE

Home Farm

❸ Neuadd Farm

Rectory Cottage

❻

BRECON

farmhouse ruin

Nant-y-felin

❹

❺

Afon Llynfi

A40

Alt yr Esgair

River Usk

LLANSANTFFRAED

ABERGAVENNY

DIFFICULTY ✳✳✳

B4560

0   1 Mile

0   1 Kilometre

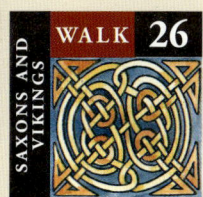

ABOUT • WINCHESTER

Even before the arrival of the Romans, Winchester was an important tribal centre, and under King Alfred's rule it became the capital of England. Winchester Cathedral was begun in 1079 and the library contains a 10th-century copy of Bede's history.

Hampshire • SE ENGLAND

DISTANCE • 6 miles (9.6km)

TOTAL ASCENT • 220ft (67m)

PATHS • well-marked throughout; some mud after rain on water meadow paths

TERRAIN • street pavements, downland, water meadows

GRADIENTS • flat, except for ascent and descent of St Catherine's Hill

REFRESHMENTS • wide choice in town

PARK • Chesil Street long-stay car park, or (Mon–Fri, 07.30–18.30, Sat 07.30–1800) Park-and-Ride from Bar End (signed from M3 Junctions 9 and 10) to King Alfred Statue, Broadway

OS MAP • Explorer 132 Winchester, New Alresford & East Meon

Up the River Itchen to Saxon Winchester

❶ At King Alfred's Statue look, as he does, up the High Street, with Abbey Gardens, site of the Nunnaminster, to the left. A few yards up the street, turn left into Abbey Passage to see the excavations of the abbey church. Return to the High Street and turn right. At City Bridge, opposite City Mill, turn right into The Weirs for the Riverside Walk (look out for the remains of a Roman wall). At a signpost, turn left over the River Itchen, then right to join a road for 100yds (91m). Cross at the corner into a private road.

❷ In 50yds (46m), signed Itchen Way, turn right across the river. Continue through water meadows, with the river on your left, to a road bridge. Turn left over bridge, then right into a parking area.

❸ With the river on your right, take the path for St Catherine's Hill under the railway bridge. Where the path divides, take the left fork. Follow the clear path to a crossing of paths at the summit. Turn right to the miz-maze.

❹ Facing the maze at the point where you first reached it, turn right (the beech copse beyond the maze is now on your left). Walk to the edge of the hill for views of Winchester, right, and the Hospital of St Cross, left. Turn left and walk along the top of the hill, with the water meadows on your right. At a gap in the ramparts, take the long flight of wooden steps to the bottom of Plague Pits Valley.

❺ Turn left on to the path by the Itchen Navigation. Go under the railway bridge and at a junction turn right, signed St Cross. Cross the Itchen, then turn right on to a farm road. The footpath continues ahead through a stile.

❻ Continue straight ahead on the footpath past St Cross Hospital (detour left to visit). At the road, cross diagonally right and continue through the water meadows.

❼ At Winchester College buildings, turn right, then left into College Walk. Turn left into College Street (keep ahead for Wolvesey Palace). At the end of College Street, turn right, go through Kingsgate, then right for the Close and cathedral.

❽ With your back to the West Front and the site of Old and New Minsters, walk left of the war memorial, between trees, to the City Museum. Cross The Square for the High Street. Turn right for King Alfred's Statue.

• DON'T MISS •

Hyde Abbey Church, King Alfred's final resting place. There is nothing to see, but the information panels in the 15th-century Hyde Gate (King Alfred Place) explain the abbey's layout. A self-guided walk is available from the Tourist Information Centre.

Map labels:

FULFLOOD · site of Hyde Abbey Church · B3330 · WINNALL · BASINGSTOKE · NEWBURY · M3 · B3040 · Winchester City Museum · **1 START** · King Alfred Statue · B3404 · City Mill · A31 · Chesil St · Wolvesey Castle · Abbey Gardens · Winchester Cathedral · Winchester College · **7** · BAR END · **2** · water meadows · park & ride · B3330 · STANMORE · B3335 · M3 · A31 · Junction 10 · **3** · hospital · Itchen · ST CROSS · **6** · Miz-maze · **4** · St Catherine's Hill · N · Itchen Navigation · farm · River · water meadows · **5** · Plague Pits Valley · M3 · Junction 11 · A3090 · SOUTHAMPTON · A3090 · Twyford Down · DIFFICULTY ✷✷

0 ······ ½ Mile
0 ······ 500 Metres

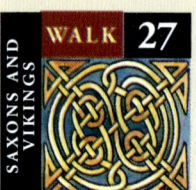

ABOUT · BURPHAM

King Alfred established over 30 burhs, or settlements, along the boundary of the Kingdom of Wessex to protect his citizens from the plundering Danes. Set near the lovely Arundel Castle, this walk explores the fortified Anglo-Saxon settlement at Burpham.

West Sussex · SE ENGLAND

DISTANCE · 5 miles (8km)

TOTAL ASCENT · 500ft (152m)

PATHS · clearly waymarked tracks and quiet lanes; some muddy sections

TERRAIN · chalk downland and forest; three stiles

GRADIENTS · gentle main ascent; shorter, steeper descent and ascent near end

REFRESHMENTS · George and Dragon, Burpham; picnic bench above River Arun

PARK · free car park by George and Dragon (not part of pub) at Burpham; plenty of roadside parking in village

OS MAP · Explorer 121 Arundel & Pulborough

Burpham: Anglo-Saxon settlement

❶ Cross the road from the car park entrance and take the path into the churchyard. Keep right of the church, and by a signpost cross steps over the churchyard wall. Follow the right edge of the field. At a road, turn right, then keep forward downhill at the next road junction.

❷ Take the next left, Coombe Lane; this becomes unsurfaced by a house and a pumping station. On emerging into a field, fork right at a waymark post, on a rising path marked with a yellow arrow, and soon climb a stile. Turn left at a junction of tracks at the top.

❸ After the track curves round to the right, keep right at the first junction and turn left at the second. Take the next bridleway off to the right, through a gate and uphill. After passing through a belt of trees and a gate, the track veers slightly right, passing to the left of the trig point (summit pillar).

❹ Do not pass through the next gate just before a major track junction, but turn sharp right keeping in the field with the trig point, along the left edge of the field. Where the fence on your left reaches a corner, turn left along a row of trees as waymarked.

❺ Beyond the next gate enter a small field surrounded by trees and keep forward at a junction as signed, picking up a woodland track alongside a fence on your right. Avoid the next signed footpath on the right, and keep to the bridleway.

❻ Turn right at a five-way junction, then immediately fork

right. Soon reach another signed junction of bridleways and keep forward downhill, on a sunken path. At the foot of the wooded slope turn left and left again.

❼ Where the main track is about to rise, fork right through a gate and follow the valley floor. Turn

right at a signpost, up through a gate. Just after, keep forward to ascend steeply where main track bends left. The path leads along a wooded strip between fields.

❽ Emerge by a gate into a field, and keep forward to a gate into woodland. Follow the woodland path downhill and turn right along the road. In Wepham village, turn left at the road junction.

❾ Where the road bends right, take the signed path rising diagonally, on the left, up the bank

· DON'T MISS ·

St Mary's Church in Burpham has two fine 12th-century Norman arches, one with a zig-zag decoration, the other with grotesque carvings of human and ape-like heads.

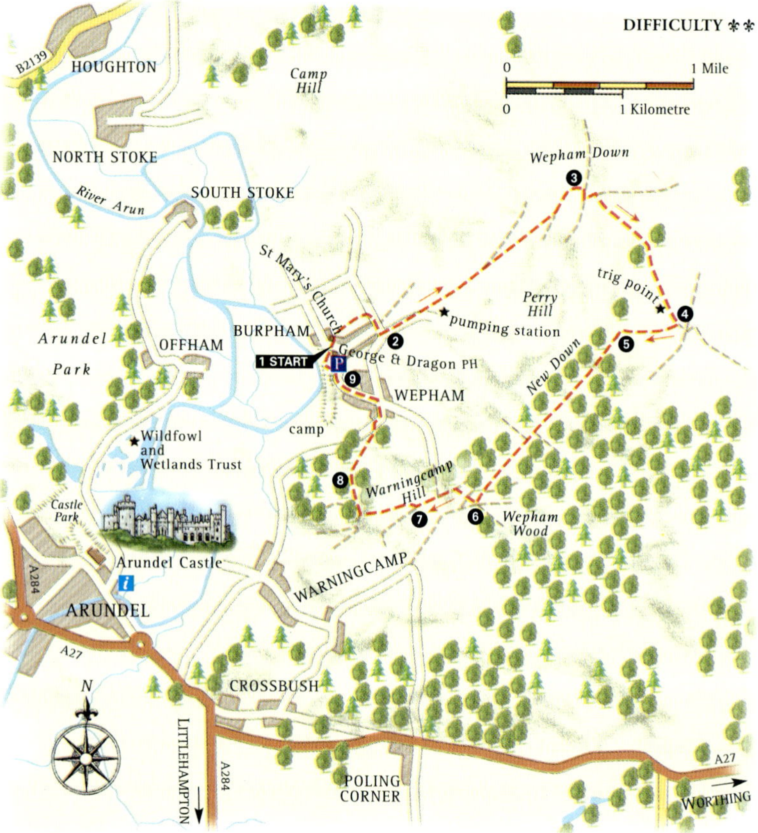

of the Anglo-Saxon camp (or burh). Enter a recreation field via a stile, cross to the stile opposite (where a picnic bench just to the left gives a fine view of Arundel Castle and the river) and turn right to return to the car park.

DIFFICULTY ✱✱

0 ——— 1 Mile

0 ——— 1 Kilometre

HOUGHTON

B2139

Camp Hill

NORTH STOKE

River Arun

SOUTH STOKE

St Mary's Church

Wepham Down

❸

trig point

Perry Hill

❹

Arundel Park

OFFHAM

BURPHAM

1 START

❷

George & Dragon PH

❾

WEPHAM

pumping station

New Down

❺

Wildfowl and Wetlands Trust

camp

❽

Warningcamp Hill

❻

Wepham Wood

❼

Castle Park

Arundel Castle

ℹ️

ARUNDEL

A284

A27

N

LITTLEHAMPTON

A284

CROSSBUSH

WARNINGCAMP

POLING CORNER

A27

WORTHING

Some time in the 1070s, Bishop Odo of Bayeux commissioned a tapestry to celebrate his half-brother William's victory at Hastings. The resulting medieval action adventure, with spies, chases and violence, is our most vivid account of the Norman Conquest.

THE NORMANS

1066–1300

Era of Conquest

In the Bayeux Tapestry, the dying Edward the Confessor bequeaths his kingdom to William of Normandy; when Harold Godwineson takes the crown instead, William invades and kills his rival at the Battle of Hastings in 1066. Over subsequent years, William stamped out a succession of revolts, confiscating English lands and awarding them to his own men. The Normans were here to stay, and they brought with them new styles – the tapestry contrasts droopy-moustachioed Saxons with their shaven-headed enemies – and a new tongue, making Norman French the language of court and nobility. Among the most immediate effects of the invasion were the hundreds of stone castles that sprouted up across the country, and the massive cathedrals that were built in Durham, Chichester, Ely, Norwich and elsewhere, often on the sites of Anglo-Saxon cathedrals. The Scottish king, Malcolm III, had submitted to William at Abernethy in 1072, but continued to raid the Northumbrian territories; and the English-Welsh border or Marcher lands provided another flashpoint, where Norman lords were installed to make repeated inroads into Powys and Gwynedd. But by 1086 England, at least, was secure and William could survey his possessions in the Domesday Book.

CRUSADES AND CONFLICT

The Norman dynasty held fast until another squabble over the crown turned into Civil War between William's grandson, Stephen, and cousin Matilda, wife of Geoffrey of Anjou. Matilda's son won the day, in 1154, for the Angevin cause, taking the crown as Henry II. His marriage to Eleanor of Aquitaine created a vast empire stretching from the Pyrenees to Scotland. Nevertheless, he's chiefly remembered for his long-running feud with Thomas Becket, Archbishop of Canterbury, whose insistence on clerical independence led to his brutal murder in the cathedral.

Richard the Lionheart, Henry's heir, spent most of his time fighting Turks in the Holy Land. Along with pilgrimages, crusades were the main mass events of the time: crowds flocked to answer the rallying calls of churchmen such as Giraldus Cambrensis, whose chronicles provide a colourful glimpse of 12th-century life. The crusaders brought back Oriental materials and fashions – women began wearing Mohammedan veils or wimples, hiding their faces, while still showing off their figures in tightly bodiced dresses.

Richard was succeeded by his brother John, whose bad press stems from the loss of his French lands and excessive cruelty to opponents. To keep the peace with his increasingly dissatisfied barons, John signed the Magna Carta in 1215, laying down the limitations of royal power and the rights of subjects.

By the 13th century Britain was an uneasy balancing act of feudal kingdoms and principalities, with the English king as overlord. This status was challenged in Wales by Llywelyn the Last, who refused to pay tribute to Edward I. Edward's response was rapid and devastating: his troops forged through Wales, leaving a ring of mighty fortresses. The principality was divided into English-style counties and the king's heir, Edward, was made their nominal prince.

In Scotland, Edward set about championing John Balliol, his candidate for the throne, in the face of opposition from Robert the Bruce. Although Edward's was successful in taking the Scottish 'stone of destiny' from Scone, the Scots were not beaten, and Britain entered the 14th century simmering with rebellions and resentments.

HISTORIC SITES

Oxford University, Oxon: founded by French scholars in 1167.

Cambridge University, Cambs: founded by breakaway members of Oxford University in 1209.

Lincoln, Lincs: Norman-Gothic cathedral and the 12th-century Jew's House.

Caernarfon, Gwynedd: Edward I's imposing fortress.

Windsor Castle, Berks: built by William the Conqueror in 1070.

Dunfermline: ruins of 12th-century abbey founded by Malcolm III and palace where he married his queen, Margaret.

• ABOUT •

Above the River Wear sit the imposing cathedral and castle – once the centre of power of the prince-bishops. In the 11th century William I conferred wide-ranging powers on the bishopric – effectively making them kings of the north.

Durham • N ENGLAND

DISTANCE • 1½ miles (2.4km)

TOTAL ASCENT • 300ft (91m)

PATHS • city pavements and riverside paths

TERRAIN • fortress rock with castle and cathedral, and ravine of the River Wear

GRADIENTS • moderate climbs from Market Place to Palace Green and from river bank to St Oswald's Church; otherwise easy

REFRESHMENTS • available throughout the centre of Durham, including on Palace Green and in the cathedral

PARK • city centre car parks in Durham, the Prince Bishop car park is the most convenient

OS MAP • Explorer 308 Durham & Sunderland, Chester-le-Street

The mighty prince-bishops, overlords of the North

❶ From the statue of Lord Londonderry in the Market Place, follow his horse's nose to pass the Nationwide building society and go up Saddler Street. Ascend the hill for 164yds (150m) and turn right up Owengate, signed Cathedral and Castle, and on to Palace Green.

❷ At the top of the hill, turn right, to follow the wall for 55yds (50m) to the entrance of the castle. After visiting the castle return to the entrance and keep ahead to enter the cathedral by the north door.

❸ After your visit, leave by the door opposite the one you entered by. Walk ahead down the cloisters. The treasury is to the right at the

end. After visiting, continue around the cloisters and go right, signed Norman Undercroft Exhibition, into an irregular square, The College.

❹ Follow the wall on your left until you reach the arch. Go through the arch and turn right on to South Bailey. Descend slightly for 273yds (250m) to Prebends Bridge. Do not cross, but turn right along the lower riverside path.

❺ Follow the path for 328yds (300m) passing the Old Fulling Mill Museum of Archaeology. Continue ahead for another 328yds (300m) and ascend a slope then steps up on to Silver Street. Turn left and cross Framwellgate Bridge. Over the bridge, turn left down steps by the Coach and Eight pub to the banks of the River Wear.

❻ Go straight ahead, passing behind the riverside buildings to reach the end of Prebends Bridge. Do not cross, but continue beside the river for 600yds (656m) until the path ascends into St Oswald's churchyard. Go through the churchyard on to Church Street and turn left.

❼ At the traffic lights continue on the main road – New Elvet. At the next crossroads turn left over Elvet Bridge and ascend the slope at the end. Turn right, back to the Market Place.

DIFFICULTY ✳

Map labels

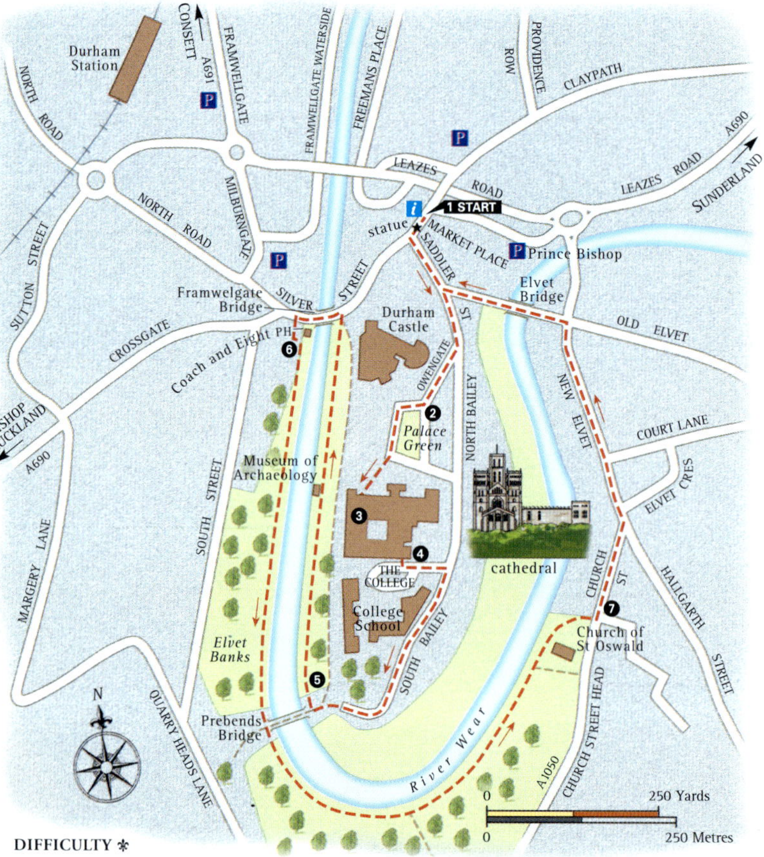

Durham Station
CONSETT A691
HILTON ROAD
NORTH ROAD
SUTTON STREET
MILBURNGATE
FRAMWELLGATE
FRAMWELLGATE WATERSIDE
FREEMANS PLACE
PROVIDENCE ROW
CLAYPATH
A690
LEAZES ROAD
LEAZES ROAD
SUNDERLAND
1 START
statue **MARKET PLACE**
Prince Bishop
Elvet Bridge
SADDLER ST
SILVER STREET
Framwelgate Bridge
Durham Castle
OWENGATE
NORTH BAILEY
OLD ELVET
NEW ELVET
COURT LANE
CROSSGATE
Coach and Eight PH
❻
❷ Palace Green
Museum of Archaeology
❸
ELVET CRES
BISHOP AUCKLAND A690
MARGERY LANE
SOUTH STREET
THE COLLEGE
College School
❹ cathedral
CHURCH ST
HALLGARTH STREET
❼
Church of St Oswald
Elvet Banks
❺
SOUTH BAILEY
QUARRY HEADS LANE
Prebends Bridge
CHURCH STREET HEAD
A1050
River Wear
N

0 .... 250 Yards
0 .... 250 Metres

ABOUT · LEWES

Lewes has a long and rich history. Shortly after the Battle of Hastings William de Warenne, brother to William I, built Lewes Castle. Close by is the Battle of Lewes site where Simon de Montfort's victory over Henry III eventually led to the first parliament.

East Sussex · SE ENGLAND

DISTANCE · 7½ miles (12km)

TOTAL ASCENT · 900ft (274m)

PATHS · waymarked paths and defined tracks; sheep runs can be muddy

TERRAIN · town and downland

GRADIENTS · an initial steep ascent, two gentler climbs later

REFRESHMENTS · plenty of pubs, cafés and restaurants in Lewes

PARK · Lewes rail station car park or pay-and-display car park on the other side of the rail line

OS MAP · Explorer 122 South Downs Way – Steyning to Newhaven

Lewes – town of the conquerors

❶ Leave the station car park by the way you entered. Turn right at immediate junction by the White Star Inn, then left before All Saints Centre (former church), up Church Twitten. At the top, turn right, down the High Street. Go forward at the traffic-lights through the precinct to the far end of town.

❷ Go forward at the road junction, up Chapel Hill (width restriction sign). Climb steeply and after a stone seat on your left and before a golf course sign, turn left. Before a gate with Cuilfail Estate sign, turn right, up the path. Emerge on to the golf course, go forward to tallest post (yellow arrow and 'take care' sign), with a memorial obelisk on the left, and continue ascending gently following posts.

❸ At far end of golf course, avoid descending but take a stile into pasture, over another stile and continue to a stile on the skyline where the view opens out ahead. Go forward towards trees as waymarked, to go down a track with a fence and woods on left.

❹ At the bottom, by a large concrete-based pond (usually dry), do not go through the gate but turn right, uphill (licensed path to Mount Caburn, landowner allows public use). Avoid two forks to the right, to follow a wide grassy path to view Mount Caburn that is soon joined by a fence on the left and head towards to the mound.

❺ Reach the gate and sign for Mount Caburn National Nature Reserve. Walk around the ramparts or climb the mound for a magnificent view and return to the

DIFFICULTY ✽✽

gate. Retrace 200yds (183m), then left over the stile and follow path downhill. At the bottom, cross a stile and follow the valley floor.

❻ Pass to the left of the concrete-based pond, cross two waymarked stiles (may be muddy) and in 75yds (70m) go diagonally right, up past marker post. Continue uphill to the golf course car park and turn left on the road to descend into Lewes.

Follow main route back through town and up the High Street.

❼ Beyond the war memorial and traffic lights, turn right into Castle Gate, passing under two castle archways. Go left at the viewpoint by the railings, down Castle Lane. At New Road, take steps up on the left (Pipe Passage). Turn right on High Street, then left down cobbled Keere Street (quite steep).

❽ Go forward at the road junction at the bottom (pass Southover Grange and gardens on the left), and right along Southover High Street. Turn left after the church into Cockshut Road. Turn left after the rail bridge on the path past the priory ruins and Battle of Lewes Memorial, left around the sports field and left on the path past the mound to road. Turn left, then right to the station car park.

From Brockenhurst explore the once-exclusive royal hunting preserve of William the Conqueror. Established by William in 1079, the New Forest is still a magical place and the natural habitat for a wide variety of flora and fauna.

DISTANCE • 6 miles (9.6km)

TOTAL ASCENT • 33ft (10m)

PATHS • paths and tracks, well-defined in places. Can be wet in winter

TERRAIN • village streets, heath and woodland. Keep dogs on leads at all times

GRADIENTS • one very gentle climb

REFRESHMENTS • Brockenhurst has a choice of inns and hotels

PARK • free car park in Brookley Road, Brockenhurst

OS MAP • Outdoor Leisure 22 New Forest

The New Forest: king among deer parks

❶ From the car park turn right and follow Brookley Road to the Watersplash, a local landmark. Bear right and pass railings. On the right are the entrances to Overbrook and Brocket Green, beyond them take a kissing gate by the entrance to Brookway and join a footpath alongside a stream.

❷ Pass a row of houses and gardens. Go through two kissing gates and turn left at the next road. Follow Butts Lawn and head for the next junction by a telephone box. Bear left for a few paces, then swing right on a track signed access to allotments.

❸ Approaching the allotments, veer a little to the right, continuing across heathland known as Black Knowl, keeping woodland to your right. Continue between gorse bushes and at a clear path, turn right towards trees. When the path ends, keep left to a wide track, turn right and head for Bolderford Bridge.

❹ Cross the bridge and swing left in front of the gate by the sign for Lyndhurst. Keep right at the fork and follow the path to cross a footbridge, keeping the fence close to your right-hand side.

❺ Turn left at the next junction, by a bridge. Follow the track across open heath to a gate by silver birch trees. Continue for several hundred yards, turn sharp left at the junction. Follow the grassy track by pine trees to a stile.

❻ Head diagonally right, following the clear path through the heather, towards an opening in the trees. Cross the river at the bridge with wooden handrails. Continue ahead using small footbridge (no handrails) then swing right towards Aldridgehill Cottage.

❼ Keep the cottage on your right and follow the drive for 50yds (46m). Take the left fork and follow the woodland path down to the footbridge over Ober Water. Continue ahead following the path up the gentle slope to a bend in the road. Go straight on alongside a car park to the next junction.

❽ Turn right, then left by Ober Lodge. Follow the track towards the Burley road. As you approach it, veer left to a parallel track which joins the road. Continue along the path parallel to the road. Make for Brookley Road on the right and return to the car park.

• DON'T MISS •

*Brockenhurst's **Church of St Saviours**, originally built as a private chapel for nearby Rhinefield House in 1905. Look out for **mink** – animal rights protesters released a number of these rarely seen animals from a New Forest mink farm in the late 1990s. Mink are most commonly seen by water, so keep a sharp eye out on the riverside sections.*

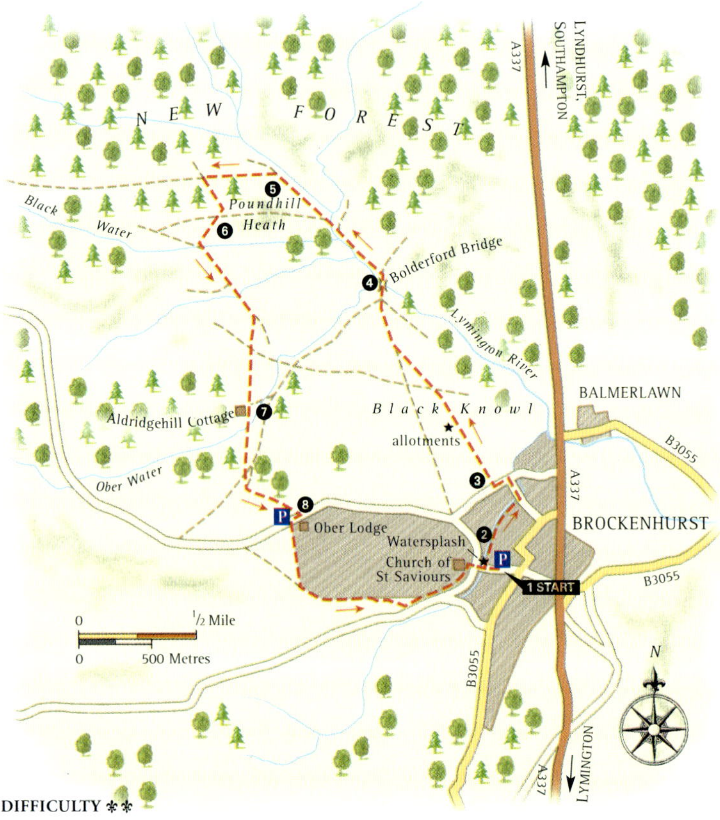

DIFFICULTY ✱✱

0 — ½ Mile

0 — 500 Metres

BROCKENHURST

BALMERLAWN

N E W   F O R E S T

Poundhill Heath

Black Water

Bolderford Bridge

Lymington River

Aldridgehill Cottage

Black Knowl

allotments

Ober Water

Ober Lodge

Watersplash

Church of St Saviours

1 START

A337 LYNDHURST, SOUTHAMPTON

B3055

A337

B3055

B3055

A337 LYMINGTON

ABOUT • LAXTON

Laxton, a tiny village east of Ollerton, is a survival of the open-field system of agriculture, common during the Middle Ages. All the village farmers can use the land and the system is still administered by the Court Leet, which meets annually at the Dovecote Inn.

Nottinghamshire • C ENGLAND

DISTANCE • 2½ miles (4km)

TOTAL ASCENT • 33ft (10m)

PATHS • field paths and lanes

TERRAIN • the deep hollow ways can be very wet and muddy after rain

GRADIENTS • none of any note

REFRESHMENTS • the Dovecote Inn, Laxton

PARK • Laxton village car park, next to the Dovecote Inn and Laxton Visitor Centre

OS MAP • Explorer 271 Newark-on-Trent, Retford, Southwell & Saxilby

Farming medieval-style in Laxton

❶ From the village car park walk past the Dovecote Inn and turn left on the road, passing the site of the pinfold (for stray animals) down the Kneesall road for about ½ mile (800m), bearing right at the junction with the Moorhouse road.

❷ After about 200yds (183m), turn right by the second wooden footpath sign on to the broad, muddy trackway of the Langsyke. This leads up through a gate and an avenue of young beeches into a hollow way and out on to Mill Field, the largest of the three great open fields of Laxton. In summer, if the field is in arable use, you will be able to see different crops growing in the strips.

❸ Ascend the broad green headland for about 500yds (457m), turning sharp right at a prominent interpretative sign on to a metalled farm track which leads out to the Ollerton road. After crossing the road, follow a grassy, often wet hollow way, turning right at the junction with another towards the end of the main street of the village, with the church tower ahead.

❹ Just before reaching the street, turn left on to a farm track. After about 150yds (137m), leave the track, turning right over a stile by a notice board which is partly hidden by the hedge.

❺ Cross another stile which leads across the West Field via Hall, or Back, Lane, a muddy, deeply-hedged lane. Follow the lane for about 500yds (457m), where a gate and sign on your left leads across a field towards the motte and bailey castle, following

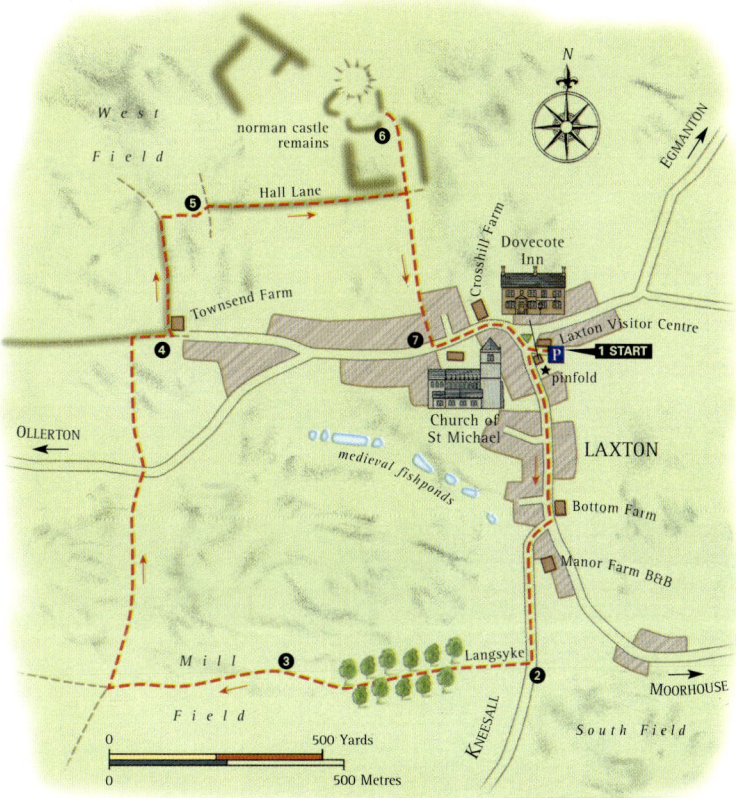

DIFFICULTY ❋

the green arrows of the former MAFF (Ministry of Agriculture, Fisheries, and Food) conservation walk.

❻ Retrace your steps back to the lane, where you go straight ahead arriving back in the village almost opposite the church.

❼ Turn left to walk down the main street and back to the car park.

• **DON'T MISS** •

*It is worth stopping at the visitor centre in Laxton, which offers lots of information on the open-field system of farming. And don't miss the beautiful, mainly 13th-century, decorated parish **Church of St Michael, the Archangel**. The church had fallen into disuse and 'impious neglect' until it was remodelled by Earl Manvers, the lord of the manor, in 1854. He dismantled and rebuilt the tower, and shortened the nave by one bay. You'll also find the well-preserved mound of a motte-and-bailey castle in the village.*

Sarum's Cathedrals

Follow the Avon from New Sarum's majestic cathedral to fortified Old Sarum, Salisbury's medieval forerunner

Iron Age Hill Fort to Medieval City

Set on a bleak hill overlooking Salisbury stands the deserted ramparts and earthworks of the original settlement of Old Sarum. People lived on this windswept hilltop for some 5,000 years: the outer banks and ditches were part of an Iron Age hill fort, and several Roman roads converge on the site. The Saxons followed and developed a town within the prehistoric ramparts.

Normans built the inner earthworks and, within them, a royal castle and two palaces. In 1075 Bishop Osmund, William the Conqueror's nephew, constructed the first cathedral. Old Sarum rapidly developed and for 150 years it was a thriving medieval city, well placed at a major crossroads. However, lack of space, shortage of water, tensions between clergy and royals and the exposed site led to a gradual decline during the late 12th century, and a new cathedral was built at New Sarum in 1220.

The Rise of Christianity

Norman rule had a profound effect on English society, in particular upon the Church, remodelling its structure, giving a new impetus to the building or reconstruction of parish churches. The Normans' policy towards religion differed radically from that of the Anglo-Saxons.

Bishops were ordered to transfer their headquarters from Saxon rural minsters to more populous centres, part of a centralisation that enabled the Normans to control the population. The rapid growth of Old Sarum from 1070 led to the transference of the rural see of Sherborne to the emerging city in 1075. Old Sarum was closer to the geographical centre of the huge diocese and, more importantly, the new bishop was Osmund, William the Conqueror's nephew and former chancellor.

Bishop Osmund built a fine cathedral close to the castle and palace. It set new standards, which were widely adopted in cathedrals throughout England. Instead of being run on monastic lines, it was served by 36 canons under the direction of four officers. Architecture was Romanesque and characterised by its lavish scale and rich library. Following Osmund's death in 1099, Bishop Roger was responsible for building elaborate palaces and the rebuilding of the cathedral.

As the cathedral grew more powerful, friction developed between the clergy and the military governor at Old Sarum. This eventually led to the removal of the cathedral to a new city, Salisbury, in the early 13th century. Building began in 1220 and was largely completed by 1250. Set within a spacious close, this new building provided a model for parish churches throughout the area.

WALK 32 — ALONG THE AVON TO OLD SARUM

❶ Enter the shopping area close to Sainsbury's and turn left to follow the Riverside Walk sign before the covered walkway. Walk beside the Avon, cross the car park access road and continue beneath two bridges. Cross a road and keep to the tarmac path beside a green. Ignore the footbridge on the right, cross a bridge over a side channel and bear right along the raised riverside path.

❷ Keep to the river bank along a boardwalk to a metal gate. Continue beside the river. Soon, bear half-left away from the river to a gate. Turn right between a hedge and fencing to reach a pitted tarmac path. Turn right, cross a footbridge over the Avon and soon bear right along a metalled track to the road in Stratford-sub-Castle.

❸ Turn right along the pavement, then just beyond Old Forge Cottage, cross the road to join a wide path beside Dairy Cottage, that gradually climbs to Old Sarum. At a T-junction of paths, keep left along the base of the hill fort; then, at a fork, bear right and ascend on to the outer rampart. Bear left around the fortifications, eventually descending to a stile by the access road. Follow the road right to tour the earth fortifications and to visit the inner bailey.

❹ Retrace your steps through the outer earthwork and go right to pass through a gate. Go through another gate and, just before the road, turn right, signed Stratford, by the hedge. Go through a gate and keep left, downhill to another gate by the Parliamentary Tree memorial. Turn right and enter Stratford-sub-Castle. Keep ahead and, shortly, cross by the right-hand bend to follow the path beside houses, signed City Centre.

❺ Reach a wide track and in a few paces cross the tiny footbridge on your right. Keep right along a gravel path through the grounds of the Sports Centre, the path bearing left alongside the river. Soon cross the footbridge to join the outward route back to the city centre and your car.

Distance: 5 miles (8km)

Total ascent: 230ft (70m)

Paths: mostly good; metalled close to the city centre; can be wet and muddy beside the Avon

Terrain: water meadow, city centre and farmland

Gradients: mainly flat; one gradual climb to Old Sarum

Refreshments: plenty of choice in Salisbury; The Old Castle opposite entrance to Old Sarum

Parking: main car park close to Sainsbury's; signed off Ring Road, west of city centre

OS Map: Explorer 130 Salisbury & Stonehenge

Difficulty: ✱✱

ABOUT • FOUNTAINS ABBEY

Founded in 1132, Fountains Abbey rose to become the richest monastery in England. The substantial ruins offer one of the most complete pictures of the life of a Cistercian monk and the walk approaches the abbey ruins through the beautiful grounds of Studley Royal.

North Yorkshire • N ENGLAND

DISTANCE • 7 miles (11.3km)

TOTAL ASCENT • 443ft (135m)

PATHS • field paths, tracks, metalled drives and garden paths

TERRAIN • estate grounds and gardens, with some farmland and woodland

GRADIENTS • moderate, but a stiff climb from and to the visitor centre. Alternative

parking for disabled people at west end of estate avoids this climb

REFRESHMENTS • Fountains Abbey visitor centre and in the Lakeside tea room

PARK • Fountains Abbey visitor centre, signed from the B6265

OS MAP • Explorer 299 Ripon & Boroughbridge, Easingwold

Holy orders and riches at Fountains Abbey

❶ From the visitor centre pay desk go through the door and turn right. Follow the path towards the abbey. After a metal gate, turn left, signed Abbey and Water Garden. Go steeply downhill to a metalled path by the abbey ruins.

❷ After exploring the abbey ruins, return to this path. Pass Fountains Hall and leave the estate through the gate. Turn left up the road, bearing left at the junction. Just after the road bends right, go left over a signed stile beside a gate.

❸ Follow the path to a waymarked gate in a crossing wall. The track beyond curves right then left through two gates to a farmhouse. Turn right alongside the shed. Follow footpath signs, going left then right, to a metal gate and on to a track.

❹ Where the hedge ends, go ahead down the field to a gate into the wood. Follow the track to a ruined archway. Go through the kissing gate left of the arch and follow the track ahead, winding downhill and bending right to the valley.

❺ Just before reaching a weir, turn sharp right down the valley, and follow the track over three bridges to a kissing gate. Continue through woodland, passing a footbridge and winding left uphill. The track passes Plumpton Hall on your left, and continues to the Studley Royal Estate entrance.

❻ Turn left up the drive towards the church. At the crossroads turn left towards the lake and follow the road, with the lake on your right, to the entrance gate. Just

beyond the pay kiosk (show your membership card or entrance ticket to regain admission), turn left and cross the canal.

❼ Follow the canalside path almost to the Temple of Piety, turning sharp left uphill before it,

signed High Ride. The path goes through a tunnel and then bends right, passing the Octagonal Temple and winding through woodland. By the Temple of Fame, the path bends left.

❽ Continue past Anne Boleyn's Seat to turn sharp right, downhill, to another lake. Turn left and continue. Follow the path beside the canal and then slightly uphill. Go right, into the abbey ruins, and retrace your steps back uphill to the visitor centre.

• DON'T MISS •

Ripon is only 3 miles (5km) from Fountains Abbey. It is a cathedral city with a history that dates back to 886 when it was granted a charter by Alfred the Great. The cathedral has a crypt constructed by St Wilfrid in AD 672 – more than 450 years before the monks arrived at Fountains. In the handsome market square is England's oldest free-standing obelisk.

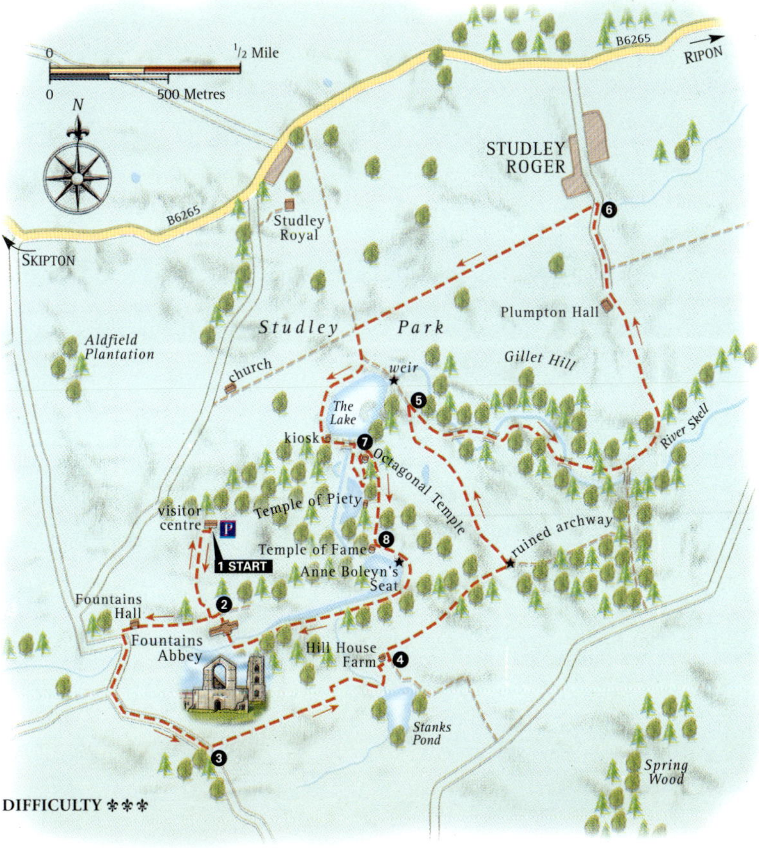

DIFFICULTY ✱✱✱

ABOUT DUNDRENNAN ABBEY

Mary, Queen of Scots, spent her last night in Scotland in this abbey, founded in 1142 by a Cistercian order of monks from Rievaulx in North Yorkshire. No early written records of the abbey have survived but the remains suggest a wealthy past.

Dumfries & Galloway • SCOTLAND

DISTANCE • 6 miles (9.6km)

TOTAL ASCENT • 98ft (30m)

PATHS • good, but can be very muddy in wet weather

TERRAIN • country lanes, farm tracks, fields and a section of A-road

GRADIENTS • gentle

REFRESHMENTS • none on route. The Selkirk Arms, Kirkcudbright

PARK • car park, Dundrennan Abbey

OS MAP • Explorer 312 Kirkcudbright & Castle Douglas

A simple life at Dundrennan Abbey

❶ From the car park in Dundrennan village return to the A711 and turn left. Take the first turning on the left, signed Port Mary, and continue along this road. At the next junction go left again avoiding the military road.

❷ Follow this road as it winds round the farm steading and past the entrance of Port Mary House. Stop for a moment and consider the fate of Mary Queen of Scots. She fled here after her disastrous defeat at Langside in 1568 and

• DON'T MISS •

Kirkcudbright is one of the most colourful towns in Scotland, with streets of brightly painted Georgian houses. The town has a rich history which dates back to the 13th century when the fortress of Castlemains came into the possession of John Balliol, the Lord of Galloway, and Edward I is believed to have stayed here during this time. In the late 19th and 20th centuries, Kirkudbright prospered under a new trade – brought by the artists of the day – and quickly gained a reputation as an artists' haven for the quality of its light. A number of famous artists were attracted to the town, including EA Hornel, who donated his home at Broughton House to the town – the house is now a museum.

**DIFFICULTY **

Map showing the walking route around Dundrennan Abbey, with labels including Abbey Burn, Barend Hill, Bar Hill, Dundrennan House, DUNDRENNAN, Heart Moss, A711, DALBEATTIE, START, Fagra Hill, Upper Rerrick, Dundrennan Abbey, Fagra, Brown Hill, cemetery, Orroland, Dropping Craig, KIRKCUDBRIGHT, Rerrick Park, forts, farm, Port Mary House, Port Mary, Abbey Burn Foot, N compass, scale 0–1 Mile / 0–1 Kilometre.

set sail from here for England, hoping to receive the protection of Elizabeth I, but she was never to return. Go through the gate at the end of the road, along a farm track and through a second gate.

❸ Walk ahead for approximately 100yds (91m), then turn right and cross a small burn. Head across the field parallel to the telegraph poles and look for the gate in the far side. Go through it.

❹ Turn left and follow the line of the burn then turn left again, cross the burn and enter the steading at Rerrick Park farm. Turn left on to the road, which runs up the side of the farm house and then turns sharp right.

❺ At the crossroads, beside a cemetery, go forward on the middle road. Pass the entrance to Upper Rerrick on the left and follow the road as it turns first right and then left to end at a T-junction.

❻ Turn left and at the junction with the A711 turn left again. Continue along this quiet road for about 2 miles (3.2km) to reach the village of Dundrennan (note that the stone from the ruined abbey was used in the construction of the village) and return to the abbey car park.

ABOUT • LOSTWITHIEL

In the 13th century, Bodmin was the centre of Devon and Cornwall's thriving tin industry and Lostwithiel, as a result, developed as an important seaport. Then, in the 13th century Restormel Castle became the seat of the feudal government of the area.

Cornwall • SW ENGLAND

DISTANCE • 4½ miles (7.2km)

TOTAL ASCENT • 410ft (125m)

PATHS • woodland tracks and fields

TERRAIN • mixed woodland and farmland; short stretch of pavements through the town

GRADIENTS • gradual; one short steep ascent from Restormel Farm to Hillhead

REFRESHMENTS • café at Lanhydrock House; The River pub and Duchy Coffee Shop both in Fore Street, Lostwithiel

PARK • National Trust car park by Respryn Bridge (honesty box) for Lanhydrock House (signed off the A38 just east of Bodmin, and off the A390 west of Lostwithiel)

OS MAP • Explorer 107 St Austell & Liskeard

The rise and fall of Lostwithiel

DIFFICULTY ✱✱

❶ Leave the car park via the exit and turn right. Take the first lane left by Station Lodge, signed Lanhydrock. At the Lodge and gates to The Avenue, turn left down Newton Lane, signed permitted footpath only. Continue to a wooded track which descends for ¾ mile (1.2km); veer left to meet two dark red gates, ahead and right.

❷ Turn right through the gate, signed footpath to Restormel Castle, and cross the field. Go through the next gate, and then another by the waterworks to join a lane then continue for 1¼ miles (2km). Where the lane bends right, keep straight on along the farm lane (dead end), with views to the castle ahead. The lane runs through Restormel Farm to meet another lane.

❸ Turn right uphill (in summer the gates are open; in winter climb over the stile) to reach the car park; turn right for the castle.

❹ On leaving the castle go through the car park, over a stile in the far left corner, and up the field, keeping the hedge on your left. Cross the wooden ladder stile and pass through a gap in the hedge. Continue uphill, keeping the hedge on your right. The path veers left, ignore the first stile on the right. At the top, turn right over a stile, then left at the footpath post near Barngate Farm. Cross the next ladder stile and pass through a gate to meet the road opposite Hillhead Cottage.

❺ Turn left; descend Bodmin Hill for ¾ mile (1.2km) to meet the A390 in the centre of Lostwithiel.

Cross the road and continue down Fore Street to the museum, St Bartholomew's Church and the River Fowey. Retrace your steps to the A390 and turn right to pass the Royal Talbot, on your left, and Tourist Information Centre, on your right.

❻ Turn left along Restormel Road (unmarked), following the brown tourist signs to the castle. At the entrance to Restormel Farm keep straight on to retrace your steps past the waterworks and through the fields to reach the red gate at Point 2 of the walk.

❼ Go through the gate and turn right to pass almost immediately through another red gate. Follow the woodland path to meet the River Fowey; the path bends left to meet a wooden footbridge.

❽ Cross the footbridge and turn left to walk along the river bank. The path ends at a kissing gate; turn left to cross Respryn Bridge, then turn right into the car park.

DON'T MISS

*The 18th-century **Restormel House**, just below the castle, has superb battlements in the Gothic style.*

Map labels: BODMIN B3269, Hart Wood, CUTMADOC, Lanhydrock House, Station Lodge, **1 START**, Bofarnel Downs, Great Wood, Respryn Bridge, TREBYAN, ❽, ❷ ❼, waterworks, River Fowey, LISKEARD, SWEETSHOUSE, Restormel Castle, Barngate Farm, ❹, Restormel Farm, Druid's Hill, B3268, Hillhead Cottage, ❺, B3269, N, A390, LOSTWITHIEL, Church of St Bartholomew, ❻ i museum, PENHALE, Beacon Hill, LANLIVERY, A390, ST AUSTELL, 0 — 1 Mile, 0 — 1 Kilometre

ABOUT • CONWY

This walk starts at Conwy Castle, built by Edward I after his conquest of Wales. The route then wanders along the estuary and up on to Conwy Mountain, a vantage point from where the tactical positioning of the castle is most evident.

Conwy • WALES

DISTANCE • 7¼ miles (11.7km) .

TOTAL ASCENT • 985ft (300m)

PATHS • minor roads, A-roads, rough tracks and paths

TERRAIN • remote farmland and hill country

GRADIENTS • road mostly flat; paths steep in places

REFRESHMENTS • Liverpool Arms in Conwy, many cafés and take-away food bars in town centre

PARK • Vicarage Gardens car park, inside the castle walls

OS MAP • Outdoor Leisure 17 Snowdonia – Snowdon & Conwy Valley

In the shadow of the mighty Conwy Castle

❶ From the car park turn right to reach the Guild Hall. Cross the road, turn right, then left, following signs for the Quay. Pass through a small archway and walk along the harbour front. Continue through another archway and bear right on to the signed North Wales Path (NWP).

❷ Continue alongside the Conwy estuary, parallel with Bodlondeb Woods. At a T-junction, turn left and walk to a main road. Go into the road opposite, and cross the railway by a footbridge. Continue past the drive to Beechwood Court, soon bearing right at the T-junction (waymarked). Just past the last houses on the right, branch right again at the fork to follow the NWP, and climb to a wooden stile giving access to Conwy Mountain. Ascend through bracken and gorse, eventually to follow a more level course across the flanks of the mountain.

❸ Continue for just over a mile (1.6km) to a waymark. Leave the NWP and bear left, descending to a more pronounced path beside a wall. Further on, rejoin the NWP and continue to a lateral farm track. Cross this and go forward on to a broad track to the parking area at Sychnant Pass.

❹ Cross the road and go up to a gate. After a short distance, take an obvious track turning sharp right on to higher ground. Shortly, bear left on a green track following waymarked NWP. Further on, as you pass under power lines for the third time, the track forks directly under them. Branch left here and continue along the track to a ladder stile over a wall.

❺ Beyond the stile, descend a little across the western slopes of Maen Esgob, and when the main track bears right, turn left through a pronounced pass between low hills, now leaving the NWP. Follow a track past a small lake (Llyn y Wrach), and shortly turn left, roughly parallel with a wall. Follow the track (which doesn't always stay by the wall and finally leaves it), to reach a group of walled enclosures. Bear right. Shortly the path descends quite steeply, and meets a surfaced road. Turn right.

❻ Soon, just before Y Bwthyn (The Cottage) and 109yds (100m) before the cattle grid, turn left through a gate on to an enclosed path to a field. Bear left across the field towards a stile, then follow an obvious route across two fields. In the next field, the route is less obvious but aims for the right-hand corner of a fence. From here, walk alongside a stream, aiming to the right of a red-roofed house, near which you meet a road. Turn right and follow the road passing Oakwood Hall Park on the right. At a T-Junction turn right and soon turn left at a footpath sign. Continue through three fields, pass through a kissing gate then bear left along a field edge to meet another road. Turn right.

❼ Head towards Conwy and enter the town by passing through a pedestrian archway in the Town Walls. Turn right on to the main street to return to the start point of the walk.

DIFFICULTY ✱✱✱

For most people, life in medieval Britain was hard work but reasonably predictable, within a fairly rigid social order. But in the mid-14th century the old world was changed beyond recognition – by the bite of a flea.

MEDIEVAL
1300–1485

Plague & Conflict

Britain in the first half of the 14th century was familiar enough with upheaval and war. The enmity between England and Scotland had rumbled on, exploding into battle at Bannockburn in 1314, where Edward II's troops were routed by Robert the Bruce. In 1337 the more warlike Edward III sent his knights across the Channel to enforce his claim to the French throne, setting in train the Hundred Years' War. Still, in most communities the daily routine was predictable, if tough – until, in 1348, an epidemic swept in from Europe that seemed to herald Judgement Day itself.

The Black Death was a form of bubonic plague, carried by fleas on the rats that infested ships and towns. The first signs of infection were swellings, or 'buboes', on armpits or groin, followed by coughing, chills and delirium. Victims were usually dead within days. By the time the epidemic had run its course Europe's population had been halved, Britain's reduced by a third. Estates and villages were left to rot, with no one to plant or harvest crops, tend or slaughter cattle, produce or sell goods. Those still capable of work found that the old feudal rules tying them to their lord's land no longer applied: they could move around, selling their labour to the highest bidder. When the crown tried to rein in this burgeoning wage economy, imposing a poll tax on everyone over the age of 14, the peasants revolted, only retreating from all-out confrontation with the young King Richard II when their leader, Wat Tyler, had been cut down by his bodyguard.

Faced with the uncertainty of earthly existence, people turned in their thousands to the comforting rituals of religion, and trekked to pilgrimage centres in the hope of sharing in the miraculous powers of holy relics.

With their stalls and souvenirs, inns and religious sites of interest, pilgrimage routes were as much a holiday as a journey of faith – as is clear in Geoffrey Chaucer's rumbustious *The Canterbury Tales*, started in 1387.

POWER STRUGGLES
The ravages of plague and food shortages continued to have their repercussions. A minor Welsh noble, Owain Glyndwr, indignant at the loss of a legal dispute over land rights, attracted a huge following of disaffected countrymen when he took arms against the king, Henry IV. At its height the rebel movement was calling its own parliaments and signing international alliances, but in 1413 the English gained the upper hand and Glyndwr vanished into hiding.

Two years later, the English celebrated another victory – against the French in Agincourt; and in 1420 the Treaty of Troyes pronounced Henry V heir to the throne of France. But the English kingdom's future was far from settled. The tussle over the crown between major political players was about to spark off 30 years of intermittent fighting between the houses of Lancaster and York, while families, towns and castles across England and Wales declared and sometimes shifted their loyalties.

In 1485 the Lancastrian claimant, Henry Tudor – son of Margaret Beaufort, the great-granddaughter of John of Gaunt, Duke of Lancaster – returned from exile in Brittany and marched to Bosworth to face the Yorkist king, Richard III.

After a fierce and arduous battle, Richard was finally unhorsed and killed. Having chased Richard's demoralised soldiers across the marshes, the new king's followers performed an impromptu crowning ceremony in the field, and the Tudor era was under way.

HISTORIC SITES

Bosworth battlefield, Leicestershire: site of the clash between Richard III and Henry Tudor.

King's College, Cambridge: founded by Henry VI.

Bannockburn, near Stirling: site of Robert the Bruce's famous victory.

Caernarfon Castle, Gwynedd: built by Edward I to be the seat of Welsh government in North Wales.

Berkeley Castle, Gloucestershire: Edward II abdicated at Kenilworth Castle, before being taken to Berkeley where he was imprisoned, tortured and finally murdered.

MEDIEVAL

WALK 37

ABOUT • GLEN TROOL

This walk takes you to southern shores of Loch Trool where Robert the Bruce and his 300 men routed the superior force of the English troops. Their victory marked the turning point in Scotland's fight for independence and their ultimate goal, the Crown.

Dumfries & Galloway • SCOTLAND

DISTANCE • 5 miles (8km)

TOTAL ASCENT • 150ft (46m)

PATHS • good; firm footing even in wet weather

TERRAIN • forest paths, gravel paths and single-track roads

GRADIENTS • moderate

REFRESHMENTS • House of Hill, Bargrennan, 4 miles (6km) southwest off the A714

PARK • car park at entrance to Caldons Campsite

Robert the Bruce, ambitious patriot

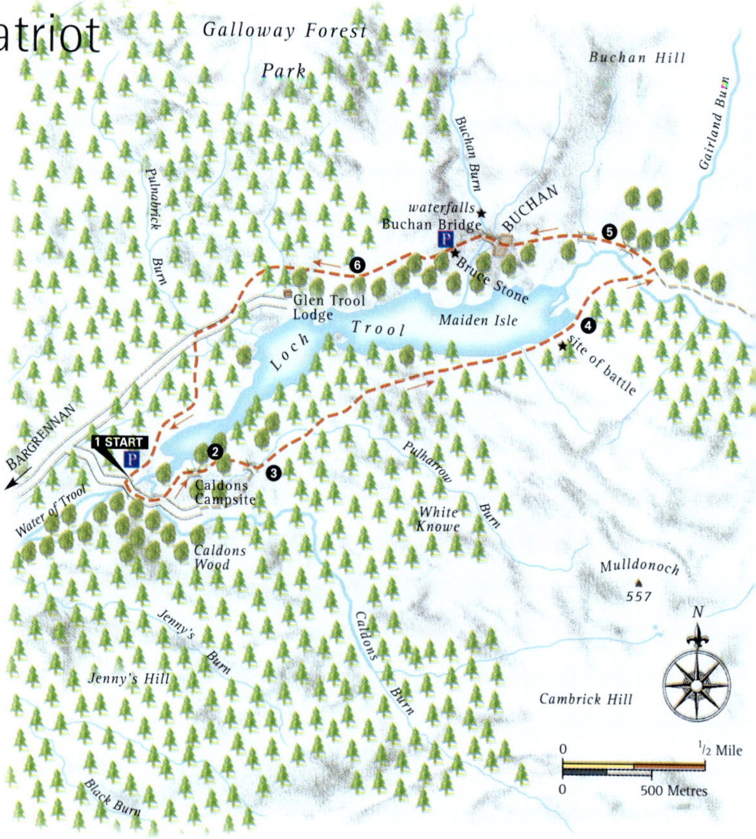

❶ From the car park at the entrance to the campsite, turn left following the waymarks for the Loch Trool Trail. Go over a bridge, enter Caldons Campsite and turn left on to the path which follows the river. Cross another bridge and pass between two toilet blocks.

❷ Continue following the waymarks as the trail winds round a picnic area and crosses a green metal bridge. Continue on the path then veer right across the grass to join a trail which heads uphill into the forest.

❸ Keep on this path as it goes uphill and crosses a bracken covered clearing. Go through a kissing gate, continue through the clearing, re-enter the wood and keep walking to the interpretation board marking the site of the battle. It is at this point you can imagine Robert the Bruce's men lying in wait to ambush the 1,500-strong English force. When the English were lured to the southern shores of Loch Trool, and unable to form a tight battalion, then Bruce's soldiers attacked, blocking their escape route and hurling boulders from the slopes above.

❹ Continue on the path from the interpretation board as it emerges from the woods and go downhill towards the end of Loch Trool. Turn left, cross a stile and a footbridge on to the Southern Upland Way and turn left.

❺ Go through two gates and cross a wooden bridge. Soon after the stone Buchan Bridge, look out for a track branching off to the left and go uphill toward the Bruce Stone and one of the best views of the loch.

DIFFICULTY ✳✳

❻ Continue on the track past the Bruce Stone – laid in memorial for one of Scotland's greatest warriors – and turn left on to the road through the car park. Keep going until you see a waymark on the left then turn left on to a forest trail to eventually return to the start of the walk and your car.

• DON'T MISS •

St Ninian founded the first Christian church in Scotland in the 5th century at nearby **Whithorn**, which thus became known as the Cradle of Scottish Christianity. Archaeologists have recently uncovered his church and can be visited at the dig. There are also the remains of a 12th-century priory. The archaeological visitor centre offers guided tours and exhibitions, and the museum contains the 5th-century Latinus Stone, Scotland's oldest Christian artefact and memorial. St Ninian's cave lies to the south, with 8th-century carvings, once used as his retreat.

MEDIEVAL

WALK 38

ABOUT • PASS OF BRANDER

Enjoy fine views over the Pass of Brander, as you follow the route taken by Robert the Bruce in 1308 into the territory of the Macdougall clan to settle a blood-feud. The successful ambush demonstrated Bruce's skills as a guerrilla fighter and as a tactician.

Argyll & Bute • SCOTLAND

DISTANCE • 11 miles (17.7km)

TOTAL ASCENT • 320ft (98m)

PATHS • mainly firm, but some very muddy sections around Tervine

TERRAIN • woods and mountain moorland

GRADIENTS • gentle

REFRESHMENTS • Kilchrenan Inn (erratic winter opening)

PARK • pull-in on roadside below Kilchrenan church

OS MAP • Pathfinder 345 Loch Awe (North)

Guerrilla warfare in the Scottish hills

❶ From Kilchrenan church, follow the road down to Kilchrenan Inn and turn left up the lane to Ardanaisaig. After passing modern forestry plantations, the road enters a wood (about 3 miles/ 4.8km from the start) where huge oaks tower above a lower canopy of hazel, silver birch and alder. Such forests covered almost all the Highlands at the time of Bruce.

❷ At the end of the public road, turn left in front of the gatehouse of Ardanaisaig Hotel to take the private road towards Tervine. Soon, you will see the Pass of Brander up ahead, with the steep, scree-covered slopes of Ben Cruachan plunging down into the loch.

❸ Just beyond the second white cottage on your left, turn left through a gate (faint marker for Fank's Cottage) over rough ground. Turn left through a gate towards a sheepfold, then immediately right through another gate on to a muddy track beside a drystone wall. At the end of the wall the track swings downhill to the right and fords a shallow burn.

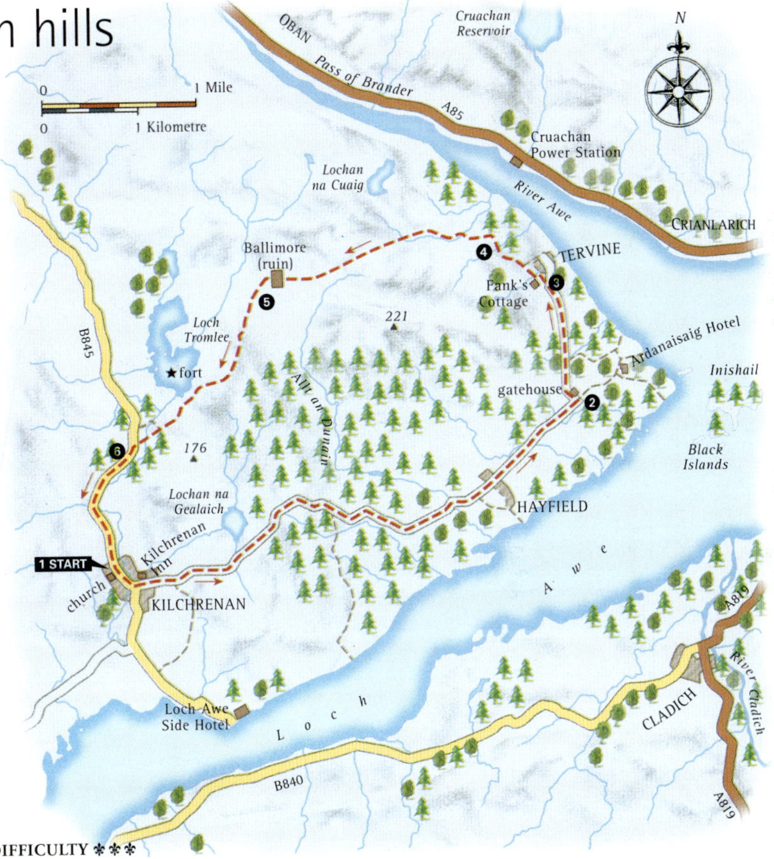

• DON'T MISS •

Kilchrenan Church, an attractive building dating from the early 18th century, contains the grave-stone of Sir Colin Campbell, who was killed in a skirmish with the clan of the Macdougalls in 1294. His descendants were given vast tracts of their territory by Bruce and the Campbells eventually became the most powerful clan in Scotland.

DIFFICULTY ✱✱✱

❹ Passing a small clump of fir trees, the track swings to the left. There are stepping stones across a burn, which the track then follows upstream. The path is very faint across the grassy hillside, but is marked by a slight embankment. Stay close to the burn. Beyond a gated fence the path rises to the watershed with dramatic views

towards the west, then swings round to the right below a craggy hill. Beyond another gate, it drops down to a ruined farmhouse.

❺ From the shell of Ballimore there is a firm, clear track to Loch Tromlee. On an island in the loch are the remains of a small medieval fortress, stronghold of the

MacCorquodales of Phantilands, sacked by the Macdonalds in 1646. The track continues through a forestry plantation before reaching the Kilchrenan road.

❻ Turn left down the road, which was once an important route to a ferry on Loch Awe, to return to the village of Kilchrenan.

Map labels:

OBAN Pass of Brander A85 Cruachan Reservoir N

Cruachan Power Station

River Awe CRIANLARICH

Lochan na Cuaig

0 1 Mile

0 1 Kilometre

Ballimore (ruin) ❺ ❹ TERVINE ❸ Fank's Cottage

B845 221

Loch Tromlee ★ fort

Ardanaisaig Hotel Inishail

gatehouse ❷ Black Islands

Allt an Dunain

176 ❻

Lochan na Gealaich HAYFIELD

1 START church Kilchrenan Inn Awe

KILCHRENAN

Loch Awe Side Hotel Loch h e CLADICH River Cladich

A819

B840

ABOUT • DUNSTANBURGH

This walk offers a wealth of history: from 14th-century Dunstanburgh Castle, part of the fortifications built to defend England against the attacks of Robert the Bruce, to 20th-century pillboxes, where troops awaited German invaders in World War II.

Northumbria • N ENGLAND

DISTANCE • 5 ¼ miles (8.4km)

TOTAL ASCENT • 460ft (140m)

PATHS • field paths, roads and farm tracks

TERRAIN • undulating farmland and fine coastland with grassy dunes

GRADIENTS • moderate

REFRESHMENTS • Bark Potts café and Robson's fish restaurant, Craster; Cottage Inn, Dunstan

PARK • signed car park at entrance to Craster

OS MAP • Explorer 332 Alnwick & Amble, Craster & Whittingham

Dunstanburgh Castle: a mighty fortress

DIFFICULTY ✱✱

❶ From the car park, take the path behind the tourist information centre signed Craster South Farm. Fork left near a bench and at a kissing gate bear half-right across the field and uphill. Go through another gate on to a lane.

❷ Turn right, then right again at a crossroads. Go through the archway across the road then turn left through a gate, signed to Dunstan (the nearby Dunstan Hall is believed to have been the birth place of Duns Scotus, a famous 13th-century philosopher). At the next gate go half-left, through another gate and past the row of houses to the road.

❸ Turn right and follow the road as it bends left. Go straight on at the next junction, towards Embleton. Take the next lane right, signed Dunstan Square. Pass the houses then bend left though the farmyard. Go straight on through a gate, signed Dunstan Steads.

❹ Follow the farm road for a mile (1.6km). As you approach the hamlet of Dunstan Steads, go

• DON'T MISS •

Craster is a picturesque fishing village, set on the rugged Northumbrian coast, and is known throughout the world for its fine smoked kippers. They have been processed in the village for more than 150 years, and are cured for up to 16 hours above fires of whitewood shavings covered with oak sawdust in smoke houses.

through a gateway and wind between farm buildings to a road. Turn right, and follow the road as it bends left to reach a lane.

❺ Turn right, following a sign to Dunstanburgh Castle. At the bottom of the lane, go through a gate and turn right beside the golf course. The path goes alongside a green to a kissing gate by a National Trust sign.

❻ Go through the gate and follow the path inland round the castle rock, to arrive at the gatehouse entrance. After visiting the castle, leave the gateway and continue

straight ahead along the ridge to reach a kissing gate.

❼ Continue ahead along the coast, through another kissing gate to enter Craster village by a gate on to a lane. Pass the houses to reach a T-junction above the harbour, and turn right, to the car park.

Map labels:
B 1339 BAMBURGH
EMBLETON
DUNSTAN STEADS
Embleton Bay
Dunstanburgh Castle
golf course
Castle Point
Queen Margaret's Cove
Embleton Burn
B 1339
dunes
Scrog Hill
Spitalford Bog Plantation
DUNSTAN SQUARE
Cushat Stiel
Stamford Cote
N
Hoddleton Plantation
Dunstan Hall
DUNSTAN
The Heughs
Little Carr
CRASTER
harbour
Craster Tower
P
1 START
i
0   ½ Mile
0   500 Metres
B 1339 ALNMOUTH
Craster South Farm
Black Hole

ABOUT • ABBOTSBURY

The Benedictine monastery at Abbotsbury was founded in 1044 and demolished during the Dissolution of Monasteries, ordered by Henry VIII. The tithe barn is all that remains but it is a powerful reminder of this gentle order of monks.

Dorset • SW ENGLAND

DISTANCE • 6½ miles (10.4km)

TOTAL ASCENT • 650ft (198m)

PATHS • well-marked throughout; ascent to Abbotsbury hill fort and some paths can be muddy and difficult after prolonged rain; otherwise firm; road-walking in village

TERRAIN • village roads, grassland, short stretch of shingle, tarmac track and fields

GRADIENTS • gradual climb to St Catherine's Chapel, short steep climb to Abbotsbury hill fort

REFRESHMENTS • choice in Abbotsbury

PARK • village car park

OS MAP • Outdoor Leisure 15 Purbeck & South Dorset

The monastic complex at Abbotsbury

❶ With your back to the entrance to the village car park, take the path in the far right corner of the car park. Turn left at a ruined gable wall, part of an abbey outbuilding, turn right at the pond, and then left on to the lane. The tithe barn is ahead of you. Continue to a fork. Take the right-hand road, signed Swannery Pedestrians.

❷ At a low stone waymarker, turn right on to a track to St Catherine's Chapel. Keep ahead over a footbridge and skirt the hill. Join the track that climbs 437yds (400m) to the chapel.

❸ From the stile behind the chapel, walk to the brow of the hill and then go downhill, aiming right and following the line of a copse. At the foot of the slope, reach a stone waymarker. To visit the Swannery (Mar–Oct), keep straight ahead for just over ½ mile (800m). Retrace your steps to this point.

❹ From the waymarker, follow signs for the Sub-Tropical Gardens, skirting the hill with the sea on your left. Turn left along the coast path (may be muddy), signed Chesil Beach, for ½ a mile (800m).

A short stretch (800ft/250m) on shingle brings you back to the beach car park.

❺ Continue on the tarmac path, with Chesil Bank on your left. Pass the drive to Lawrence's Cottage, and at a low stone waymarker turn right uphill, for the hill fort. Go round the back of East Bexington Farm and diagonally right uphill towards a cottage in trees. Over a stile turn immediately right, with the hedge on your right. Enter an area of scrub and trees and follow the sign to the hill fort. The path is steep and can be muddy and slippery. At the top, follow the stone wall to the right. Reach the road and, across it, the double-bank Iron Age hill fort.

❻ Walk along the southern rampart with superb views over the Fleet, Chesil Beach and Portland. Past the trig point, drop down to a stile and cross a lane. Continue along Wears Hill.

❼ Just beyond a gate, reach a signpost. Following directions for Abbotsbury village, walk diagonally right downhill for 328yds (300m), through old stone quarries, and continue for 875yds (800m) to join Blind Lane. Turn right into Back Street and left on to the main road through the village for village car park. If you used beach car park, continue from Point ❶.

stone circle

BRIDPORT

B3157

Abbotsbury Hillfort

trig point

❻

cottage

tumuli   Wears Hill   ❼   tumuli

Inland Coast Path

White Hill

East Bexington Farm

quarry

Abbotsbury Plains

South West Coast Path

Lawrence's Cottage

ABBOTSBURY

1 START

Abbotsbury Sub-Tropical Gardens

Castle Hill Cottages

Abbotsbury Castle (ruins)   ❺   P

St Catherine's Chapel

❸   ❷   tithe barn

B3157

WEYMOUTH

Linton Hill

Chesil Bank

tea rooms   ❹

Abbotsbury Swannery Ticket Office

N

Lyme Bay

Chesil Beach

The Fleet

0 ────── 1 Mile

0 ────── 1 Kilometre

DIFFICULTY ✹✹

Warwick's Medieval Castle

When not at war, England's 14th-century knights were stars of the country's favourite spectator sport: the tournament

An Impregnable Stronghold

After the 17th century, Warwick Castle evolved into a stately home, whose lavish house parties often included the monarch among the guests. Earlier, it had served more utilitarian purposes and, well before the Normans arrived, there had been a Saxon fort to defend against Viking raiders. Henry de Beaumont, one of William the Conqueror's vassals, built the first stone castle, but that was largely destroyed during the Barons Revolt in 1264. Today's castle dates mostly from 14th- and 15th-century rebuilding and was designed to be both imposing and impregnable. Seemingly both objectives were achieved, for the only assault on its formidable defences was an unsuccessful attack by Royalist forces during the Civil War.

Entertainment Medieval Style

Despite the disturbances of the 14th century, there was some comfort within the castle's spartan exterior and, for the nobility at least, life had many pleasurable diversions. Knights were the superstars of the day and, when not seeking honour on the battlefield, spent their time practising combat or competing in tournaments. These were great spectacles, the champions and their horses clad in shining armour and colourful liveries, which, besides adding glamour to the occasion they served a practical purpose on the battlefield by identifying the combatants. Jousting and single combat contests were popular, with prizes for the victor, the possible bonus of the loser's forfeited armour and horse, and favours from lady admirers. More unruly was the mêlée, a mock battle between opposing teams. Although the objective was victory through surrender, by unseating, knocking down or disarming opponents, things often got well out of hand.

Hunting parties were more civilised. These, too, gave an opportunity to demonstrate skills with horse, bow and sword, and to display favourite hunting birds and dogs. Many castles had menageries, with collections of hawks and dogs, but there were also more exotic animals, such as bears and lions. It is said that Richard the Lionheart had a crocodile, before it escaped into the Thames.

Little excuse was needed for a feast, and while the poor were lucky to have coarse bread, pottage and weak beer, the tables of the rich were a gastronomic delight. Beef, mutton, venison and boar were served, together with fish and game birds and such delicacies as peacock and heron. Rich and spicy sauces often flavoured the dishes, to disguise the taints of over-ripe food. Pastries, sweets and puddings were also popular, all washed down with imported wine. Jesters, jugglers and acrobats provided a floor show to a musical background from the minstrel gallery and, once the tables had been cleared, it was time to dance.

WALK 41 — A WANDER AROUND WARWICK

❶ Walk through St Nicholas' Park to the river and turn left. Past a footbridge beyond the park, continue along a wooded riverside path. After a railway bridge and then the Grand Union Canal, carried high above on a three-arched aqueduct, turn left and climb steps to the canal's towpath. Instead of crossing the bridge, turn right and follow the canal around the town's northern edge, passing old warehouses and workshops that exploited the canal's cheap and relatively swift transport. After some 2 miles (3km), immediately before bridge number 51, leave the canal and climb on to the road above. Turn left over the bridge and then go right into Budbrooke Road. Walk through a small car park on the left and carry on, following a short length of canal, the Saltisford Arm.

❷ Forced back to the road beyond its far end, pass beneath a railway bridge and immediately go right, crossing a redundant canal bridge. Over a gate/stile on the right, climb left up a tree-planted bank on to Warwick Racecourse and keep going between a driving range and golf course. Where the range ends, turn left past the club house and continue off the course.

❸ Carry on ahead up Linen Street and then turn right, down to the main road. At the main road, go left through West Gate, past the Lord Leycester Hospital and along the High Street. At Castle Street, turn right and then fork right beside Oken House. Cross the road at the bottom and enter a gate to the Warwick Castle. Its entrance is to the left.

❹ When you have visited the castle, leave the courtyard by the opposite gate and turn right down a flight of steps. Go left at the bottom and walk out to the main road. The car park is down to the right.

Distance: 5¼ miles (8.5km)

Total ascent: minimal

Paths: riverside and canal paths may be muddy; otherwise well surfaced-paths and tracks

Terrain: river and canalside paths; town paths in Warwick

Refreshments: plenty in Warwick and at the castle

Parking: car park off A41, by St Nicholas' Park and the River Avon

OS Map: Explorer 221 Coventry & Warwick, Royal Leamington Spa

Difficulty: *

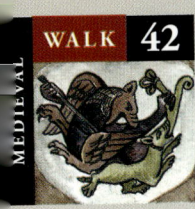
ABOUT • CANTERBURY

Birthplace of Christianity and mecca for pilgrims, Canterbury is famous for its association with the poet Geoffrey Chaucer, author of The Canterbury Tales. *After your walk, step back in time with a visit to the Canterbury Tales Visitor Attraction.*

Kent • SE ENGLAND

DISTANCE • 3 miles (4.8km)

TOTAL ASCENT • 66ft (20m)

PATHS • surfaced roads

TERRAIN • city streets

GRADIENTS • level; short ascent to city walls

REFRESHMENTS • cafés, pubs and restaurants in the city centre

PARK • long and short stay car parks (fee) around the city walls

OS MAP • Explorer 150 Canterbury & the Isle of Thanet

The tale of Canterbury

DIFFICULTY ✳

❶ With your back to Westgate Archway and Museum, walk along the pedestrianised St Peter's Street towards the town centre. Cross the River Stour and pass Eastbridge Hospital (Pilgrims Hospital) on your right. Continue past the library and Guildhall Street, turn right along St Margaret's Street.

❷ Pass the Canterbury Tales visitor attraction and the Tourist Information Office, then turn right down Hawks Lane, signed to Canterbury Heritage. At Stour Street, turn left, pass the Canterbury Heritage Museum and at the end of the street, keep ahead along Church Lane to pass St Mildred's Church.

❸ Before the ring road, turn left between metal bollards and walk past the Norman castle. At Castle Street, turn right then left along the pavement by the ring road. In a few paces, bear left along Castle Row, then right by the toilets into Dane John Gardens. Keep right, climb on to the city walls.

❹ Climb the path to the monument on top of Dane John

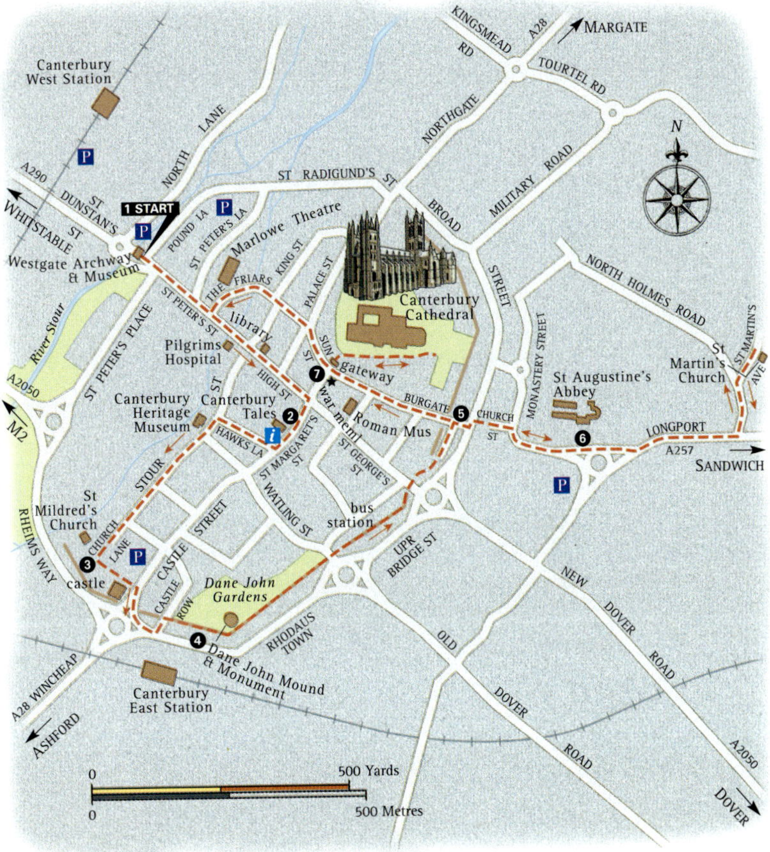

• **DON'T MISS** •

*Stroll beyond St Augustine's Abbey to visit **St Martin's Church**, the oldest parish church in England still in constant use. Believed to date back to Roman times, St Augustine worshipped here before he established his own monastery. Also you can walk through reconstructions of Roman buildings at the **Roman Museum**, set underground at the level of the Roman town.*

Mound for the fine city view. Continue along the walls above the bus station and descend to cross St George's Street. Continue to Burgate.

❺ Turn right, cross the pedestrian crossing over the ring road and walk along Church Street to the junction with Monastery Street.

Cross over to the fine gatehouse, turn right and follow Longport left to reach St Augustine's Abbey.

❻ To visit St Martin's Church, keep left at the roundabout, turn first left, then right into St Martin's Avenue. Retrace your steps back to the pedestrian crossing over the ring road and walk ahead along

Burgate to the war memorial and the cathedral gateway.

❼ Turn right through the gate to visit the cathedral. Go ahead along Sun Street, then over a junction into Orange Street. Continue along The Friars to pass the Marlowe Theatre. At St Peter's Street, turn right back to Westgate Archway.

MEDIEVAL

WALK 43

ABOUT • WHARRAM PERCY

The discovery of Wharram Percy in 1948 led to extensive excavations revealing a 5000-year-old community. The village was deserted during the 15th century due to the Black Death which ravaged many settlements in England between 1338–79

North Yorkshire • N ENGLAND

DISTANCE • 8 miles (13km)

TOTAL ASCENT • 1,640ft (500m)

PATHS • field paths and track, some roads

TERRAIN • undulating chalk landscape

GRADIENTS • one steep climb through fields, one on road

REFRESHMENTS • Middleton Arms, North Grimston

PARK • roadside parking in North Grimston, near the church, or in the Wharram Percy car park near Bella Farm

OS MAP • Explorer 300 Howardian Hills & Malton

Plague and pestilence in the Yorkshire Wolds

❶ Follow the main road south, past the Middleton Arms pub. Just beyond the speed derestriction sign take a track left over a cattle grid, towards Wood House Farm. Cross two more cattle grids. On the rise beyond, turn right at the Wolds Way sign.

❷ Go downhill and cross a bridge between two stiles. Bear slightly left and ascend the valley to a signpost. Turn left, going over a stile at another signpost. Then continue along the side of the field. At the next signpost go right, then go through the hedge on to a track.

❸ Follow the track across a road and downhill. At the next road turn left and walk uphill through Wharram le Street. At the crossroads turn right, towards Birdsall. Just beyond the houses on your left, go over a stile, signed Wolds Way.

❹ Follow the field edge to a road, then go straight ahead, passing Bella Farm. Beyond the farm, follow the sign for Medieval Deserted Village. Go through the car park and down the track. After the second kissing gate veer right to another gate.

❺ Go through the gate and down the steps on to the former railway line. To visit Wharram Percy, cross and follow the lane opposite. Return to the same point and turn left (not under the bridge). Follow the disused line to a road.

❻ Go straight ahead, and follow the road to a crossroads. Turn right, signed North Grimston. Follow the road, turning left at a T-junction by the entrance to Wharram Grange Farm. Go over a cattle grid, and right at a T-junction near Luddith Farm.

❼ After the next cattle grid turn right, signed CW. Follow the field edge then go through a gate and ahead, left of the stream. After another gate, pass under the railway bridge. Follow the path on to the road. Turn left to return to the start point.

DIFFICULTY ✶✶

ABOUT • HARLECH

Built of local grey sandstone by Edward I in 1283–90, Harlech Castle has served as both a fortress and a refuge. In the Wars of the Roses it was besieged by Yorkists for nearly eight years, and the struggle is remembered in the song 'Men of Harlech'.

Gwynedd • WALES

DISTANCE • 5 miles (8km)

TOTAL ASCENT • 200ft (61m)

PATHS • rocky track through woods – can be muddy; sandy track through dunes

TERRAIN • surfaced roads, steps, gravel track, sand dunes and beach, woodland track. **Make sure you complete the walk during low tide.**

GRADIENTS • steep steps to sea level; steep climb (rocky track and steps) to castle rock

REFRESHMENTS • cafés and pub in Harlech

PARK • castle forecourt; Upper Bron y Graig car park in town

OS MAP • Outdoor Leisure 18 Snowdonia – Harlech, Porthmadog & Bala

Song of the 'Men of Harlech'

• DON'T MISS •

Barmouth, a popular beach resort about 12 miles (19km) south of Harlech, was the port used by Jasper Tudor and the other Lancastrian rebels. Jasper and his ally, Griffith Vaughan, plotted their assault on the throne in a house on the harbour, Ty Gwyn, now largely rebuilt.

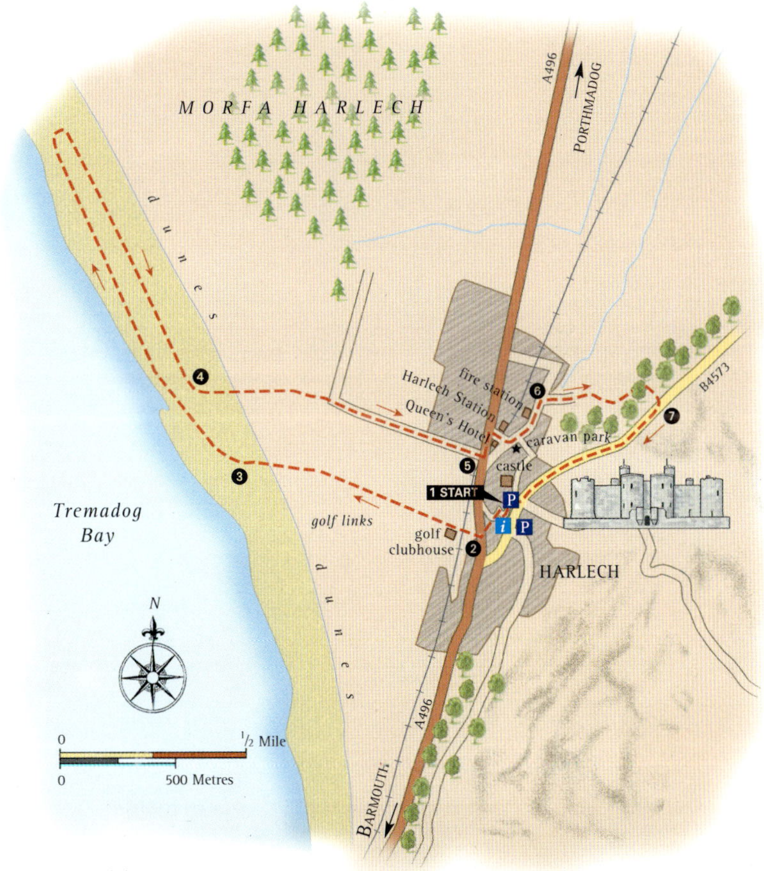

❶ Start at the top castle entrance. With your back to the castle, turn right. Following the sign towards Harlech railway station, take the road that snakes downhill. Part way down, take the public footpath, left, down a flight of slate steps.

❷ Cross the road and follow the public footpath opposite. Cross the railway line with care and go through the metal gate. Follow the path, keeping the wire fence to your right. As you leave the golf course, ignore the track which forks right and take the sandy path between the dunes to the beach.

❸ Turn right and walk along the beach for about a mile (1.6km). From here you can enjoy magnificient sweeping views of the castle and bay. Then turn back and retrace your steps as far as the red-and-white striped pole (lifebelt point H7).

❹ Turn left along the marked sand path, which soon becomes a surfaced path. Go through the metal kissing gate and continue ahead to the main road.

❺ Cross the road. Turn left, then right (just past the Queen's Hotel) towards the railway station. Cross by the level crossing and turn left. Pass the turning to Woodlands Caravan Park and continue beyond the fire station to the public footpath sign.

❻ Turn right to go through the woods. Continue ahead, presently climbing quite steeply. Climb the gap in the stone wall and continue up a rocky slope to the more

clearly marked path. Turn right, uphill, and climb the steep steps.

❼ At the top of the steps climb over the metal bar. Turn right, and

follow the road back into town. At the crossroads, turn right, following the sign to return to the castle where it is worth leaving plenty of time to explore.

DIFFICULTY ✸✸

MORFA HARLECH

dunes

Tremadog Bay

golf links

A496

PORTHMADOG

B4573

Harlech Station
Queen's Hotel
fire station
caravan park

❻

❼

❺
castle

1 START

❹

❸

golf clubhouse ❷

HARLECH

dunes

A496

BARMOUTH

N

0 — ½ Mile

0 — 500 Metres

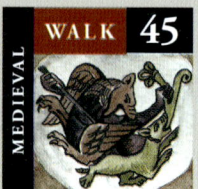

ABOUT • LUDLOW

Ludlow found fame in A E Housman's A Shropshire Lad, but in the 15th century it was better known as a seat of power. In 1473 Edward IV sent his son to take control of the feudal marches and it marked the beginning of the end of Welsh independence.

Shropshire • C ENGLAND

DISTANCE • 5 miles (8km)

TOTAL ASCENT • 330ft (100m)

PATHS • mostly defined tracks; can be very muddy in wet weather. A little safe road walking

TERRAIN • some cultivated fields and forestry tracks

GRADIENTS • very gentle

REFRESHMENTS • numerous in Ludlow, but none on walk

PARK • car park off Castle Square, Ludlow. Larger car park behind Feathers hotel on Corve Street (follow signs to railway station)

OS MAP • Explorer 203 Ludlow, Tenbury Wells & Cleobury Mortimer

The seat of power in Ludlow

DIFFICULTY ✳✳

❶ Start at the Tourist Information Centre and museum, opposite the car park in Castle Square. Turn left out of the TIC and walk to Ludlow Castle at the end of the square. A full tour of the castle can take an hour

❷ From the castle walk back past the car park exit and down a cobbled arcade. Turn left when you see narrow College Street, then turn right to explore St Laurence's parish church, the largest in the county. The west window shows several of the Marcher Lords.

❸ Walk back down College Street, turn left and in 5yds (4.5m) turn right through the arches of The Buttercross (now Ludlow Town Council offices) and down Broad Street to Ludford Bridge. Beyond the bridge turn left into Park Road and follow it to the end. Cross the stile and walk ahead, keeping the wall/hedge on your right.

❹ At a driveway turn right, pass through a gate, and continue down to the main road (B4361). At the road turn left, continue for 383yds (350m) and, beyond three houses, take the driveway to Mabbitts Horn. Just beyond this house reach a stile.

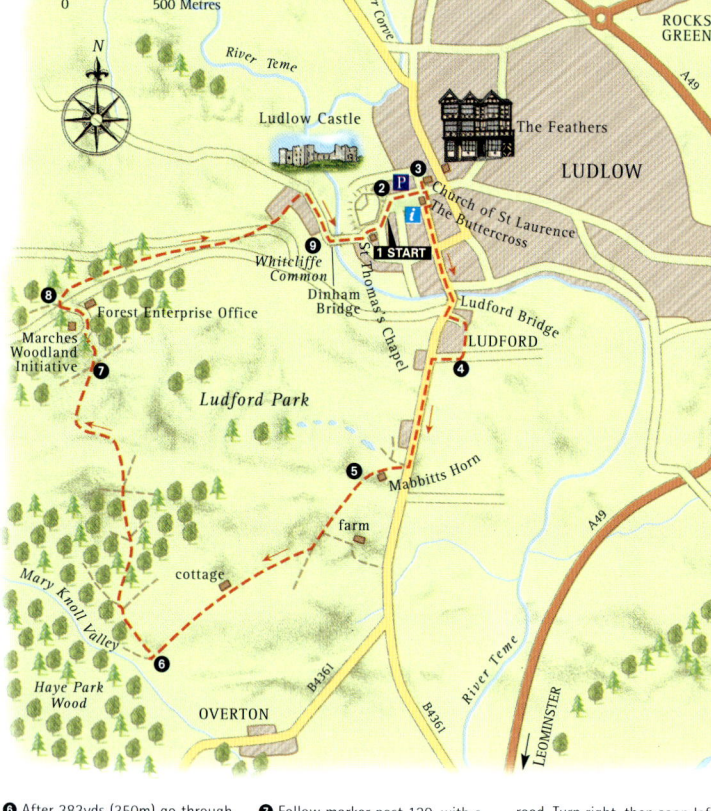

❺ Cross the stile. After 219yds (200m) the path becomes a track with hedgerows on both sides. After a track marked 'Private', which leads to a farm on the left, take the right fork (waymarkers). Continue between hedges along this sunken lane for 437yds (400m). Pass through a gate into a field and in 109yds (100m) go through another gate in front of a cottage on to a track.

❻ After 383yds (350m) go through a tall gate before a hairpin bend on a gravel forestry road; turn right here, uphill, signed Mortimer Trail, permissive route. In 219yds (200m), at a bench, take a footpath at marker post 106. Follow these sequentially numbered marker posts carefully, later through a felled area, until, when in trees again, reach a rutted junction and post 119.

❼ Follow marker post 120, with a dense coniferous plantation on your left. At the main track turn right, pass the Forest Enterprise Office on your right, and reach the main road.

❽ Cross the road and take footpath signed Ludlow, which goes left then turns back to the right. This track has Mortimer Trail waymarks on it, follow these to a

road. Turn right, then soon left, downhill, at a hairpin bend on the main road. Eventually continue round a right-hand bend to Dinham Bridge.

❾ Just before the bridge is Whitcliffe Common, on the right. Cross the bridge and walk uphill back to the castle, bearing left in front of St Thomas's Chapel, the oldest building in Ludlow.

The Tudors reigned for only 118 years, but their dynasty has captured the British imagination more than any other. From the accession of Henry VII until the death of the Virgin Queen, Elizabeth, theirs was an era of unforgettable characters and profound social change.

THE TUDORS

1485–1603

Building a Dynasty

With Henry VII's marriage to Elizabeth of York, the Wars of the Roses were effectively brought to a close. When the King died, his young heir – the sporty, musical, dashing Prince Henry – was welcomed as a bright new star. Henry VIII made an impact on the European stage, too: his mentor, Cardinal Wolsey, arranged the magnificent peace summit with France at the Field of the Cloth of Gold, near Calais; and the King's anti-Lutheran pamphlet earned him the Pope's gratitude and the title 'Defender of the Faith'.

Domestic matters soon cast their shadow over Henry's reign – specifically the absence of a male heir. Henry had married Catherine of Aragon in 1509, but by 1527, with only a daughter, Mary, surviving, he was seeking a way out. Having failed to gain a Papal annulment, Henry took direct action, declaring himself Supreme Head of the Church of England and pronouncing his own marriage invalid. Within a year of marrying the vivacious Anne Boleyn in 1533, he had another child: Elizabeth. Three years later Anne was dead, executed on trumped-up treason charges. Henry's third wife, Jane Seymour, died giving birth to his longed-for son, Edward. There followed three more wives, but no more children.

Henry took full advantage of his new role as head of the reformed Church, dissolving and looting hundreds of monasteries. By the end of the 1530s the countryside was littered with the disintegrating shells of religious buildings, and the previously Catholic population found itself abruptly converted to the Protestant cause.

AFTER THE HENRIES

Edward VI was a sickly child of nine when he became king, and reigned for only six years, guided by staunchly Protestant courtiers. The crown then passed to the devoutly Catholic Mary, who, to her subjects' alarm, married the Spanish king, Philip II. The 'pregnancy' that she celebrated in the same year turned out to be early symptoms of the dropsy that would eventually kill her. Taking this as divine retribution for heresy, Mary became a ruthless persecutor of Protestants, instigating the infamous 'turn or burn' policy.

When Elizabeth succeeded Mary she was already an old hand at the political game, having survived in spite of her half-sister's jealousies. As queen, she aimed for a middle course, avoiding religious extremes. She also resisted parliament's pressure to marry her off and secure the dynasty's future. The succession was a particularly thorny issue, as Mary, Queen of Scots, claimed the English throne as granddaughter of Henry VII. After her Scottish opponents had forced her to abdicate, Mary fled to England, where, for nearly 20 years, she was moved from place to place, a potentially dangerous figurehead for Elizabeth's enemies. Eventually, a plot was uncovered to snatch the crown for Mary, and she was executed – sparking the wrath of Catholic Spain. When the Spanish Armada, sent to wreak vengeance, was battered by the English and foundered in rough seas, Elizabeth's popularity hit an all-time high.

Elizabeth's long reign was a golden age in many ways: music flourished, with composers such as Byrd and Tallis making their names; Shakespeare was a leading light of English drama; Francis Drake and Walter Raleigh typified the spirit of adventure and exploration; and in the absence of civil war, the building and woollen trades boomed. Gloriana, the Virgin Queen, would long remain a charismatic symbol of the Tudor age at its best.

HISTORIC SITES

Little Moreton Hall, Staffs: half-timbered manor house built 1440–1589.

Burghley House, Lincs: exotic home of Elizabeth I's adviser.

Mary Rose, Portsmouth Historic Ships, Hants: glimpse of the Tudor sailor's life, and the remains of Henry VIII's flagship.

Hampton Court, Surrey: Tudor palace complete with Henry VIII's real tennis court.

Shrewsbury: wool-trade centre with many surviving half-timbered houses.

Stratford-upon-Avon: site of Shakespeare's birthplace.

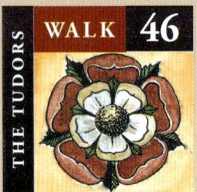
ABOUT • LAVENHAM

The timbered façade of Lavenham offers the perfect image of a Tudor wool town, at its peak during the reign of Henry VIII. Lavenham offers some superb 16th-century architecture including the Guildhall of Corpus Christi and the Swan Inn.

Suffolk • SE ENGLAND

DISTANCE • 5 miles (8km)

PATHS • mostly firm, but sections can be muddy; keep dogs under strict control in the town and through farmyard and fields

Terrain • town, former railway, open farmland, quiet lanes

GRADIENTS • some gentle slopes, but mostly fairly level

REFRESHMENTS • Swan Inn, Lavenham; National Trust tea rooms in Guildhall, Market Square

PARK • in the car park, Lavenham, signed near the church; other parking available in the town

OS MAP • Explorer 196 Sudbury, Hadleigh Dedham Vale

Lavenham – a timbered treasure

❶ Turn right out of the car park and head down hill into the town centre. Turn right just before the timbered Swan Inn into Water Street. Turn into the bottom of Lady Street to admire the old guildhall, now part of the inn but once one of four guildhalls around the town. Continue down Water Street. Pass the bottom of Barn Street, pause to admire its houses.

❷ Turn left up Shilling Street, passing Shilling Grange and other splendid timbered and plastered houses. Nos 22-24 are particularly fine. Turn left at the top into Bolton Street, and bear right into Market Square, passing a memorial to US airmen of World War II.

❸ After exploring the square, with its magnificent timbered Guildhall, little houses, butter cross and Angel Hotel, leave via Market Lane and turn right on the High Street. Continue over the brow of the hill, admiring the lovely old row of houses, Nos 61-63.

❹ At the bottom, just before the railway bridge, take the muddy path down to the left, signed Lavenham Walk. This bends left to join the route of the old railway line (which can be followed all the way to Long Melford), a lovely walk with occasional benches. Continue along this for about a mile (1.6km), with the big square tower of Lavenham church looming to your left, and trees forming a natural arch overhead.

❺ Cross the road via two metal gates and continue along the railway path for about a mile (1.6km). Go through the banks of a cutting, and through a squeeze gate under a brick road bridge. Stay on the line, to pass a Site of Special Scientific Interest with

unusual chalk downland vegetation. After another area of woodland the path deteriorates, emerging on to an open field. Keep straight ahead along the lower edge of the field to meet a junction of tracks.

❻ Turn left up the farm track, back over the hill. Stay on this track and follow the yellow waymarkers as it bends right, towards the farm, then left

between two old black barns. Follow the road round to the right, and at the junction with the track, keep left down the main drive towards Lavenham.

❼ At the end, turn right along the road for a short distance. A fingerpost indicates the path left. Follow it straight across the field towards the barred wooden gate. Cross the stile and keep straight on, with the hedge on your right.

Cross another stile, and go straight on to meet the lane.

❽ Turn right here towards the church, and turn left up the stone steps below the tower. Walk round three sides of the church, keeping on your left, and take the little path in the bottom corner through the wooden kissing gate.

❾ Head down the grassy path towards the pond. Go through the gate and over the bridge, and at the end of the lane turn right into Hall Road. Where this meets High Street, turn right to return to the car park.

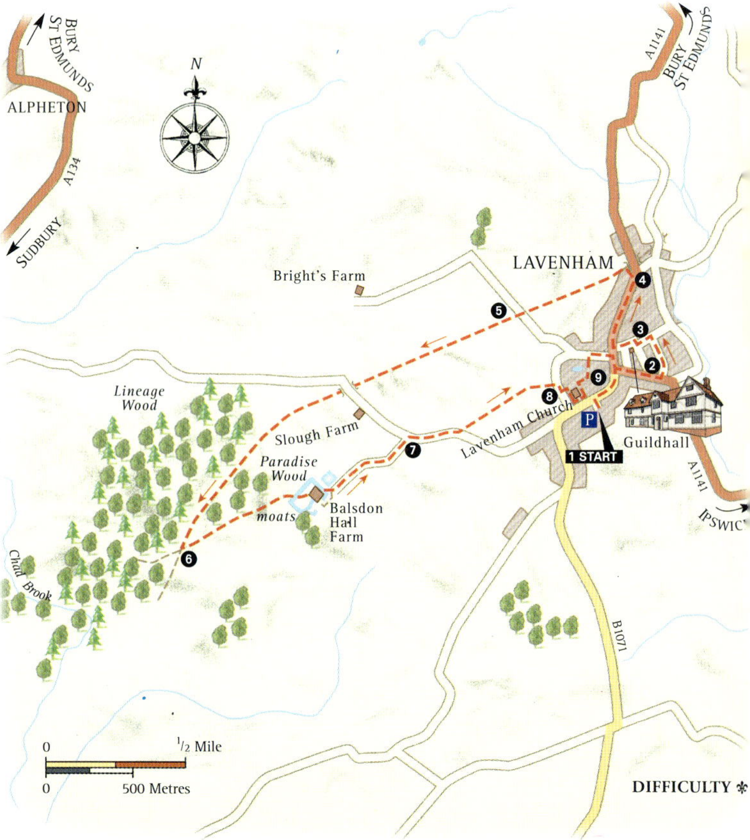

DIFFICULTY ✱

[Map of walk route around Lavenham, Suffolk, showing locations including Alpheton, Bright's Farm, Lineage Wood, Slough Farm, Paradise Wood, Balsdon Hall Farm, Chad Brook, Lavenham, Lavenham Church, Guildhall, with waypoint markers 1-9, a compass rose, and scale bars of ½ Mile and 500 Metres]

ABOUT • ST CATHERINE'S CASTLE

This walk starts from the old pilchard-fishing hamlet of Polkerris and leads you along the cliffs to the lovely St Catherine's Castle, which is actually more of a fort. It was built by the town's residents in 1510 to protect them from attacks from France.

Cornwall • SW ENGLAND

DISTANCE • 6 miles (9.6km)

TOTAL ASCENT • 246ft (75m)

PATHS • coast path, woodland and field tracks (some muddy after wet weather), and country lanes

TERRAIN • cliffs, farmland, wooded valleys

GRADIENTS • some short, steep ascents/descents on coast path and inland valleys

REFRESHMENTS • Rashleigh Arms, Polkerris; café at Readymoney Cove; pubs, cafés and restaurants in Fowey

PARK • free parking in Polkerris; unsurfaced, unmarked car park on right, before village, descending lane signed off the A3082 Fowey to St Austell road just east of Polmear

OS MAP • Explorer 107 St Austell & Liskeard

Henry VIII's coastal fort of St Catherine's

❶ From the car park entrance turn right and head for the Rashleigh Arms by the beach. Turn left (signed public toilets), and follow the coast path signs up concrete steps, and zigzag steeply up through woodland. At the T-junction turn left away from the sea to reach a coast path post at the field edge.

❷ Turn right; follow the coast path along the field and through a gate. Pass through another gate, then climb for 2 miles (3.2km) up to a gate/stile. Just past the National Trust sign for The Gribbin the path divides; keep right to reach the daymark.

❸ Follow the coast path downhill for ¾ mile (1.2km) to reach Polridmouth. Ignore the footpath left (to Menabilly); follow the path behind the beach past the house and lake, to cross the weir on stepping-stones.

❹ Continue up steep steps on to Lankelly Cliff (NT). Pass through the next gate, go round the field edge, and drop down steeply to a stile. Walk up the next field. Descend through a gate to Coombe Haven. Continue over a stile to enter Alldays Fields, then through a small gate into Covington Wood.

❺ Turn sharp right to reach St Catherine's Point; take the next path, right, to the castle. Retrace your steps and turn right to rejoin the coast path, descending to a T-junction behind Readymoney Cove.

❻ Turn left, uphill, for ½ mile (800m) following the deeply banked Saints' Way (signed with a cross), to meet a lane. Turn left to reach Coombe Lane. Turn right to to lead into Prickly Post Lane.

❼ Follow signs left through a drive and down a narrow footpath. Go through a gate and downhill over a stream, under a bridge and uphill over a stone stile. Continue downhill, over a stile, to reach Trenant; cross the drive and the stone stile. Go through the next gate, then downhill and over a stream on a railed footbridge. The path continues over a stile by a ruined cottage, then uphill through a gate into Tregaminion farmyard. Walk through the farmyard, turn right, then left at the farmhouse to reach a T-junction.

❽ Turn right along the lane; after 200yds (183m) turn left on a footpath to rejoin the coast path post at Point 1. Go ahead and retrace your steps downhill to Polkerris.

DIFFICULTY ✳✳

0 _____ 1 Mile

0 _____ 1 Kilometre

N

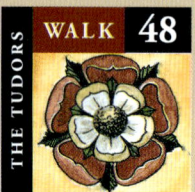

This walk takes you along a drovers' road before visiting the cave of the 16th-century outlaw Twm Sion Catti, thief, highwayman and master of disguise. He was a popular figure of the day and often protected from the king's officers in return for an evening's entertainment.

DISTANCE • 6 miles (9.6km)

TOTAL ASCENT • 300ft (91m)

PATHS • minor roads and forest trails. Paths very muddy and slippery in wet weather

TERRAIN • woodland, farmland

GRADIENTS • undulating roads. Tarmac tracks mostly flat or slightly uphill. Paths can be steep in places

REFRESHMENTS • Rhadirmwyn Bridge and Rhandirmwyn (nearest villages to the walk)

PARK • ample car parking spaces at start point by the dam

OS MAP • Explorer 166 Rhondda & Merthyr Tydfil

Along a drovers' road to the cave of Twm

❶ Facing Llyn Brianne, bear left down a road, and at a T-junction turn right. Further on where the road forks branch left and after about 1/2 mile (800m) turn right into a car park serving the RSPB Dinas Reserve just entered.

❷ Head for a wooden kissing gate at the left-hand side of the car park. Follow a raised wooden pathway leading through woodland. When the boardwalk forks, branch right and follow a nature trail which runs parallel to the river.

❸ Taking care, follow the path through an ancient oak woodland and pass the cave and sometime home of Twm Sion Catti. (A path does lead from the nature trail to the cave, but it is not obvious and may be dangerous in wet weather.)

• DON'T MISS •

*The **drovers' roads** which you walk along this route have played an important part in history. Welsh drovers were the cowboys of their day, driving vast herds of cattle, sheep, pigs and flocks of geese to English markets in the hope of a good sale. They also acted as bankers, delivering and returning the locals' investments, and as an unofficial postal service. Their regular routes through Wales were punctuated with resting places and inns; one of the most remote and spectacular is the road over the hills from Tregaron to Llandovery.*

Craig Cnwch-glas

Afon Doethie

Craig Ddu

Pen Rhiwbie

392

Troed-rhiw-ruddwen

Carreg y Gath

405

Craig Clungwyn

Afon Tywi

Llyn Brianne

dam

1 START

TREGAR

Nant y Ffin

38

Twm Sion Catti Cave

Dinas RSPB Reserve

Ystradffin

Craig Alltyberau

440

Afon Tywi

LLANDOVERY, RHANDIRMWYN

0 — 1/2 Mile

0 — 500 Metres

DIFFICULTY ✱✱

❹ Branch right when the woodland path forks and pass through a large wooden gate. Turn right on to a tarmac road and follow this for about a mile (1.6km). Then turn right on to a single-track road heading for Troedyrhiw and, passing over a bridge, press on, climbing gently.

❺ Cross a metal bridge and then continue until the surfaced road ends in front of a farm and bears sharply right, gently climbing a rough-surfaced vehicle track leading up a narrowing valley.

❻ Near the top of the valley, the path runs through a forest and,

beyond its high point, emerges on the other side, bearing sharp right. A short way on, climb gently to the left on a broad track parallel with the shore of Llyn Brianne, and eventually return to the dam. Cross and walk back to the car park and your car.

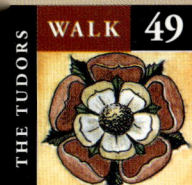

ABOUT • FURNESS ABBEY

Like so many other monasteries in England, Furness was a victim of Henry VIII's split with the Catholic Church. Abbot Roger Pele and his monks rose up against the king but were quickly forced into submission and the abbey looted and destroyed.

Cumbria • N ENGLAND

DISTANCE • 6 miles (9.6km)	
TOTAL ASCENT • 260ft (79m)	
PATHS • field paths, lanes and tracks	
TERRAIN • rolling farmland, can be muddy in winter	
GRADIENTS • easy	

REFRESHMENTS • cafés and inns at Dalton and the Farmers Arms at Newton

PARK • Goose Green car park at the bottom of Church Street opposite Furness Park Garage

OS MAP • Outdoor Leisure 6 The English Lakes – South Western area

The Abbot of Furness

❶ Turn left out of the car park, signed Public Footpath, Mill Wood, and pass through a gate at the end of the lane, signed Public Footpath to Broughton Road. Take the raised path beyond, following a beck and passing under a railway bridge before continuing through three tall gates into another field. At the far side, turn left across a footbridge, go under another railway bridge, and follow an enclosed path to the road.

❷ Cross the road before turning right along a field-edge path through the Vale of Nightshade. Pass under another railway bridge and left along the road to abbey.

❸ Swing left at the junction beyond the abbey. Pass the car park and just beyond a left-hand bend, follow a clear but unsigned path on the right. Cross the railway with care and turn right by the cottage to follow a Mill Beck. Cross the beck on a slab bridge, before recrossing it at Bow Bridge.

❹ Turn left along the lane. After 300yds (274m) a footpath sign points the way uphill over two fields to Newton. Turn half-right past The Village Inn, then left, passing the Farmers Arms and out of the village.

DIFFICULTY ✳✳

❺ Go left at the T-junction. After 200yds (183m) take the path on the right, which cuts diagonally northeast across fields, crossing primitive stiles before coming out on to another lane. Continue along an enclosed muddy track, which is staggered slightly right across the road, to pass Malkin Hall. Turn right along the next lane for 50yds (46m), then left up a gravel track.

❻ Beyond some outbuildings, climb a raised bank on the left of the track and head north on an old mine railway trackbed. Continue through a bush-lined cutting past a water-filled mining hollow, then descend beside a hedge towards Standing Tarn.

❼ Turn left though a squeeze stile above the tarn and head diagonally away from the tarn at the top right-hand corner of a large field. Staggered to the right, across a rough farm track, the next path begins at a squeeze stile and continues by a field edge. Turn left beyond the next stile and descend on a winding lane past some cottages, then pass beneath the railway to reach the main street in Dalton.

❽ Turn left up the main street, past the shops and the castle. Turn left along Church Street, descending past the Brown Cow Inn back to the car park.

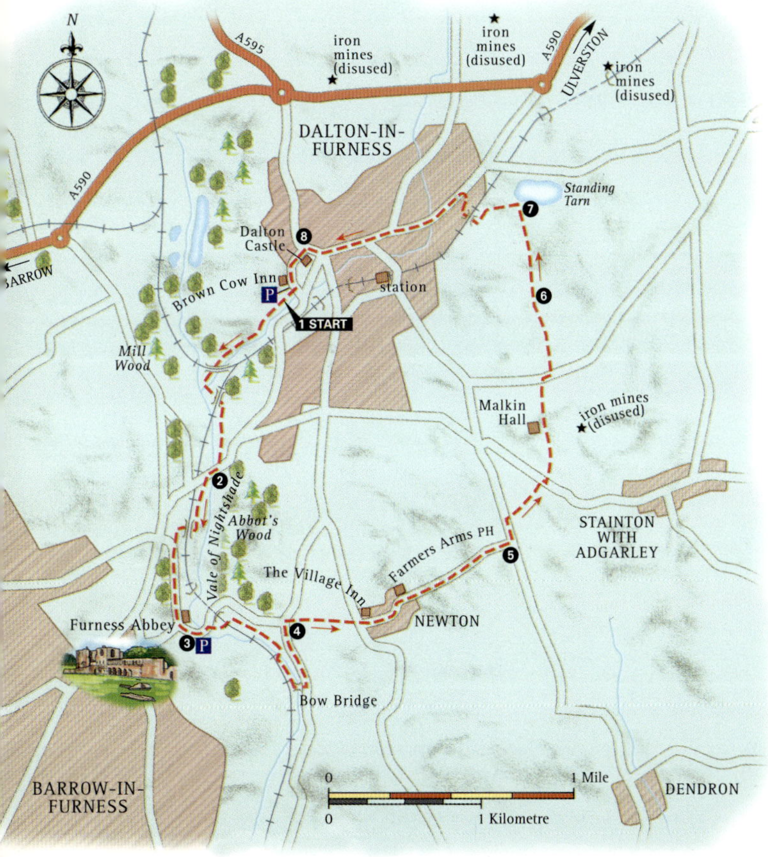

• DON'T MISS •

Dalton Castle where you can view a display of restored armour from the Civil War. Built by the monks of Furness Abbey, following 14th-century raids on their territories by the Scots (including one by Robert the Bruce), the castle has been both a courthouse and a prison. Today, it is in the care of the National Trust.

N

iron mines (disused)

iron mines (disused)

A595

A590

ULVERSTON

A590

iron mines (disused)

DALTON-IN-FURNESS

A590

Standing Tarn

Dalton Castle ❽

Brown Cow Inn
P

station

❼

❻

1 START

Mill Wood

Malkin Hall

iron mines (disused)

STAINTON WITH ADGARLEY

❷

Abbot's Wood

Vale of Nightshade

The Village Inn

Farmers Arms PH

❺

NEWTON

Furness Abbey

❸ P

❹

Bow Bridge

BARROW-IN-FURNESS

DENDRON

0   1 Mile

0   1 Kilometre

BARROW

Shakespeare's Globe

Discover London's thriving riverside and visit the world-famous Globe Theatre on this fascinating walk along the South Bank

Elizabethan London

Extending from Vauxhall Bridge downstream to Tower Bridge, this riverside walk shows how much the South Bank has changed since William Shakespeare came to London, joined a theatre company as an actor and performed many of his plays on the stage of the historic Globe. It was on this stretch of the Thames, at the Hope, Swan, Rose and Globe open-air playhouses, that the world's finest drama was staged.

During the latter part of the 16th century, Southwark was a rowdy place littered with taverns and brothels and renowned for bawdy entertainment. The Globe overlooked a river and a city teeming with life. River wherries ferried passengers from one bank of the Thames to the other; heavy goods were transported by water and the only way to cross the river on foot was via London Bridge.

The scene today is very different, but one landmark, the Globe, remains. It may be a replica but it serves as a lasting memorial to the genius of one man – William Shakespeare (1564–1616).

A Sumptuous Stage

In 1576 actor-manager James Burbage established the first purpose-built playhouse, near the Lord Mayor's Reach. He called it The Theatre, and it prospered for the next 20 years. As the 16th century drew to a close, Burbage's lease expired forcing him to look for new premises. He found a suitable venue in the Blackfriars below St Paul's but the local inhabitants opposed the project.

Burbage died in 1597 and his sons, Cuthbert and Richard, leased a plot of land across the river in Southwark, using the materials from the old Blackfriars theatre to construct the new building on Bankside in 1599.

For the next 14 years the Globe, 'the glory of the Banke', gained an enviable reputation for its drama and for the skill of William Shakespeare, its most talented actor and playwright. But in 1613, during a performance of Henry VIII, a cannon spark set fire to the roof and the building quickly burned to the ground. The only casualty was a man whose breeches caught fire. Undeterred, the company rebuilt the Globe, this time with a tiled roof.

More than 370 years later, in 1989, archaeologists discovered the remains of the Globe's foundations, confirming that part of it is buried under Southwark Bridge Road and part of it under nearby Anchor Terrace. One engraving survives, indicating that the second Globe was built on the foundations of the first.

Arriving in London in 1949, American actor Sam Wanamaker was appalled to find that the only reference to the Globe's existence was a blackened bronze plaque on a brewery wall. Wanamaker rebuilt the Globe, and the project was completed in 1994 (sadly Sam Wanamaker died shortly before its completion), close to its original site, using authentic materials and building methods.

The 21st-century Globe is a 20-sided building built with 36,000 hand-made bricks and thatched with 6,000 bundles of Norfolk water reed. The rebirth of this, the first building in London since 1666 to have a thatched roof, is the result of the hard work of many people – and the dream of one man.

WALK 50
ALONG THE RIVERSIDE TO THE GLORY OF THE BANKE

❶ Approach Vauxhall Bridge from the underground station, keeping the eye-catching MI6 building on your right. Bear right and follow the Thames Path along Albert Embankment towards Lambeth Bridge. Pass under it: now Big Ben and the splendid Gothic façade of the Palace of Westminster dominate the north bank of the river. Pass St Thomas's Hospital and take the subway under the road at Westminster Bridge.

❷ Keep the old County Hall building on your right and walk beneath the London Eye. Make for Hungerford Bridge, pass the Royal Festival Hall and approach Waterloo Bridge, with the National Film Theatre on the right. Beyond it lies the National Theatre with Blackfriars Bridge and St Paul's Cathedral ahead. Walk along to the Oxo Tower, with its design shops, cafés and coffee bars, and pass through the subway at Blackfriars Bridge.

❸ Walk alongside Tate Modern to reach the Millennium Bridge. Just beyond it is the Globe Theatre. Turn the corner by the Anchor Inn and follow Clink Street, passing the museum and the remains of Winchester Palace, once part of the medieval town house of the Bishops of Winchester. Continue along Pickfords Wharf to the reconstruction of the Golden Hinde and keep right here for Southwark Cathedral.

❹ Keep left of the cathedral and look for the Mudlark pub. Walk to a sign on the left for London Bridge, City Pier and Thames Path East. Return to the river and turn right. Pass HMS *Belfast* and head for Tower Bridge. Cross and make for Tower Hill underground station or Fenchurch Street station.

Distance: 3 miles (5km)

Terrain: riverside promenade and pavements

Refreshments: plenty on route

Park: South Bank car parks. Alternatively, use the train and underground

OS Map: Explorer 173 London North, the City, West End, Enfield

Difficulty: ✳

ABOUT • KENDAL CASTLE

Climbing Castle Hill leads to Kendal Castle, home of the ruling barons of Kendal from the 13th century. The Parr family lived here and their long and intriguing history only became known when Catherine Parr became the only wife to outlive Henry VIII.

Cumbria • SW N ENGLAND

DISTANCE • 7½ miles (12km)

TOTAL ASCENT • 650ft (198m)

PATHS • well-defined, firm paths

TERRAIN • limestone hills and town streets

GRADIENTS • steady climb from the town back to Kendal Scar

REFRESHMENTS • Castle Inn, Castle Street; the 1657 Chocolate Shop, off Finkle Street

PARK • Scout Scar car park, Underbarrow Road

OS MAP • Outdoor Leisure 7 The English Lakes South Eastern area

Kendal Castle

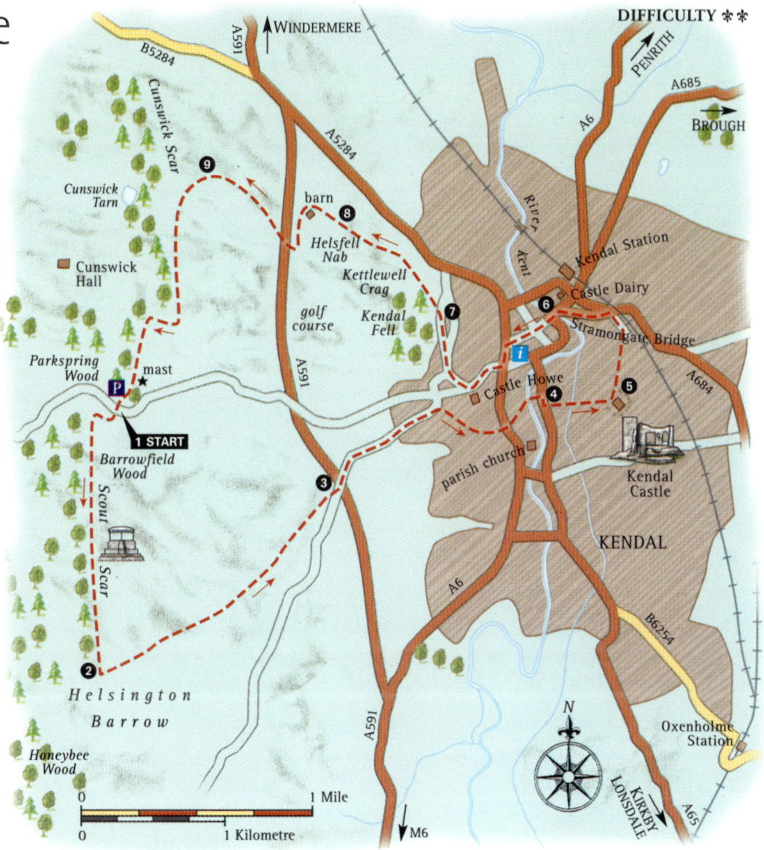

❶ Go through the kissing gate across the road from the signed car park and climb through scrub hawthorns towards Scout Scar. Follow the edge path south.

❷ Turn left at a large cairn and follow the limestone path across the plateau. Beyond the second access (a kissing gate) through crosswalls, the path traverses a field to reach a country lane.

❸ Turn left along the lane over the by-pass down towards Kendal. Take the right fork on the edge of town, then turn right down Gillinggate. Go straight across the main road at the bottom, into Dowker's Lane, and through the arched stone gate into the recreation ground. Take the left-hand path through the recreation ground and cross the footbridge spanning the River Kent.

❹ Cross the road, turn right then go left up Parr Street (which becomes Sunnyside) before climbing the path to the castle.

❺ Head north along the grassy ridge back into Kendal. Turn left along Castle Road, then left again along the A684. Where this bends right go straight ahead to cross the river at Stramongate Bridge.

❻ Continue along Stramongate and Finkle Street, then turn left along Stricklandgate. Turn right by the Tourist Information Centre to climb up Allhallows Lane and Beast Banks. Turn right by the triangular green in to Mount Pleasant (leading to Serpentine Road). At the main road turn right, then take the left fork into Queens Road.

❼ Go left up a narrow tarmac lane, signed footpath to Helsfell

Nab. Half-way up the hillside this becomes a gritty track heading northwest on the slopes of Kendal Fell.

❽ Beneath Kettlewell Crag the path turns right over a stile (look for a small yellow arrrow) and follows the right-hand field edge beneath Helsfell Nab. Beyond an old barn swing left on a path parallel to the by-pass. Cross two ladder stiles before reaching a third to cross the footbridge over

the by-pass. Cross another ladder stile to leave the footbridge and then cross one more over the wall to the right. Continue on the faint footpath across the field, aiming for the grassy hilltop ahead.

❾ Beyond the stile in the left corner of the field, swing half left to the edge of Cunswick Scar. Head south along it, crossing a stile, then turn right, following the permissive route signed to Scout Scar. Go over the stile into the

woods and take the right fork back to the car park.

• DON'T MISS •

*The 14th-century **Castle Dairy** on Wildman Street is Kendal's oldest building. It was probably part of a dowry given by Sir Thomas Parr to his daughter Agnes on her wedding to Sir Thomas Strickland in 1455.*

DIFFICULTY ✷✷

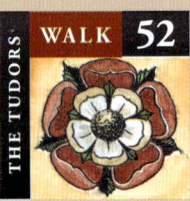
ABOUT • SHERBORNE

Founded by the Saxons and set amid green valleys and wooded hills, Sherborne is a lovely, mellow-stoned town. It was also home to one of the most famous figures of the Elizabethan court, Sir Walter Raleigh, who lived here from 1592 until his death in 1618.

Dorset • SW ENGLAND

DISTANCE • 5½ miles (8.8km)

TOTAL ASCENT • 400ft (121m)

PATHS • good, but field paths can be waterlogged after heavy rain

TERRAIN • parkland, farmland, town streets

GRADIENTS • gradual; one steep ascent

REFRESHMENTS • choice of pubs and cafés in Sherborne; tea room in Sherborne Castle

PARKING • main long-stay car park accessed off Long Street or Ludbourne Road (close to Sainsbury's). Alternative parking at station

OS MAP • Explorer 129 Yeovil & Sherborne

Sir Walter Raleigh

DIFFICULTY ✳✳

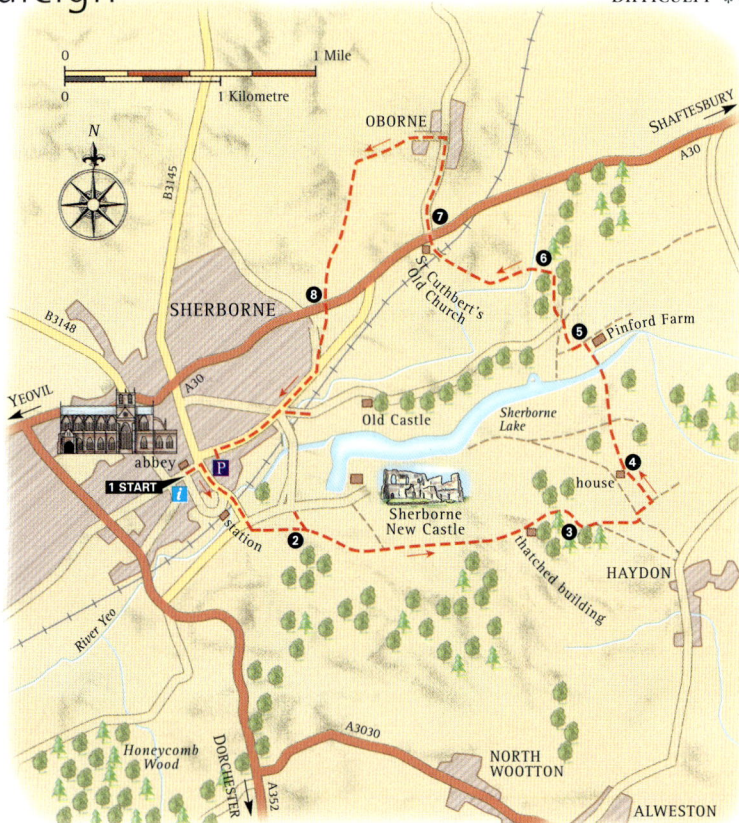

❶ With your back to the abbey, turn left along Half Moon Street, then right down South Street. Fork left past Sainsbury's and cross the railway to a T-junction. Cross over and take the waymarked path left, diagonally uphill. Bear left beside railings down to a turnstile gate and right along the drive to visit Sherborne New Castle.

❷ Return along the drive to the turnstile gate and go uphill. Bear left and beyond the gate take the grassy path between fields to a gate. Bear right on a track to a gate and go uphill towards a thatched building in trees. Go through a gate and go steeply uphill into the deer park. Bear right at the top to a gate into woodland.

❸ Shortly, follow the path left, and disregarding the concrete path right, keep ahead to farm buildings. Turn right along the access road to a drive. Turn left, then right with a yellow marker down a track along the field edge. At a junction of paths, cross the stile on your left and walk beside woodland to a gate (house left).

❹ Enter the deer park and proceed straight ahead, downhill along the line of telegraph poles, towards a farmhouse. Keep ahead beyond a gate to cross a bridge over the River Yeo. Continue along the right-hand field edge to a gate beside Pinford Farm.

❺ Turn left along the drive, then just beyond a gate, turn right through a gate into a field. Head uphill towards an ornate drive entrance and a gate. Turn right through the gateway and take the second path left. In a few paces, bear right following yellow markers along a path through a copse, eventually reaching a stile.

❻ Head straight across the field to a gate, then bear half-left to double stiles in the hedge. Proceed diagonally right to a gate and pass beneath the railway bridge. Just beyond, bear off right to a stone stile and walk to the A30, beside St Cuthbert's Old Church.

❼ Cross and follow the lane to Oborne. Cross the small bridge on your left, pass the church and keep ahead, uphill along a cobbled path. Remain on the path to the A30.

❽ Follow the bridleway opposite, beside Four Acres, to a stile and descend to a gate. Keep ahead to a gate and go through the farmyard to a lane. Turn left, then right at the T-junction into Sherborne. For the Old Castle take the first road left; otherwise, keep ahead along Long Street into the town.

• DON'T MISS •

St Cuthbert's Old Church in Sherborne, is an enchanting small stone building between the A30 and the railway station. Only the chancel survives of the 1553 church. Note the 14th-century slip-tiles, the rustic, 17th-century communion rails, and the medieval pillar piscina.

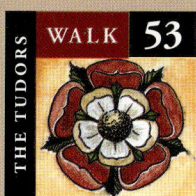

A steep, demanding climb is rewarded with panoramic views over Fife, with the Highland mountains on the far horizon. The moor is a wild place and not so very different from when Mary, Queen of Scots, rode the hillside with a falcon on her wrist.

DISTANCE • 5 miles (8km)	
TOTAL ASCENT • 1,148ft (350m)	
PATHS • mostly good, but some stretches muddy in wet weather	
TERRAIN • woods and open moorland	
GRADIENTS • steep on East Lomond Hill	

REFRESHMENTS • tea rooms, restaurants and pubs in Falkland

PARK • near the town hall

OS MAP • Explorer 370 Glenrothes North, Falkland & Lomond Hills

Favourite home of Mary, Queen of Scots

❶ Follow the lane out of the car park and turn left up Back Wynd. Bear right at the factory entrance gates, then turn left at the crossroads into East Loan. Continue uphill where the road turns into a track with the factory entrance on the left.

❷ After 60yds (55m) fork right on to the signed track. Soon take the signed footpath left to climb a long flight of steps, with a handrail, cut into the hillside through trees.

❸ Continue up the steps to an attractive area of beech wood. The route, now a path, levels off slightly. As you gain height the path becomes steeper entering coniferous pines. The woodland clears to reveal an expanse of moorland and heather. The path is well-defined until near the summit where it becomes steep and demanding. Look back for views of Falkland and its palace almost directly below.

❹ The only evidence of the Pictish hill fort is the ramparts which encircle the site. Ben Lomond can be seen to the west, the Grampian Highlands to the north, the North Sea and the East Neuk of Fife to the east and the Firth of Forth and Edinburgh to the south. From the far side of the summit follow a faint path downhill to the left to join the straight clear track that can be seen further down the slope, cutting across the moorland.

❺ Pass through a kissing gate, bear right along the clear track, an old limestone-burners' road enclosed by drystone dykes. In August and September the heather moorland is a purple blaze of colour. The track (take care in wet conditions as the track can be muddy and boggy) leads down to a minor road.

❻ At the junction with the road turn right. Here there are toilets, a picnic area and car park. Continue on the road downhill, with woodland on your left, for 2 miles (3km) into Falkland. Enter the town and pass a number of well-restored cottages dating back to the 17th and 18th centuries. One, the Old Room, opposite Mill Wynd, is now a cunningly disguised electricity sub-station. Many cottages have 'marriage lintels', engraved with initials, hearts and dates above their doors.

❼ Having visited the palace, then turn right into Beck Wynd to return to the car park.

• DON'T MISS •

Just after reaching the main track at Point ❺, a signed path to the left leads to a large, early 19th-century lime-kiln. In the days before artificial fertilisers, lime was essential for improving acid soils. The flooded quarry pits around the kiln are now an attractive nature reserve.

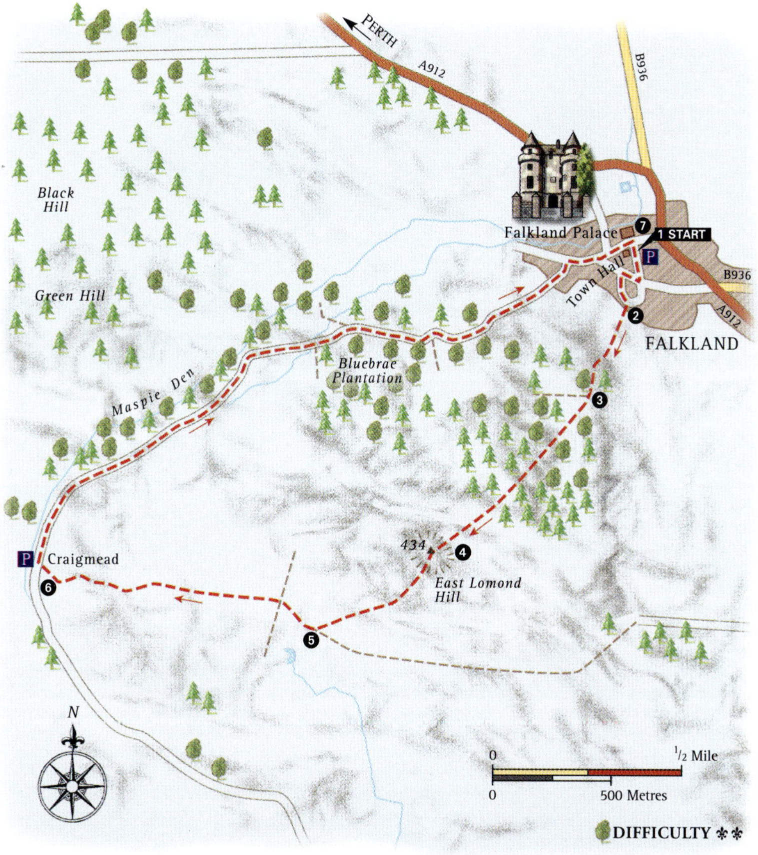

PERTH · A912

B936

Black Hill

Falkland Palace

❼ 1 START

Town Hall

B936

A912

❷

FALKLAND

Green Hill

Bluebrae Plantation

❸

Maspie Den

P Craigmead

❻

434

❹

East Lomond Hill

❺

N

0   1/2 Mile

0   500 Metres

◆ DIFFICULTY ✱✱

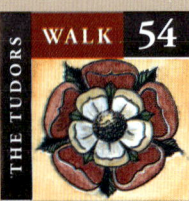

THE TUDORS

WALK 54

ABOUT • HARDWICK HALL

Discover one of the most fascinating women in British history in this walk around Hardwick Hall. Born in 1527, Bess wed four wealthy men, outlived them all and inherited their estates to become one of the richest women in England, only outdone by Elizabeth I.

Derbyshire • C ENGLAND

DISTANCE • 6 miles (9.6km)

TOTAL ASCENT • 584ft (178m)

PATHS • mostly wooded, or surfaced; open fields can be muddy in wet weather

TERRAIN • dense woodland opening out on to agricultural pastures. Note: keep dogs on the lead whilst in the park

GRADIENT • gradual and comfortable

REFRESHMENTS • Hardwick Inn, café in the Old Hall

PARK • Hardwick Information Centre (signed)

OS MAP • Explorer 273 Lincolnshire Wolds South, Horncastle

Bess of Hardwick

DIFFICULTY ✱✱

❶ In the car park at the Tourist Information Centre, face the lake and take the wooded track to the left alongside Miller's Pond. Cross the bridge and at the end of the pond, bear left after passing through a kissing gate. Follow the grassy track to another kissing gate, and continue to Blingsby Gate on the left.

❷ Turn left, passing through Blingsby Gate and follow the firm gravel road. Pass a farm on the right and a blue sentry box on the left. Very soon pass through blue gates (entrance to Hardwick Park) to meet the road. Turn left, on the right is Stainsby Mill.

❸ Retrace your route back through Blingsby Gate, continue on the road and pass through the next gate. Immediately turn left and climb up over the meadow following the wire fence on the left which leads to another blue gate.

❹ Pass through the blue gate and take the right fork which leads to the village of Ault Hucknall. Emerge from the track immediately opposite the Church of St John the Baptist. Turn right along the road until a bend reveals a bridlepath, signed Rowthorne Trail, on your right. Cross cultivated fields to a stile and a road.

❺ Turn right, then right again to the entrance gates of Hardwick Park. Walk towards Hardwick Hall. At the main entrance to the house, and just before the Old Hall, turn right down a wide grass track. Pass through the kissing gate and immediately turn right, hugging the fence downhill.

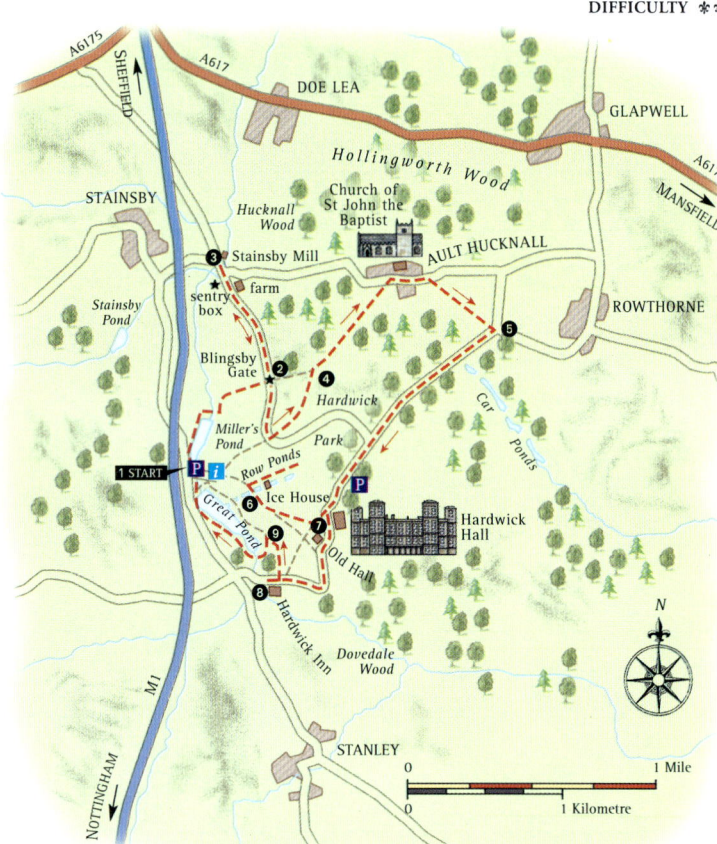

❻ Pass through another gate to the five historic Row Ponds. The Ice House can be seen between the third and fourth pond. Retrace your steps back to the Old Hall.

❼ Return to the road in front of Hardwick Hall, turn right and follow the road down through trees to another gate. This is another entrance/exit to the Park. On the left is Hardwick Inn.

❽ At the Park gate bear sharp left and walk across the field, hugging the fence as it circles round woodland. Eventually pass through a gate in the fence.

❾ Follow the path through the woodland, leading to the Great Pond on your right. Continue to the road and turn right to return to the car park and the start of the walk.

• DON'T MISS •

The church of St John the Baptist at Ault Hucknall holds the tomb of Thomas Hobbes (1588–1679), political philosopher and tutor to the 2nd and 3rd Earls of Devonshire. On its pews you will find rows of beautifully embroidered kneelers, each one crafted by one of the locals.

During the 17th century Britain endured a roller-coaster ride through religious and political controversy, and was nearly torn apart by civil war. By the dawn of the 18th century, the foundations of a modern nation state had been laid.

THE STUARTS

1603–1714

Gunpowder to Wig Powder

James VI of Scotland, son of Mary, Queen of Scots, became James I of England when Elizabeth died without an heir. He left Calvinist Edinburgh to take up his throne in London, where Puritans were pushing to get rid of all remnants of Catholic ritual in the Church. Their bid to abolish bishops went too far for the new king, but when, in 1605, Guy Fawkes and his Catholic conspirators tried to blow up the Houses of Parliament, James hardened his stance and reimposed anti-Catholic penalties.

James was a big spender and patron of the arts. Shakespeare's *Measure for Measure* was written in his honour; during his and his son's reigns drama and poetry flourished under Webster, Jonson, Donne, Milton and many others; royal funds were splashed out on the construction of the Banqueting House in Whitehall Palace, designed by Inigo Jones. Asked to vote him money to cover these costs and to pay for war with Spain, Parliament presented its 'grievances'.

Charles I found himself in similar difficulties, seeking funds for wars with Spain and France, and alienating Parliament with his 'High Church' views. In 1629 the Commons passed resolutions condemning the King, while the Speaker was held down in his chair. For the next 11 years Charles ruled without calling a Parliament. The interlude ended with the King's defeat by Scottish Presbyterians resisting the English-style religious practices. Parliament returned, in defiant mood, and the wrangle continued.

In 1642 Charles entered the House of Commons with troops to arrest the ringleaders, only to find that 'his birds had flown'. Neither side was prepared to yield, so both prepared for war.

The Civil War is still a vivid popular memory, as are the long-haired, droopy-hatted Royalists, or Cavaliers, and the helmeted Roundheads

who took prominence under Puritan general Oliver Cromwell. Seven years of bitter fighting devastated the country, dividing families and destroying crops, buildings and lives. After Charles' execution in 1649 the nation was left in a state of exhaustion and shock. In 1651 the political philosopher Thomas Hobbes called for a 'Leviathan' – a strong sovereign – and reflected the general post-war despair. Enter Oliver Cromwell as Lord Protector. His vicious campaigns in Ireland and his Puritanical domestic policies made him a hate-figure to many, and after his death Charles II was restored to the throne to widespread acclamation.

AFTER THE RESTORATION

Theatres reopened in 1660 for the first time since 1642, but religious conflicts continued, and a split between the King's supporters and opponents – Tories and Whigs – marked the beginnings of a political party system. In the mid-1660s two disasters hit – the Plague and the Great Fire of London. But despite all this, parts of Britain, at least, were prospering. American and West Indian colonies supplied tobacco, cotton, rice and sugar in a closed trade system that excluded Scotland altogether. Fortunes were made; money opened doors to power and influence. Even the Great Fire had benefits, providing Christopher Wren with the opportunity to make his architectural mark.

In 1688 the Glorious Revolution took place. The Catholic king James II was deposed in favour of William of Orange, and Parliament established a constitutional, Protestant succession. Everywhere, the old certainties of religion, power and knowledge were being challenged. Two years before the Glorious Revolution, Isaac Newton had put forward his laws of physics, changing man's view of the universe for ever.

HISTORIC SITES

Hatfield House, Herts: superb Jacobean mansion.

Parliament House, Edinburgh: built for the Scottish Parliament in the 1630s.

Queen's House, Greenwich: Inigo Jones's masterpiece.

Eyam, Derbyshire: village struck by the plague in 1665 and put into voluntary quarantine.

Lancaster Castle, Lancs: ten witches were tried and sentenced here in 1612, and executed on Gallows Hill near by.

Audley End, Essex: built for the Lord Treasurer in 1614; at the time, England's largest house.

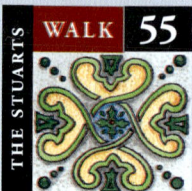
ABOUT • NORDELPH

From the village of Nordelph, you explore the man-made landscape of the Fens, which caused deep controversy in the 17th century. With the permission of Charles I, Dutch engineers drained huge tracts of bog land to create a fertile landscape.

Norfolk • SE ENGLAND

DISTANCE • 5 miles (8km)

PATHS • mostly good, but field path can be very muddy; some road walking

TERRAIN • village, fields, river bank

GRADIENTS • mostly level walking; a climb up the bank, and two awkward stiles and bridges to negotiate

REFRESHMENTS • Chequers Inn, Nordelph

PARK • car park by phone box, just over bridge off A1122, signed Welney.

OS MAP • Explorer 228 March & Ely, Chatteris & Littleport

The wide skies of a man-made landscape

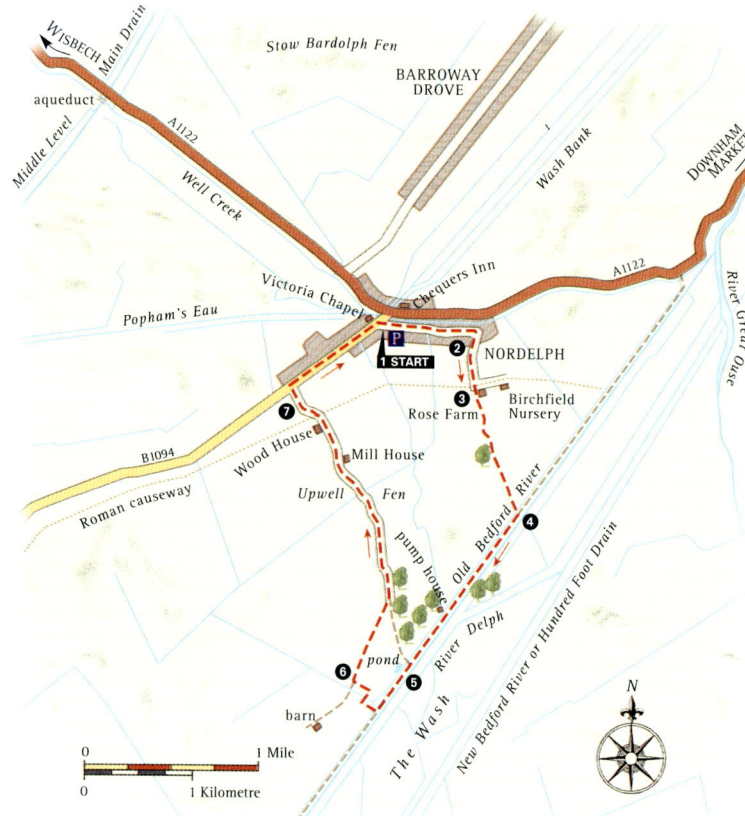

❶ From the car park and picnic area by the landing stage opposite the Chequers Inn, turn away from the bridge and walk down the High Street, parallel with Well Creek, which is on your left. Pass a row of terraced cottages, and the church (due for demolition at time of writing). Pass the village hall and war memorial on your right. Continue past a squat pepper-pot house, and a row of modern housing.

❷ Follow the main road as it bends sharp right and continues as Birchfield Road, away from Well Creek. A ditch, or lode, on your right separates you from the expansive fields.

❸ Where the road bends left, follow the footpath sign straight ahead along a grassy path by the lode. Stay along the field edge, following the course of the lode, heading for a lone poplar tree. At the tree, where the lode disappears underground, keep straight on, following the line of concrete fence posts.

❹ At the end of the field, cross the reedy drain via a footbridge. Cross the stile, climb up the river bank and turn right. Walk along the grassy river path of the Old Bedford River for about a mile (1.6km), with excellent views over the flat fen landscape. Note the flood meadow between the river and the parallel line of the New Bedford River.

❺ Descend near the oblong artificial fish pond on to the lower path, continuing through a gate. Shortly after passing under the pylons, look for a stile and

footbridge with a handrail down to your right – stepped access may be slippery. Cross over, and turn right on the opposite bank, bearing left with the field edge along the lode.

❻ At the concrete bridge, turn right on to the farm track. This becomes a tarmac road, passing through farm buildings and scattered houses. Just past Wood House farmhouse, look out for the

track off to the right (private) – this is the line of an old Roman causeway. Stay on the road, to reach a junction.

❼ At the junction, turn right and walk on the verge back towards the village. Where Coronation Avenue opens up on the left, cross over and continue into the village on the footpath. Turn right by the Victoria Chapel to the car park.

DIFFICULTY ✳✳

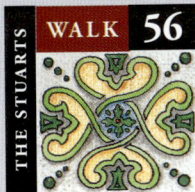
This walk visits Appleby Castle, restored in 1651 by the extraordinary Lady Anne Clifford. She won fame as a great adversary of Cromwell and for her prolific building and restoration work, including St Anne's Hospital and St Michael's in Bongate.

DISTANCE • 6½ miles (10.4km)

TOTAL ASCENT • 375ft (114m)

PATHS • field tracks and farm lanes

TERRAIN • pastureland and town

GRADIENTS • no steep ascents

REFRESHMENTS • several pubs and tea shops in Appleby. The Royal Oak on Bongate is next to the start of the walk

PARK • roadside parking by the war memorial and St Michael's Church at the top of Mill Hill on Bongate

OS MAP • Outdoor Leisure 19 Howgill Fells & Upper Eden Valley

The indomitable spirit of Lady Anne Clifford

❶ Walk down Mill Hill to cross Jubilee Bridge over the River Eden by Bongate Mill. Walk up the hill and turn right at the top for 200yds (183m). Cross the road to the shop opposite, go along Colby Lane for 15yds (14m) to a footpath on the left signed Bandley Bridge.

❷ Cross the stile and go along the left-hand edge of the field to another stile. Turn right down a green lane for 10yds (9m) and turn left at a metal stile. Go over the rise in the field, cross the stile and turn right on to a green lane. As the track turns right, turn left over a stile along the edge of a field. Soon turn right over next stile.

❸ Continue through the middle of the next field, aiming for a gate just below the horizon. Cross the stile by the gate and continue through the middle of the field. Over the brow of the hill, descend to the right-hand corner to cross a beck at the bottom. Turn right through a gate in a wall then left to cross Bandley Bridge. Cross a stile by a gate, turn right through a grassy field and a gate. After a

ruined wall, bear left up the bank towards a marker pole. At the top, bear left through a gate, then right on to a track to Nether Hoff.

❹ Go through the farmyard, then along the lane over a bridge and past some modern houses. At the junction with a road, cross to a footpath through a garden diagonally opposite, signed Village Green and Colby Hall. Go through a gate and across a field to a footbridge then, bearing right, cross over two stiles. Bear left, round the base of the bank on your left and at the end of the field go through a gate on to an access road. In 30yds (27m) turn right over a bridge to follow a concrete track over the hill. As Colby Laithes comes into view turn right up a footpath signed Appleby.

❺ Follow this track as it turns sharp right, then left, and becomes indistinct. Go through several fields and join a track coming in from the left. As the track bends right through a gate, cross a stile and turn left. By bungalows at the field corner join a path behind gardens. Pass a playground and turn left on a snicket (alley) into Appleby. Turn left on Holme Street, pass the fire station and cross Holme Bridge. Turn right through a metal gate signed Sands. Another gate leads to a woodland path, which eventually drops down to join a metalled road. Continue to the Sands (the road by the river) and turn right over the Eden.

❻ Walk along Bridge Street into Boroughgate, turn right through the Cloisters to St Lawrence's Church. After visiting the church return to walk up the left-hand side of Boroughgate. Pass the Hospital of St Anne, left, to the castle gates then follow Shaws Wiend, descending to Scattergate. Pass the rear entrance to the castle, retrace your steps down to Jubilee Bridge and Mill Hill.

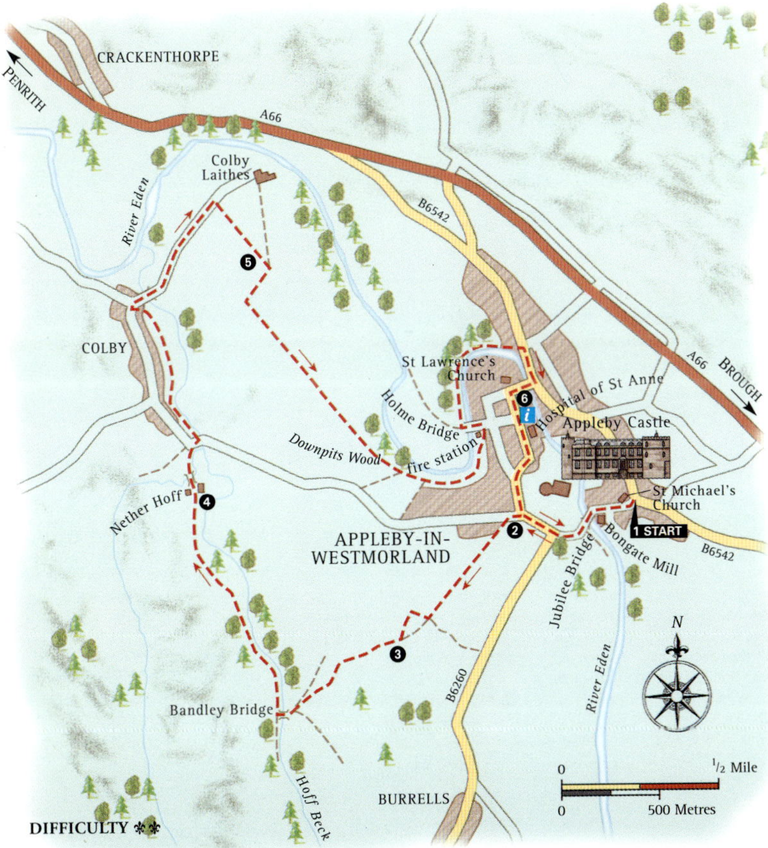

CRACKENTHORPE

PENRITH

A66

Colby Laithes

B6542

River Eden

❺

COLBY

St Lawrence's Church

Holme Bridge

❻

Hospital of St Anne

Appleby Castle

Downpits Wood

fire station

i

A66 BROUGH

Nether Hoff ❹

APPLEBY-IN-WESTMORLAND

St Michael's Church

❷

1 START

Jubilee Bridge

Bongate Mill

B6542

River Eden

B6260

❸

N

Bandley Bridge

Hoff Beck

BURRELLS

0 ½ Mile

0 500 Metres

DIFFICULTY ✽✽

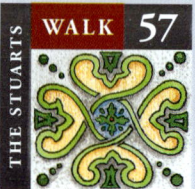
ABOUT • BOSCOBEL HOUSE

After defeat at the Battle of Worcester Charles II fled to Boscobel House. To avoid Cromwell's troops, who were searching the grounds, the King hid in an oak tree for 14 hours before fleeing to France where he stayed until the Restoration in 1660.

Staffordshire • C ENGLAND

DISTANCE • 8 miles (13km)

TOTAL ASCENT • 135ft (41m)

PATHS • minor roads (one fairly busy but with wide verges), tracks and paths, some wet and muddy at times

TERRAIN • rolling countryside, arable fields, woodland

GRADIENTS • very gradual; mainly flat

REFRESHMENTS • two pubs passed on the route: The New Inns (sic) at Kiddemore Green and The Royal Oak at Bishop's Wood

PARK • at Boscobel House (English Heritage), open daily Apr–Oct 10–6, Nov 10–4; Dec Sat, Sun 10–4

OS MAP • Explorer 242 Telford, Ironbridge & The Wrekin

The Royal Oak at Boscobel House

❶ Turn right out of the car park and right again at the T-junction. Ignore the left turn and follow the road for 1¼ miles (2km), keeping to the grass verge. About 250yds (229m) after a large, red-brick farmhouse, take the track signed bridle path, to the left.

❷ Continue, soon following a wall, and at the end turn right on to the lane. Take the track to the left to Chillington Farm. Follow the blue arrow waymarks through the yard, between two farm buildings. Follow the distinct path along the edge of a field, with a hedge on your left, then across another field.

❸ Turn right at a T-junction. Ignore drive to house with ponds on left, pass through the gate, leave the main track, taking the path to the left round the edge of the garden then across the field to a copse. Bear right to the wooden footbridge, follow the edge of the field, then a tree-lined path.

❹ At the end, turn left and follow the lane for ¾ mile (1.2km), passing Villa Farm, to reach a road, to the right, signed Black Ladies and Top Barn Farm. Follow track, curving left between The Black Ladies

(period house) and stables, bearing sharp left after the farm. Where the track forks, keep left.

❺ After Invicta Farm, follow the track to the left, ignoring bridleway signs to the right. Turn right on to the road; at the staggered crossroads go ahead into Old Weston Road. Keep left into Royal Oak Drive and follow this to the right, then left, then left again at the T-junction.

❻ Take the signed footpath to the right, between fences, in front of the school at the end. Cross the stile, cross the field diagonally up to the left (or skirt round the field to the right if the field is in crop) to a stile, which becomes visible near the corner. Cross stile, turn right on to the road. Continue, and after about ½ mile (800m), beyond the woods, take the road, left.

❼ Bear left, then right to the farm. In front of the house, follow the faded arrows through the black gate to the left, round two sides of the stable yard, through another gate, round a shed, then through another gate into open country.

❽ Follow the path along the edge of a field (hedge/fence on left), down to a gate in the corner and on to a tree-lined path (can be muddy in places). Pass the ruins of White Ladies Priory; turn left on to a lane to return to the car park at Boscobel House.

• **DON'T MISS** •

Chillington Hall was the home of the Giffard family for more than 800 years. The present Georgian house is the third to have been built on the site and was substantially rebuilt in the 18th century. The gardens and lake were laid out by 'Capability' Brown in 1770.

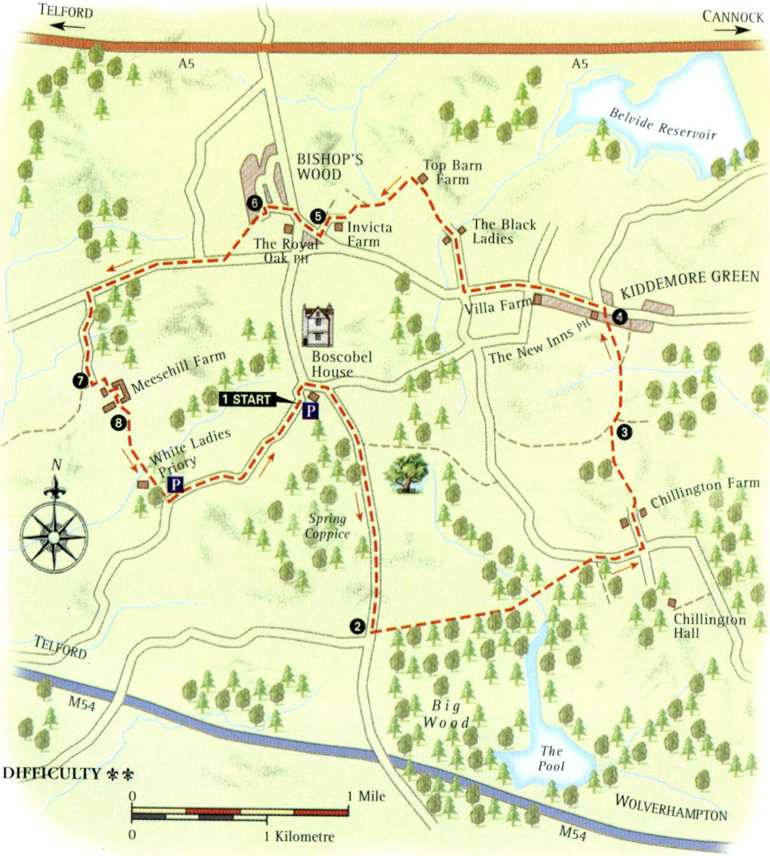

DIFFICULTY ✳✳

TELFORD

CANNOCK

A5

A5

Belvide Reservoir

BISHOP'S WOOD

Top Barn Farm

❻

❺ Invicta Farm

The Royal Oak PH

The Black Ladies

KIDDEMORE GREEN

Villa Farm

The New Inns PH

❹

Boscobel House

❼

Meeschill Farm

❽

1 START P

White Ladies Priory P

N

❸

❷

Spring Coppice

Chillington Farm

Chillington Hall

TELFORD

M54

Big Wood

The Pool

WOLVERHAMPTON

M54

0 ——— 1 Mile

0 ——— 1 Kilometre

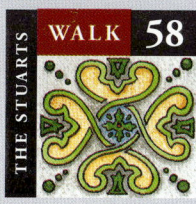

This walk celebrates the Quakers or Friends who journeyed from this small Welsh town to Pennsylvania, USA, in the 1680s to escape persecution and give voice to their faith in a new land. Don't miss the Quakers' Heritage Centre, in Eldon Square.

DISTANCE • 6 miles (9.6km)

TOTAL ASCENT • 590ft (180m)

PATHS • some rocky and muddy tracks; can be slippery

TERRAIN • surfaced roads, tracks, fields

GRADIENTS • some steep ascents and descents

REFRESHMENTS • several pubs and cafés in Dolgellau; Fronoleu Country Hotel near top of first ascent

PARK • Marian car park, Dolgellau

OS MAP • Outdoor Leisure 18 Snowdonia – Harlech, Porthmadog & Bala

A mission of faith

DIFFICULTY ✲✲✲

❶ From the Tourist Information Centre in Eldon Square, cross the square and take the left-hand road to Pont yr Aran/Aran Road. Cross the river and continue ahead, past the ambulance depot. Turn right, signed Tabor, to climb Fron Serth. Where the road forks, keep left.

❷ As the route descends, turn left in front of Tabor Cottage cottage. Shortly, turn left following public footpath sign. At the next junction pass Tyddyn Carreg farmhouse and through the metal bar gate, left. Follow the boundary wall across the field to the burial ground.

❸ Retrace your steps, pass the farmhouse and take the track to the right. Beyond Tŷ Newydd, go through the wooden gate keeping on the track ahead through *coed* (mixed woodland). Emerging from the wood, follow the track left and go through the gate.

❹ Cross the road and follow the public footpath opposite, up the drive past a house, through a farmyard and two further gates. At the top take the gate, right, and cross the field ahead. Go through the gap in the stone wall, a gate, and the next gap ahead. Bear right towards the ruined farm building.

❺ Turn right just before the cottage and follow the field boundary. Bear left to the metal gate and climb the wooden stile to its right. Follow the path between ferns, downhill.

❻ The route descends through woods bearing left at a wall above a farm. Cross two stiles, and follow the arrow to the left. Go through the metal gate (arrowed) and jump across the small brook. Continue ahead, with two houses on your right. Join the part-gravel track and cross the cattle grid; continue for 164yds (150m) to the lane.

❼ Follow the tarmac road left. Beyond the stream, take the footpath, right. At the wooden gate, follow the arrowed track, left, across a footbridge over the river. Go through the kissing gate and climb the track. Cross a stream via stepping stones, then climb the stile into woods.

❽ Where the trail forks, take the left, ascending, path. At the T-junction, turn left and climb the steep, arrowed track. At the top, go through the wooden gate. Shortly, turn left along the stony track. Continue to the tarmac road.

❾ Turn right along the road, continuing through the gate across the road and past Esgeiriau farmhouse after about ¼ mile (400m). Ignore footpath signed right. In ½ mile (800m) follow a bridleway sign, right. Take the main track round the hillside and downhill. Go through the metal gate just after a gap in the wall, left, to descend into town. At the first house, turn right. Continue ahead at the road, go straight across at the crossroads, then turn left for Eldon Square.

Map labels

LLANELLTYD • A470 • Afon Mawddach • Cymmer Abbey • A470 • BALA • Dolserau Hall • A494 • PEN-Y-COED • A4493 • Afon Wnion • A470 • B4416 • Tyddyn Carreg • burial ground • coed • ❸ • MACHYNLLETH • Tŷ Newydd • ❹ • ❷ • Tabor Cottage • DOLGELLAU • 1 START • Esgeiriau • stepping stones • ❼ • ❽ • ❺ • ❻ • cottage • ❾ • N • Afon Aran • Afon Clywedog

0 ____ 1 Mile
0 ____ 1 Kilometre

Carisbrooke's Royal Prisoner

An invigorating downland walk on the Isle of Wight with a visit to a magnificent castle to discover more about King Charles I, Carisbrooke's famous prisoner

Carisbrooke's Medieval Castle

Set on a sweeping ridge of chalk downland, 46m (150ft) on the site of a Roman fort, the majestic medieval ruins of Carisbrooke Castle are regarded as one of the Isle of Wight's finest treasures. Originally a fortified camp built by the Saxons as defence against the Vikings, and later strengthened by the Normans, who built the impenetrable stone walls, fine gatehouse and keep, overlooking Bowcombe Valley and the approaches to the central downs and the heart of the island. But the castle only experienced military action twice, in 1136 and in 1377. In the late 16th century the outer bastions were built to guard against the threat of Spanish invasion. The most important episode in the castle's long history was the imprisonment of Charles I in 1647. You can walk the lofty battlements in the footsteps of Charles I, view the bowling green created for his amusement in the outer bailey, and see the window from which he tried to escape.

The Rise and Fall of Charles I

There was an uneasy relationship between crown and parliament during the reign of James I, and after the accession of his son, Charles I, to the throne in 1625 things went from bad to worse. Charles's High Church views and demands for war funds provoked a series of crises and disputes, and in 1630 he dispensed with parliament altogether and embarked on a period of personal rule.

There was nearly a decade of relative political stability between his three kingdoms before Charles's lack of empathy, stubbornness and high-minded approach to statecraft led to the collapse of royal authority in the late 1630s and the descent into rebellion and civil war by 1642. Bitter battles between the royalist and parliamentarian armies raged across the country for four years, until major strategic errors by Charles led to crushing defeats at Naseby, Langport, Bristol and, finally, at Oxford in May 1646. A virtual prisoner of his rebellious Scottish army, Charles still considered it his divine right to rule the country as an autocrat, and he refused to negotiate a political settlement with the parliamentarians.

Rumours spread of a plot to murder him, and Charles escaped from Hampton Court Palace in 1647 and sought refuge at Carisbrooke Castle. Governor Robert Hammond was torn between his loyalty to the king and his duty to parliament, but promised to do what he could for Charles. He was treated with respect, had the best rooms in the castle and was allowed freedom to move around the island. On hearing that Charles had signed a secret treaty with the Scots in December 1647, by which they undertook to invade England and restore him to the throne, Hammond imprisoned Charles in the castle. During his ten-month incarceration Charles made two unsuccessful attempts to escape before being taken to taken to London for trial and execution in 1648.

WALK **59** | EXPLORING CARISBROOKE CASTLE'S DOWNLAND VISTA

❶ Facing Carisbrooke Priory, turn left along the road and take the footpath, opposite Quarr Business Park, to Carisbrooke Castle – built on a Roman site Carisbrooke once marked the capital of the island. At the castle walls, follow the grassy rampart right around the walls, keeping ahead at the lane to pass the castle entrance. Take the footpath, signed Millers Lane, to the right of the car park entrance and descend to a lane. Turn left, cross a ford, then at a T-junction, turn right to Froglands Farm. Pass the farm, then bear right at gates to follow a bridleway through Bowcombe Valley.

❷ After a sharp right bend, descend and cross the stile on your left. Keep straight on, following the grassy path to a track. Turn left and keep right at a fork. At the field boundary on the left, follow the field edge to a gate. Ascend through a copse to a gate, then keep to the left-hand field edge, steadily uphill to a gate. Maintain direction to a further gate. Keep to the wide track beside a coniferous plantation and take the footpath left, signed Gatcombe. Go through a gate and keep ahead, passing a dew pond to a further gate. On reaching a stile on the left, bear right downhill to a T-

junction of paths and turn left, signed Garstons.

❸ Descend off the down. Go through a gate and shortly bear right beside Newbarn Farm. Turn right along the metalled access lane into the hamlet. Keep right on merging with Snowdrop Lane and turn left along the Shepherds Trail, signed Carisbrooke.

❹ Ascend a concrete drive and pass a house. Then, at the top, keep to the main path (Shepherds Trail) across fields via gates. Disregard the path merging from the left and shortly follow the sunken path gently

downhill to Whitcombe Road. Keep ahead back to the car park.

Distance: 5½ miles (8.8km)

Total ascent: 600ft (183m)

Paths: generally firm but some bridleways can be muddy in wet weather

Terrain: farmland and open downland

Gradients: undulating; one steep ascent and one long steady climb

Refreshments: Coach House tea room at Carisbrooke Castle

OS Map: Outdoor Leisure 29 Isle of Wight

Difficulty: ✳✳

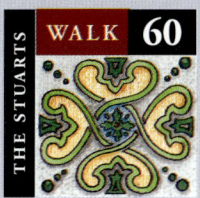
ABOUT · LONDON

Discover 17th-century London – the plague, the Great Fire and the beginning of banking and commerce. At this time, London was undergoing enormous changes, and mostly at the hands of one man, architect Sir Christopher Wren (1623–1723).

Greater London · SE ENGLAND

DISTANCE · 3 miles (4.8km)

TOTAL ASCENT · nil

PATHS · city streets

TERRAIN · pavements, cobbles, streets and alleyways

GRADIENTS · level

REFRESHMENTS · numerous inns and coffee shops along the way

PARK · plenty of car parks in London, though it can be expensive and the streets are often congested. Nearest underground station – Monument

OS MAP · Explorer 173 London North, The City, West End, Enfield

London: churches and commerce

❶ From The Monument walk along Monument Street. Approach the junction with Lower Thames Street, bear left into cobbled Lovat Lane. Pass The Walrus and Carpenter pub and look for Church of St Mary at Hill. Visit the church, leave by a different door and turn left to the junction with Eastcheap.

❷ Turn right and follow it into Great Tower Street. Pass St Dunstan's Hill, approach All Hallows-by-the-Tower, cross over into Mark Lane and turn right into Hart Street. Pass Seething Lane and continue into Crutched Friars. Pass under the railway and turn left into Lloyds Avenue. Bear right along Fenchurch Street towards St Botolph's Church.

❸ Keep left, go to the rear of the church, and take the subway to Houndsditch. Soon turn left into St Mary Axe. The Baltic Exchange is ahead. Turn right along Camomile Street, cross Bishopsgate and Old Broad Street to pass All Hallows London Wall Church. Pass Great Winchester Street, Blomfield Street and Finsbury Circus, and turn left into Copthall Avenue.

❹ When the road bends left, veer right down an alley to Telegraph Street. Turn left at Moorgate and walk along to the back of the Bank of England. Turn right and follow Lothbury to Gresham Street and continue to Guildhall Yard. See St Lawrence Jewry, and cross to turn left into Milk Street.

❺ Bear right at Cheapside and walk to St Paul's Cathedral. Retrace your steps briefly along Cheapside and look for flower beds and an arch on the right between

two banks. Through the arch turn immediately left to reach steps (gardens and fountains to the right), and cross Bread Street to a alley leading to St Mary-le-Bow.

❻ Keep to the right of the church, bear right at the junction and walk along the narrow pedestrianised street for a few paces, turning left into Well Court. Follow it round to the right. Cross Queen Street into Pancras Lane, then cross Queen Victoria Street to Bucklersby. Keep to the left of the Saxon church of St Stephen Walbrook and take the alley, St Stephen's Row, next to it.

❼ Look for the little churchyard, hemmed in by buildings, and turn right at the next junction. Bear right into St Swithins Lane. At Cannon Street, turn left and left again into Abchurch Lane. Pass St Mary Abchurch and, at King

William Street, bear left and walk to the Bank of England and the Royal Exchange.

❽ Keep right and follow Cornhill. Pass St Michael's Church, then turn right into Gracechurch Street. Swing left into Leadenhall Market and take the first right turning. Keep right at Lime Street and cross Fenchurch Street into Philpot Lane. Turn right at the next road junction, then left into Pudding Lane. Return to Monument. Monument Underground Station is on the right.

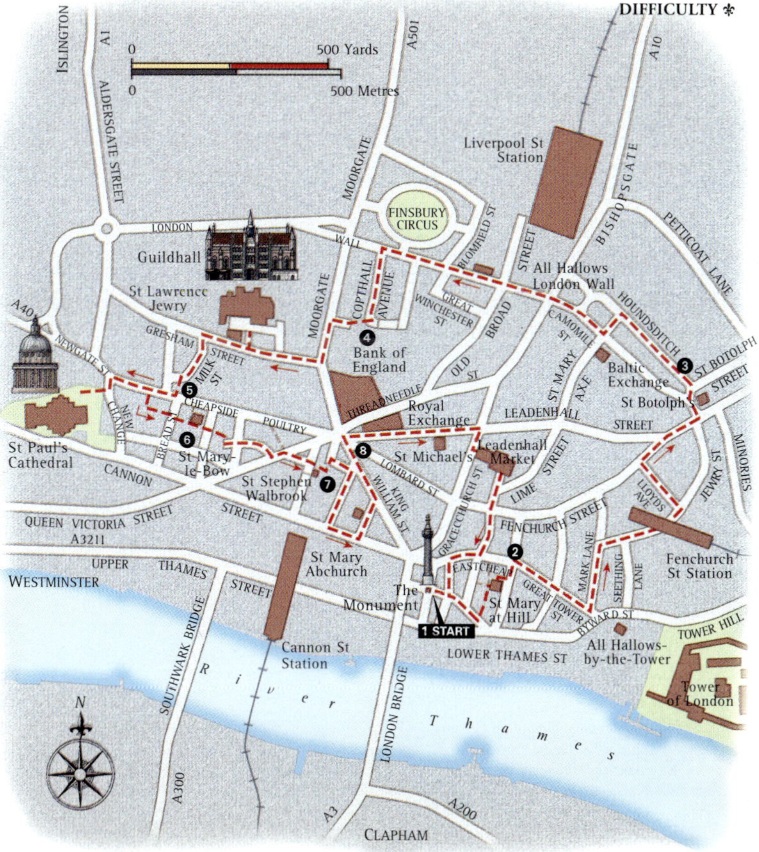

DIFFICULTY ✳

[Map of the City of London showing the walk route marked with a dashed line, with labelled streets and landmarks including The Monument, St Paul's Cathedral, Guildhall, Bank of England, Royal Exchange, Liverpool St Station, Fenchurch St Station, Tower of London and the River Thames.]

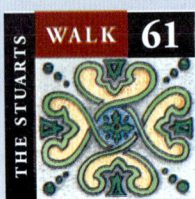
ABOUT • RULLION GREEN

The Covenanters, having refused to accept the authority of bishops or kings over church matters, were pursued here and routed by Scottish troops. The Battle at Rullion Green was part of a 30-year-long dispute, which caused the death of 18,000 men.

Midlothian • SCOTLAND

DISTANCE • 5 miles (8km)

TOTAL ASCENT • 1,300ft (396m)

PATHS • mostly well-maintained and dry, but rough descent from Turnhouse Hill

TERRAIN • mostly mountain moorland and wooded waterside. Dogs must be kept on leads. The Pentland Hills Regional Park is

grazed by sheep and a habitat for ground nesting-birds

GRADIENTS • steep on Turnhouse Hill

REFRESHMENTS • Flotterstone Inn

PARK • car park at Flotterstone Information Centre

OS MAP • Explorer 344 Pentland Hills, Penecuik & West Lothian

Church matters versus military men

❶ From the car park, follow the footpath up the glen beside the metalled drive. Glencorse Burn, which has now been tamed by dams and reservoirs further up the valley, would have been a broad, ferocious torrent at the time of the battle.

❷ At the end of the footpath cross the road and bear left through a gate on to a track signed Glencorse. At the end of the stone wall on your left, turn left and follow the path across a footbridge. This is probably the point where Dalyell crossed the burn, when he brought his army through the hills on the north side of the valley.

❸ Following the burn upstream, the path fords a shallow rivulet and then climbs to the top of the ridge. Only at this point would Dalyell's army have been spotted by the Covenanters, camped half a mile (800m) away beneath the southern slope of Turnhouse Hill. The path continues down into the valley beside a ruined drystone wall before starting on the long ascent of Turnhouse Hill.

❹ From the summit, you will have a grandstand view of the battlefield below. The Covenanters occupied the higher ground, ranged along a spur, now crowned with trees over to the right. Dalyell was attacking from the left and failed to outflank his enemy owing to the steepness of the hill. When he lost every skirmish, he quickly abandoned subtle tactics and used his great superiority in numbers to launch a sustained frontal assault across open ground.

❺ Continue along the path, to the bottom of a deep cleft in the hills. Cross a stile and turn immediately right to follow a faint path downhill beside a drystone wall. Crossing a small stream, the path drops down into the valley, where there is a footbridge, which crosses Logan Burn.

❻ Once over the bridge, turn right along the metalled drive, which runs along the shore of Glencorse Reservoir. This did not exist at the time of the battle and on his march to Rullion Green Dalyell would have passed the ruins of St Catherine's Chapel, which now lie beneath the water.

❼ Just beyond Glen Cottage, at the end of the reservoir, turn right through a gate to follow a path through pine woods and past the 19th-century filter beds. The path continues beside Glencorse Burn

• DON'T MISS •

The 19th-century filter beds used to clean the reservoir's water can now be seen as works of art, with their strange iron ventilation shafts thrusting from the roots of trees. The beds themselves have been transformed into attractive water-gardens and tree-nurseries.

to rejoin the metalled drive back to the car park.

DIFFICULTY ✳✳✳

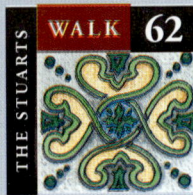

THE STUARTS

WALK 62

ABOUT • WELLS

In 1685, Wells was the centre of strife as a rebel army arrived looking for new recruits to overthrow the papist King. After the Battle of Sedgemoor, Lord Chief Justice Jeffreys arrived in Wells and condemned hundreds of rebels to death or transportation.

Somerset • SW ENGLAND

DISTANCE • 9½ miles (15.3km)

TOTAL ASCENT • 1,000ft (305m)

PATHS • streets then field tracks and farm lanes, a little road walking

TERRAIN • town, pastureland and woodland

GRADIENTS • a steep ascent up the Mendip escarpment out of Wookey Hole

REFRESHMENTS • several pubs and tea shops in Wells and Wookey Hole, none on rest of route

PARK • by the old Tythe Barn in Silver Street

OS MAP • Explorer 141 Cheddar Gorge & Mendip Hills West

Wells and the 'Pitchfork Rebellion'

DIFFICULTY ✱✱✱

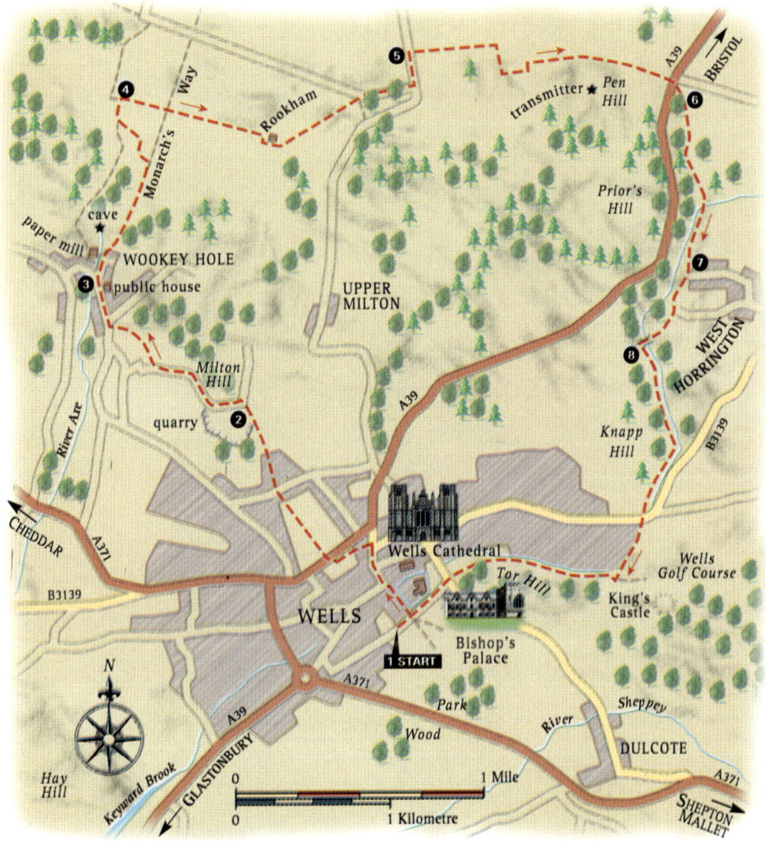

❶ Walk up Silver Street to the Bishop's Palace. Turn left by the moat, go under arch into Market Square. Turn right at the far right corner up Sadler Street. Go right on to New Street and follow it round to the left. Turn left, signed West Mendip Way, and follow the alley around to a left turn, down Lover's Walk. At the back of the sports' pitches fork right, and right over the footbridge. Go through the school grounds to a gate on the far side. Continue up the hill towards houses. Cross the road and at the top of the footpath opposite, cross to another footpath. Go through a gate to emerge on a track.

❷ In 50yds (46m) turn left on a road, uphill past a quarry. Turn left (workings on your left). Bear right through the woods at a stile just before the road bends right. By lime kilns, turn left down a lane. In 400yds (366m), as lane veers left, go through gate, right, to a fenced path, left. Go down the left edge of a field, turn right on the road into Wookey Hole, pass the pub, bear left in front of the paper mill. Turn right towards the caves.

❸ Walk up the lane until it bends round right. Cross the fields, following signs for Monarch's Way. Go half right up the field, aiming for a fence into some woods. Continue up the hill to a junction of hedges. Beyond this, turn left to meet the top of Green Lane, coming up from the other side of the Coomb. Turn right and continue up the hill.

❹ At top go right, in front of wall. Cross three fields; in fourth, aim for hedge in front of buildings. Turn right down to a gate on left. Go through and follow hedge, carry on half-left to a track. Over

cattle grid go left past a bungalow and right at junction with Durston Drove. At T-junction, go left along Old Bristol Road for 200yds/183m.

❺ Turn right, signed Pen Hill, cross two fields, a stile and turn right. Follow field edge to stile on far side. Turn right, to transmitter support. Through gate to follow a track round to the right, emerging on road in front of a white house.

❻ Go through a gate opposite to join a bridleway to the right of a field. Go through a gate in the corner and descend to the stream. Continue down through the woods then through a gate and stile on the left. Bear right with the stream and stay with the rising track.

❼ In a clearing by a white house turn right and follow the track left to a stile. Cross and follow the

left-hand field edge to a stile in the next field. Immediately beyond, turn right down to a stile. Descend steps to cross a bridge, turn left.

❽ Follow the path to Wells Golf Club. Cross the road, go through the gate to the path between the golf course and houses. Continue on this streamside path to a road. Cross, go through gate opposite and return to Silver Street.

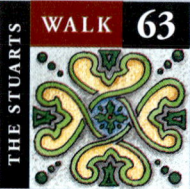
ABOUT • KILLIECRANKIE

The first victory of the Jacobite Rebellion by followers of James VII took place in 1689 in Killiecrankie. The terrifying Highland Charge overwhelmed the government troops and their leader, General Hugh MacKay, in just ten minutes.

Perth & Kinross • SCOTLAND

DISTANCE • 6½ miles (10.4km)

TOTAL ASCENT • 500ft (152m)

PATHS • good trails, metalled roads

TERRAIN • forest trails and country roads

GRADIENTS • moderate

REFRESHMENTS • Killiecrankie Visitor Centre and Boating Station

PARK • forest car park at Faskally Boating Station

OS MAP • Explorer 21 Pitlochry & Loch Tummel

Killiecrankie: the first of the Jacobite battles

❶ From the car park walk past the boating station and continue uphill following the lochside path for Killiecrankie which leads underneath both the A9 flyover and Clunie footbridge.

❷ Follow the loch, past the viewing point where the Old Bridge of Clunie stood before it was demolished for the hydro-electric scheme in 1950. Loch Faskally is a man-made feature following the deep, natural river valley.

❸ Keep left on the single-track metalled road towards Killiecrankie. Just before the entrance to Faskally House, turn left on to the signed footpath following the lochside. Pass the point where the rivers Tummel and Garry meet.

❹ Pass under the Garry Bridge and a short distance further on turn left and cross the river on a metal footbridge. Turn left up the steep slope to Garry Bridge car park. Immediately after the car park, turn right on to an unclassified metalled single-track road that climbs up past Tenandry Parish Kirk. Soon after there are views of the valley and east towards the mountains.

❺ After 1½ miles (2.4km), turn sharp right and then bear right and cross the River Garry on a stone bridge. Cross the rail bridge and turn right on to the B8079 and follow the footpath past the primary school. The path peters out and after a very short distance bear right on to a track leading downhill following the riverside, but still to the east of the railway.

❻ Continue to the Killiecrankie visitor centre (where you will find refreshments and toilets). From here continue on the path downhill, passing Soldier's Leap and the railway viaduct. You are now on the east bank of the River Garry. Continue southwards, passing Balfour's Stone, to the metal footbridge.

❼ Take the path on the left here, uphill and over the railway bridge to exit on to the B8079. Turn right and follow the B-road, continuing straight ahead as it becomes the B8019 at Garry Bridge, eventually returning to the car park.

• DON'T MISS •

The picturesque town of Dunkeld owes its present appearance to the victorious Highland army that descended on its defending Covenanting forces after Killiecrankie and all but destroyed it. The partially ruined Gothic cathedral is all that remains of that time.

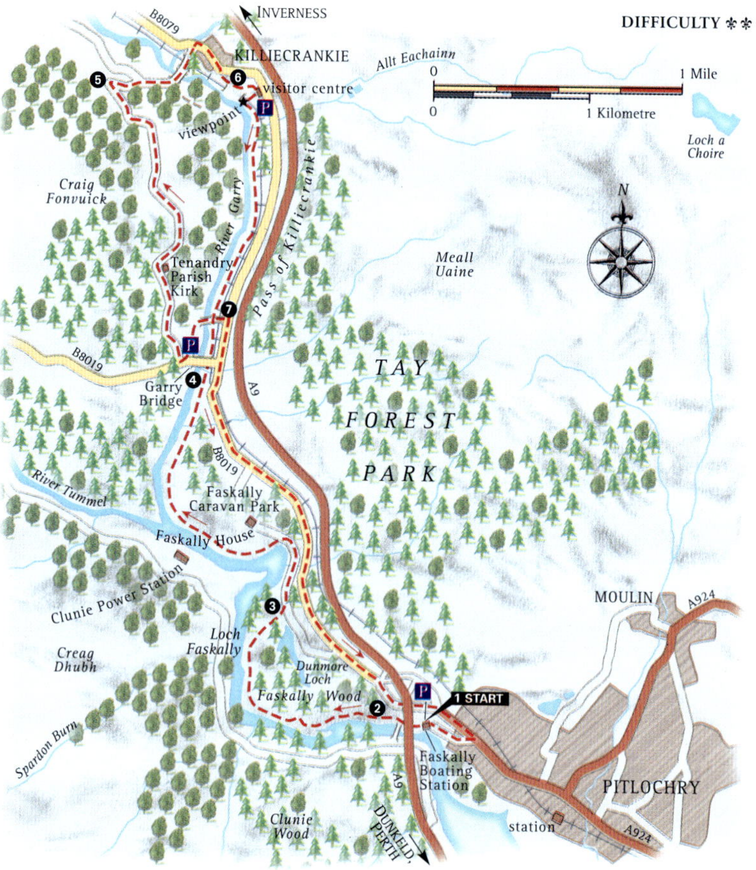

DIFFICULTY ✱✱

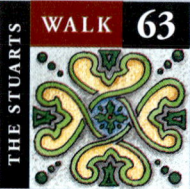

After 18 pregnancies, Queen Anne
died in 1714 with no surviving children.
A new monarch arrived by invitation:
the Elector of Hanover, George I.
The Georgian era had begun.

GEORGIAN

1714–1837

Birth of Industry

George was not universally welcomed. The 'Old Pretender', son of James II, pressed his own claim to the throne, but fled to France after the ill-fated Jacobite uprising of 1715. A few years later came a different crisis, the South Sea Bubble – an 18th-century version of the Wall Street Crash. The South Sea Company went under in 1720, and hordes of its investors, from government ministers to household servants, faced ruin. Norfolk squire Robert Walpole, who had consistently condemned the Company's fund-raising schemes, was one beneficiary, becoming the first British Prime Minister in 1721.

Britain spent much of the 18th century at war, and along the way gathered lands and gained the naval prowess celebrated in the 1740 ditty 'Rule Britannia'. At home, agriculture and industry were progressing rapidly and new inventions popped up by the hundred. Successful experiments in stock-breeding prompted landowners to turf out their tenants to make way for more sheep and cattle. In 1730 Charles 'Turnip' Townshend revolutionised farming methods with crop rotation. The textile industry was mechanised – and many spinners were put out of work – by James Hargreaves' Spinning Jenny; Richard Arkwright devised a hydraulic spinning frame in 1769, and in the same year James Watt patented his steam-engine. Improved smelting techniques increased iron production, and a network of canals carried the industrial materials from source to market.

REFORM AND REVOLUTION

London was now the financial and social hub of a growing empire. People gathered in the city's coffee-houses to read newspapers and discuss the day's issues, and satire found an eager audience. William Hogarth's prints provided graphic social comments on greed, decadence and ambition. Political corruption became a target for radicals such as John Wilkes, whose popular support foreshadowed the campaign for parliamentary reform and the 1832 Reform Act, which extended the vote to all 40-shilling freeholders.

The Jacobite threat resurfaced briefly in 1745, now led by the Young Pretender, 'Bonnie Prince Charlie'. After the terrible massacre of his followers on Culloden Moor the following year, Charles escaped to Skye, disguised in women's clothes. Both Jacobite and Hanoverian supporters had taken up a popular anthem, albeit with variations in the lyrics; today it is known as 'God Save the Queen'.

In 1763 Britain emerged from the Seven Years' War with France and the government set about replenishing its funds with heavy taxes. When a stamp duty was imposed on the American colonies, it met with an angry response, which presently escalated into war. By 1783 the former colonies had won their independence from the 'mother country'. Revolutionary ideas carried home by America's French allies contributed to the French Revolution, at first welcomed by romantic British radicals such as William Wordsworth and political philosophers such as Tom Paine. But soon revolution turned to terror, and before the end of the century Napoleon Bonaparte was leading his armies through Europe.

British patriots found their heroes in Admiral Lord Nelson, who died fending off the French at Trafalgar in 1805, and the Duke of Wellington, victor at Waterloo ten years later.

Meanwhile, the future George IV, acting as Prince Regent during one of his father's bouts of madness, commissioned John Nash to create Brighton Pavilion at the fashionable sea-bathing resort of Brighton. Thus ended the Georgian era with a fitting foretaste of the 19th century's imperial swagger.

HISTORIC SITES

Brighton Pavilion, Sussex: inimitable Regency frivolity.

Edinburgh: Georgian elegance in the New Town.

Cheltenham, Gloucestershire: spa town favoured by George III.

10 Downing Street, London: home of Robert Walpole and his successors.

Syon Park, Surrey: mansion and gardens remodelled by Robert Adam and Capability Brown.

Ironbridge Gorge, Shropshire: preserved site of early advances in the iron industry.

WALK 64

GEORGIAN

ABOUT • ARKENGARTHDALE

Lead has been mined here for thousands of years but it wasn't until the 17th century that intensive mining began and small 'frontier' towns began springing up. This walk has plenty of history to offer as it wends its way through the Yorkshire Dales.

North Yorkshire • N ENGLAND

DISTANCE • 8 miles (13km)

TOTAL ASCENT • 1,213ft (370m)

PATHS • mostly clear tracks; a little walking on heather moor

TERRAIN • steep, mined valleys and moorland

GRADIENTS • two stiff climbs, but generally gradual slopes

REFRESHMENTS • Red Lion in Langthwaite and the CB Inn in Arkengarthdale

PARK • car park at southern end of Langthwaite village

OS MAP • Outdoor Leisure 30 Yorkshire Dales – Northern & Central areas

Arkengarthdale's ancient lead-mining industry

1 From the car park, turn right, then right again. Cross the bridge, continue ahead between cottages and climb the hill. Follow the lane to the hamlet of Booze (note that hamlets in Arkengarthdale are early Norse settlements). Pass the farmhouse and a stone barn and follow the track to a gate.

2 Beyond the gate, where the track bends left, go ahead, beside a tumbled wall. Bear right to pass a ruined cottage and follow the path to the stream. Walk upstream, pass through a gate, and cross the stream on stepping stones.

3 Follow the course of the steam through moorland to a wooden hut. Turn left along the track beyond. Go straight ahead at a crossing, then turn left at a T-junction. Where the wall on your right ends, take the path, right, down to a gate.

4 Follow the gill downhill to go through another gate. Turn right along the track beyond it. Continue through a gateway and on to another track by a barn. Follow the track, which bends left by a stone wall and passes farm buildings, through two gates to a white gate.

5 Go through the gate into Scar House grounds. Bear right down the drive, over a bridge and cattle grid and turn right on to a track. Continue to a road. Turn left, then right at a T-junction. After a cattle grid, turn left on a signed track.

6 Bear right at a gravelled area and continue uphill on the track. Where it divides, go left beside slag heaps and pass the junction of two flues. The track bends right then left, uphill, to a T-junction. Turn left here. Follow the track downhill to a road.

7 Turn left. Beyond the farmhouse turn right at a bridleway sign towards the house, and turn left before reaching it. Follow the signed track though a gate. Continue downhill and turn left before a small barn. Go over four stiles to the road. Turn left back to the car park.

DIFFICULTY ✱✱✱

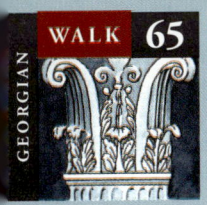
ABOUT • RAASAY

The defeat of the Jacobites at Culloden in 1746 ended all hopes to return a Stuart to the throne and led to a relentless manhunt for Bonnie Prince Charlie. This walk takes you to Raasay, one of his final hiding places in Scotland, before he fled into exile.

Highland • SCOTLAND

DISTANCE • 6 miles (9.6km)	**GRADIENTS •** mostly gentle
TOTAL ASCENT • 540ft (165m)	**REFRESHMENTS •** Raasay Hotel
PATHS • mostly good but can be muddy after heavy rain	**PARK •** parking area before the last house on the road to North Fearns
TERRAIN • green lanes, moorland, hillside and tarmac road	**OS MAP •** Pathfinder 187 Narrows of Raasay

Bonnie Prince Charlie's escape to Raasay

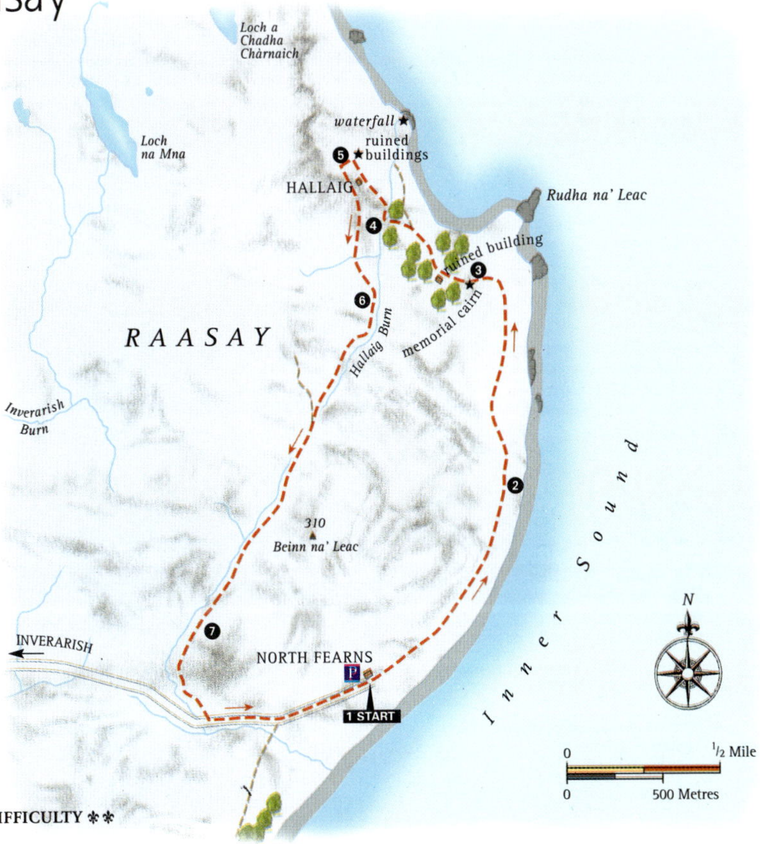

❶ From the car park at the end of the road continue along the green lane. The sea is on your right and you will have a superb view across to the islands of Scalpay, Longay and Pabay.

❷ After a mile (1.6km) look up to the left as you pass the impressive cliffs of Beinn na' Leac. Continue on past the headland of Rudha na' Leac, beyond which you will see a memorial cairn on the path.

❸ Stop at the cairn to read the inscription to the gaelic poet Sorley McLean, who was from Raasay, and also to those who were cleared from the land to make way for sheep. McLean's poem Hallaig is reproduced here. From here the path narrows, entering woodland and passing a ruined building. Follow the path out of the wood and where it forks, keep left. Re-enter woodland, go downhill and cross the Hallaig Burn where it meets the path.

❹ Climb uphill from the burn and veer right towards the top corner of a drystone wall. At the corner

Map area shows: Loch a Chadha Chàrnaich, Loch na Mna, waterfall ★, ★ ruined buildings ❺, HALLAIG, ❹, Rudha na' Leac, ruined building ❸, ❻, memorial cairn, Hallaig Burn, RAASAY, Inverarish Burn, 310 Beinn na' Leac, ❼, INVERARISH, NORTH FEARNS, ❶ START, Inner Sound, N, 0 — ½ Mile, 0 — 500 Metres

• **DON'T MISS** •

Raasay House, near Inverarish (now an outdoor adventure centre with facilities for day visitors), is the historic house where James Boswell and Doctor Samuel Johnson stayed on their tour of the Hebrides in 1773. While staying in Raasay Boswell is reported to have 'danced a Highland dance' on the summit of Dunn Cann.

DIFFICULTY ✷✷

you can see the best preserved of the houses of Hallaig township which was cleared of people in the 18th and 19th centuries to make way for sheep.

❺ Continue by following the track round the rest of the ruins, heading towards a rocky crag in the north, then turn left and head

uphill. Turn left again and with the crag behind you head south towards another crag on the distant hills.

❻ When you intersect the Hallaig Burn, turn right and follow its course uphill until it disappears. Then pick up the rough track, heading round the back of Beann

na' Leac. Eventually the track will disappear but by then you will see the road below.

❼ Descend the hill heading towards the road. When you reach the burn turn left and walk along it until it flows under the road. Turn left and return to your car.

ABOUT • HARTLAND

The coastal scenery off Hartland Point may seem spectacular but to the sailors of the 18th century it must have offered a cruel welcome. The jagged cliffs were responsible for a number of shipwrecks and, inevitably, the lives of many sailors.

Devon • SW ENGLAND

DISTANCE • 3½ miles (5.6km)

TOTAL ASCENT • 360ft (110m)

PATHS • fields, grassy coast path, quiet country lanes and farm tracks

TERRAIN • dramatic and rugged coastal scenery, rolling farmland

GRADIENTS • some short but steep climbs on the coast path

REFRESHMENTS • Wreckers' Retreat pub at Hartland Quay; cream teas available in Stoke in the summer; The Hart Inn, The Anchor and the King's Arms pubs in Hartland village

PARK • west of St Nectan's Church in Stoke, signed from Hartland

OS MAP • Explorer 126 Clovelly & Hartland

The unforgiving coastline of Hartland

❶ With the church on your right, follow the wall round to meet a footpath sign pointing left. Follow the path between the cottages and the lane, over a stile, through a kissing gate and over a stile into a field. Turn right, downhill, with views of the sea at Blackpool Mill. Walk along the lower edge of the field to enter the woods above the Abbey River, right, to reach the coast path.

❷ Turn left through a gate; follow the path uphill to Dyer's Lookout, and across Warren Cliff past the ruined tower, left. Leave the field by a stile by the Rocket House.

❸ Turn right; follow coast path posts along the cliff edge and down steps to join the lane leading to Hartland Quay.

❹ From the car park follow coast path signs on and up steps to pass along the cliff edge round the back of Well Beach. Go through a kissing gate and follow the coast path to the right passing through a five-bar gate to avoid mighty

St Catherine's Tor. Cross the stream, cross the next field and pass through a gate. The path now continues uphill, towards the coast, and over a stile before dropping down to Speke's Mill Mouth. Pause for a moment to enjoy its impressive run of waterfalls, totalling 160ft (49m).

❺ Turn left up the track, following coast path signs inland, then turn right at the next post to cross the stream on a footbridge. Turn left at the next post, signed coast path valley route. Keep straight on at the next two signposts, signed Milford. Leave the heathland over a stile into a field; walk straight to the top and out through a gate, to join a farm track that meets the lane at Milford.

❻ Turn left downhill, pass Docton Mill to reach the crossroads at Lymebridge.

❼ Turn left and continue uphill through Lymebride to reach Kernstone Cross. At the crossroads continue straight ahead along the green lane, signed unsuitable for motors. At the entrance to Wargery Farm turn left downhill and follow the track to the edge of Stoke, where it veers right. Go straight on to reach the village centre.

❽ Turn left and walk through the churchyard, turning left at the church door to return to the start of the walk.

• DON'T MISS •

Hartland Abbey (1157), situated a little inland up the Abbey River has been a family home since 1539. The gardens were designed by Gertrude Jekyll, and are delightful. The woodland walk is particularly lovely in spring and joins this route down to the sea at Blackpool Mill. The house and gardens are not open every day, so it is advisable to check the opening times in advance.

DIFFICULTY ✱✱

A walk around Bristol will reveal
the city's role in the 18th-century
slaving triangle. It is worth picking
up a booklet on the Slave Trade
Trail, from the Tourist Information
Centre, as it makes a valuable
companion as you tour the city.

DISTANCE • 4½ miles (7.2km)	REFRESHMENTS • a huge range throughout route
TOTAL ASCENT • 215ft (66m)	
PATHS • pavements throughout	PARK • Bristol Industrial Museum pay-and-display (maximum three hours)
TERRAIN • city centre, parkland, quayside and residential streets	OS MAP • Explorer 155 Bristol & Bath
GRADIENTS • very steep ascent of Constitution Hill	

On the Slave Trade Trail

❶ From the museum turn left over Wapping Bridge. Turn left on the quayside and walk around the Arnolfini Gallery, to cross Pero's Bridge. Go ahead towards the TIC then veer right by Explore@Bristol. Turn right in front of the museum and cross the road to go up some steps. Pass the cathedral on your left to emerge on College Green and turn left.

❷ Continue to Deanery Road and take the second right up York Place, opposite the Three Tuns. Cross into Brandon Hill Park up some steps and take the left-hand path. Walk through the park and emerge by Jacob's Well Road by the Wildlife Trust. Cross and walk up Constitution Hill.

❸ At the top cross Lower Clifton Hill and Clifton Road. Bear left, on the level, to Regent Street and turn right up Merchant's Road. Turn left and walk round Victoria Square. At the end of the second side, turn right in front of Lansdown Place, then left down Queen's Road. Take the first left down Richmond Park Road to Pembroke Road.

❹ Turn right and cross Queen's Road down Richmond Hill. At the bottom, turn left down Queen's Road and cross the Triangle. Turn left down Park Street and second left on Great George Street to see the Georgian House. From here the walk follows the Slave Trade Trail.

❺ Return to Park Street and turn right. Cross and take next left along Unity Street then right down Denmark Street . At the bottom, turn left on St Augustine's Parade. Go along Colston Avenue under the Centregate arch to the Three Loaves of Sugar. Continue under the arches of modern buildings to Lewin's Mead Sugar House on the left.

❻ Turn right and cross through the arch opposite to Broad Street. Take the third alley on the left to see Taylor's Court, then return to Broad Street, past the Guildhall and turn right to look at Corn Street. Turn round at the Commercial Rooms and return towards Broad Street but turn right in front of No 56, down All Saint's Lane by All Saint's Church.

Go straight ahead through the covered market and across two roads. Descend steps by St Nicholas's Church and cross to the waterfront along Welsh Back.

❼ Take the second right up King Street, past the Llandoger Trow and the Theatre Royal. At the bottom, turn left and follow the pavement round into Queen Square. From the Custom House, cross the park, turn left to the Hole in the Wall, cross the road and then the bridge on Redcliffe Way.

❽ Go right, round roundabout past the Quaker Burial Ground (left) and St Mary Redcliffe (right) on to Redcliffe Hill. Take the second right on Guinea Street, and right down Alfred and Jubilee Places. Turn right on to Redcliffe Parade East, and cross to descend a ramp to the quayside by Redcliffe Caves.

❾ Follow the quayside round to the left and cross the footbridge in front of the Ostrich. Turn right to Merchant's Wharf, Wapping Bridge and the Industrial Museum.

DIFFICULTY ✲

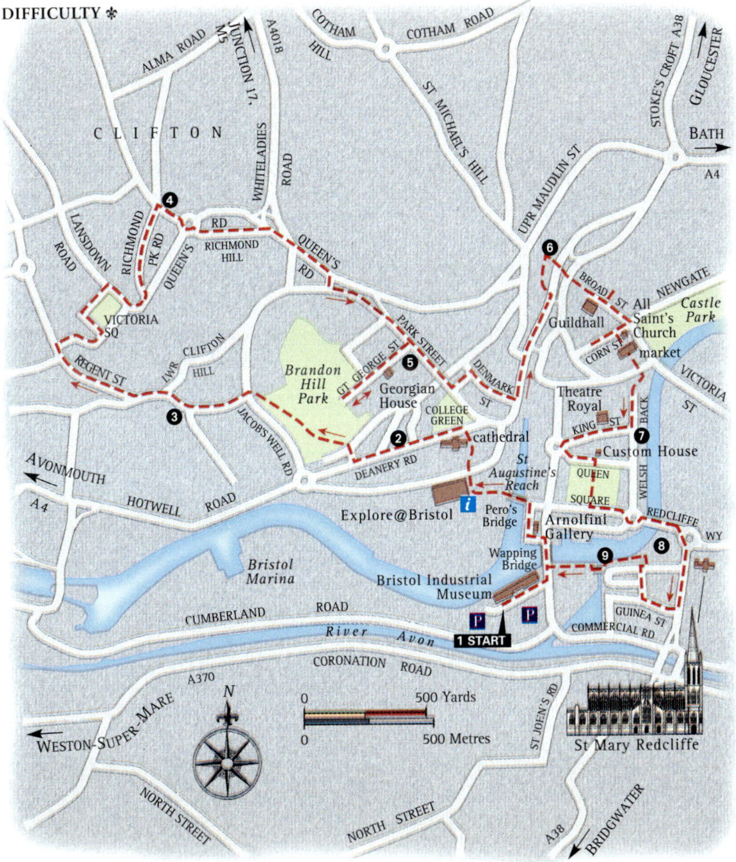

The Age of Canals

The motorway interchange of its day, Braunston's canal junction and marina,
in Rutland, are still busy with the passage of barges

Pre-industrial Britain

Before the railways, the only effective bulk transport was by boat.
After the Romans left Britain, roads fell into decline and overland
trade relied largely on packhorses. Although 18th-century turnpike
roads greatly improved mail and passenger services, the movement
of heavy loads remained a slow and laborious process, and only
towns on the coast or a navigable river grew to any significance.
Early improvements using weirs and flash locks helped, but by the
17th century, only 700 miles (1,126km) of navigable waterway
existed. Although the next 150 years added a further 600 miles
(966km), there was still little effective access for inland coalfields
and new factories. The emerging industrial revolution was seriously
threatened. Although already existing in Europe, it was not until
around 1760 that the first 'dead-water' canals appeared in Britain.
The Sankey and Worsley canals, constructed to transport coal from
the mines, were an overnight success, instantly halving the price of
coal in Manchester and Liverpool.

The Early Waterways

The impact of the canals was spectacular, prompting a massive
investment, and in less than 25 years all the major navigable rivers
had been linked. Development was rapid, with cuttings, aqueducts
and improved locks being employed to create more direct routes
and allow changes in level. Indeed, many of the first canals were
later straightened, as at Wolfhampcote, where an aqueduct now
carries the waterway across the River Leam, saving over 2 miles
(3km) against its former route. Tunnels were also excavated, and
the one near Braunston, carrying the Grand Junction, is around
1¼ miles (2km) long. Engineers also faced problems in providing
a reliable water supply to elevated sections, since a lock uses around
25,000 gallons (113,650l) of water each time a boat passes. Rivers
and streams were one source, but because mill-owners complained
about the loss of their water, reservoirs were built and, sometimes,
pumping stations employed to lift water back. The walk passes a
former pumping station beyond Braunston Marina. Another
strategy employed in the Midlands was the construction of narrow
canals, with 7ft-(2m)-wide locks rather than the standard 14ft
(4m). But as their use was restricted to narrow boats, cargoes on
boats from other parts of the country had to be reloaded and many
canals were later widened to improve their competitiveness.

Living in barges, the boatmen and their families became
a race apart, inhabiting a world perhaps 100 miles (160km)
long, but only 50 yards (46m) wide. Undertaken whatever the
weather, the work was often hard; the hours long and the living

conditions often poor. But by the 1860s the canals' heyday had
passed and competition from the railways heralded their
inexorable decline.

WALK 68

EXPLORING THE OXFORD AND GRAND UNION CANALS

❶ Join the Oxford Canal
towpath where it passes
beneath the A45 and walk south
from the bridge towards a canal
junction, which comes into view
ahead. Ignore the bridges
carrying the path over the fork
on to the Grand Union Canal
and instead turn right to pass
beneath. The two canals run
together for the next 5 miles
(8km), before the Grand Union
branches north at Napton.
However, in three quarters of a
mile (3km), beyond a dismantled
railway bridge and immediately
after passing beneath bridge
number 98, climb up the
embankment to a stile. Turn
right across the bridge and carry
on along a track towards a farm
at Wolfhampcote. There, join
another track coming from the
right and go on, crossing the
original line of the canal. Bear
right at the farm entrance and
on past a cottage and
Wolfhampcote church. In the
fields beyond, humps, hollows
and ditches are all that is left of
the abandoned medieval villages
of Wolfhampcote and
Braunstonbury.

❷ At the far end, the track rises
past cottages to the main road;
instead, go left after the last
cottage to return to the
towpath. Now on the Grand
Union, turn right and walk
beneath the road, passing Stop

House, where there is an
interesting exhibition about the
canals, to reach Braunston
Marina.

❸ Beyond the marina, the canal
climbs 35½ feet (11m) through
six successive locks and then
enters a cutting leading to the
eastern portal of the Braunston
Tunnel. There, the towpath ends;
while the boatmen 'legged' their
boats through, the horses were
led over the hill to the other
end, 1¼ miles (2km) away. You
can still follow their track,
which rises beside the tunnel
entrance. However, the return
route lies back along the canal,
past the marina and junction
and on to the bridge where you
started.

Distance: 5½ miles (9km)

Total ascent: none

Paths: sections of the towpath
can be muddy, otherwise well-
surfaced paths and tracks

Terrain: open, rolling
countryside

Refreshments: the walk passes
two canalside pubs

Park: layby beside the A45, just
beyond the canal, a quarter of a
mile (0.4km) east of Braunston

OS Map: Explorer 15 (234)
Rutland Water

Difficulty: ✻

GEORGIAN

WALK 69

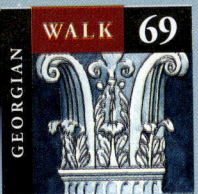

ABOUT • NEW LANARK

David Dale, a Glaswegian banker and industrialist, was the visionary behind New Lanark's town planning. In an age where the chasm between the rich and poor was largely ignored, he provided social housing and 'cradle to the grave' care of its townsfolk.

South Lanarkshire • SCOTLAND

DISTANCE • 8 miles (13km)

TOTAL ASCENT • 200ft (61m)

PATHS • mostly firm but some muddy stretches

TERRAIN • woodland and riverside gorges

GRADIENTS • steep in some sections, but with steps to ease ascents

REFRESHMENTS • Mill Hotel in New Lanark

PARK • car park above New Lanark

OS MAP • Explorer 335 Lanark & Tinto Hills, Lesmahagow & Douglas

The social reformers who built New Lanark

❶ From the car park take the path down to New Lanark, where there are a number of buildings open to the public and exhibitions of the community's history.

❷ Beside Robert Owen's School, bear left off the road along a path that continues through a gate into Scottish Wildlife Trust's nature reserve. Follow the path up steps and along the river, past the thundering Dundaff Linn and weirs that once powered the cotton mills.

❸ Turn right at the approach drive to Bonnington Power Station, which in 1927 was Britain's first hydro-electric scheme. At the power station, fork right off the drive to follow a footpath signed to Falls of Clyde. The waterfalls, Corra Linn and Bonnington Linn, are most dramatic after prolonged heavy rain, when there is more water than the power station needs, and the excess flows freely through the gorge.

❹ Keeping to the path, cross the river over Bonnington Weir, then turn right down a woodland track into the Corehouse Estate. After 200yds (183m), turn right on to a footpath down towards the river. From here there are spectacular views of the falls.

❺ Keep to the riverside path, ignoring other paths up to the left. Beyond the ruins of Corra Castle, there are views of New Lanark on the opposite bank. At a junction with a track, turn right and continue until you reach some houses on your left. Just beyond their gardens, climb the bank to your left and follow a faint path through the trees to a gap in the wall along Kirkfield Road. Turn right and then right again at the bottom of the hill into St Patrick's Lane and follow signs for Clyde Walkway.

❻ Cross the river on Clydesholm Bridge, then turn right through the gate of Old Brigend (private property). Follow the Clyde Walkway up to the treatment works, then climb steeply, with several steps, and bear right to follow a lane to Castlebank Park. Just beyond a sign to Jookers' Johnnie, turn right down the drive to Castlebank House. Follow the path signed Clyde Walkway down from Castlebank Park to river level and on to New Lanark and your car.

• DON'T MISS •

*Near by you'll find the **Falls of Clyde**, part of a Scottish Wildlife Trust reserve, which offers a full ranger service including badger watching and bat walks (between May–September). Plus, an open hide, manned 24 hours a day, offering unrivalled views of breeding peregrine falcons (telephone 01555 665262).*

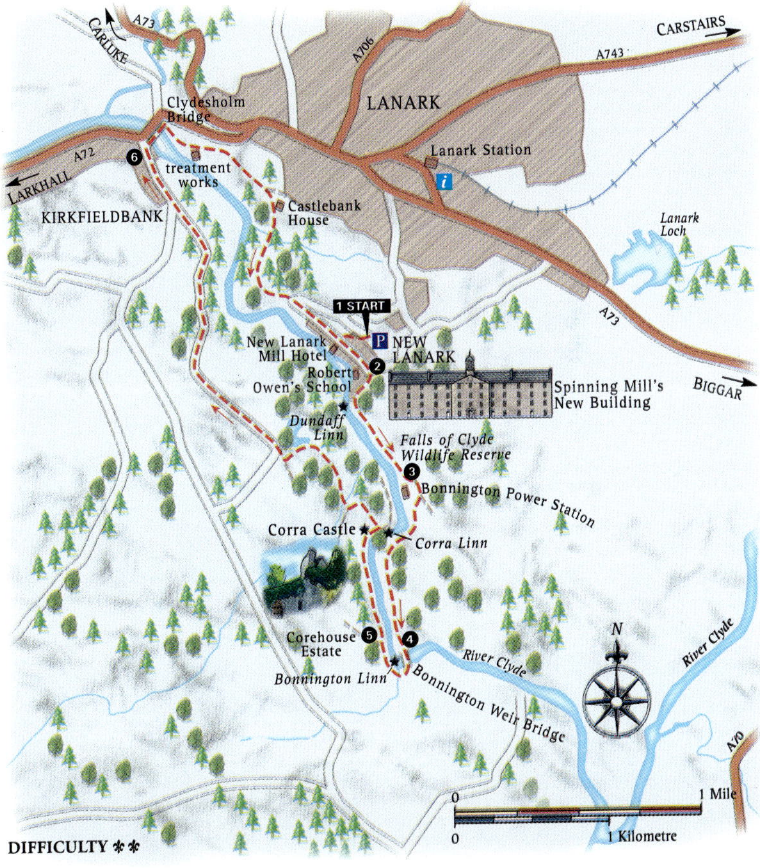

DIFFICULTY ✽✽

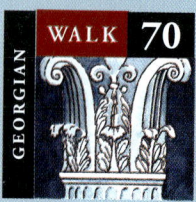
Starting near the summit, you descend through woodland to the Ackers Wood railway, crossing the plain below, and following the Macclesfield Canal before climbing up to Mow Cop, where Hugh Bourne launched the Primitive Methodist movement.

DISTANCE • 5½ miles (8.8km)

TOTAL ASCENT • 600ft (183m)

PATHS • field and woodland paths, lanes and canal towpaths

TERRAIN • paths, especially descending to the canal, can be boggy

GRADIENTS • a gradual descent, level

towpath and then a steepish ascent to Mow Cop

REFRESHMENTS • The Rising Sun, Kent Green, near Scholar Green

PARK • National Trust car park at Mow Cop

OS MAP • Explorer 258 Stoke-on-Trent & Newcastle-under-Lyme

Mow Cop and the birth of a new faith

DIFFICULTY ✳✳

❶ From the car park, head north, following the Gritstone Way and Mow Cop Trail signs, bearing left after 22yds (20m) on the broad track towards residential Wood Street. Turn right after crossing the road and then immediately left, signed Old Man of Mow.

❷ Take this track, passing the strange pinnacle of the Old Man of Mow on the right. Just before a prominent radio mast, follow a yellow waymark downhill to the left for 656yds (600m), across muddy fields (keep to the left-hand wall), and then steeply down through Roe Park Wood.

❸ Emerge from the woodland at a stile, follow the track through the field past a farm and through a gate to join a wide lane. In 109yds (100m) bear right around Wood Farm to eventually reach a metalled lane, which leads left to the Ackers railway crossing.

❹ Take care crossing the high speed line and enter Yew Tree Lane, turning right in 219yds (200m) at the junction into New Road to reach the canal bridge. Descend to the towpath on the far side of the bridge (No 85) via the steps on the right-hand side, hard against the bridge.

❺ Turn left and follow the canal towpath south for about 1½ miles (2.4km), with the tower of Mow Cop to the left and passing the fine, red-brick Georgian façade of Ramsdell Hall on the other bank.

❻ Just past the Heritage Narrow Boats marina at Kent Green, take the stile on the right before bridge No 87 and turn left on the road.

❼ Continue under the railway line and up the hill towards the village of Mount Pleasant.

❽ In 875yds (800m), at the top of the hill, Mount Pleasant Road turns sharp right. After 100yds (91m) take the track on the left (The Brake), signed Brake village.

❾ This soon becomes a footpath which goes straight and steeply up

the hill on an embankment for 547yds (500m), towards Mow Cop village. Emerge on to a rough track and turn left. In 164yds (150m) go right up steps pass the Primitive Methodist Memorial Chapel.

❿ Cross Woodcock Lane, pass the village Post Office and Stores on the left. Turn left into the High Street and return to the car park at Mow Cop in 400yds (366m).

CONGLETON

A34

Moreton Hall

moat

Little Moreton Hall

Macclesfield Canal

❺ ❹ Ackers Crossing

Roe Park Wood

Wood Farm

❸ farm

Ramsdell Hall

radio mast

The Rising Sun PH

❻ Heritage Narrow Boats Marina

❼

Old Man of Mow

❷

1 START

folly

P

post office chapel

SCHOLAR GREEN

The Brake

❽ ❾

❿

MOW COP

A34

NEWCASTLE-UNDER-LYME

MOUNT PLEASANT

0 ½ Mile

0 500 Metres

N

• DON'T MISS •

*The **Macclesfield Canal**, part of the famous Cheshire Ring of canals, was begun in 1826, and took only five years to complete. The 28-mile (45km)-long waterway linked the Peak Forest Canal in Marple to the Trent and Mersey Canal at the Hardings Wood Junction.*

ABOUT • STRATHNAVER

This walk is a reminder of the brutal clearances of Strathnaver (1785–1850). Ten thousand tenants were evicted from Strathnaver by Elizabeth, Countess of Sutherland and her ruthless factor, Patrick Sellar, to make way for intensive sheep-farming.

Highland • SCOTLAND

DISTANCE • 5 miles (8km)

TOTAL ASCENT • 50ft (15m)

PATHS • mostly good but can be a little muddy in wet weather

TERRAIN • metalled road, forest roads, moorland and forest trails

GRADIENTS • mainly flat with a few slight gradients

REFRESHMENTS • none on the route; seasonal coffee shop near the Strathnaver museum at Bettyhill

PARK • off the road at the corner of the junction of the B873 and the B871 at Syre

OS MAP • Pathfinder 64 Mid Strathnaver

The Higland Clearances at Strathnaver

❶ From Syre church head south along the B873. Look out for the memorial to Donald MacLeod on the right-hand side of the road. Rosal village is across the river from here but hidden by the forest.

❷ Continue along the road for a mile (1.6km), then cross the river via two anglers' bridges. Take great care when crossing, particularly in wet weather conditions. A forest road runs parallel to the River Naver but access is prevented by a deer fence.

❸ Turn left and continue to follow the track beside the deer fence for about ¾ mile (1.2km) until you reach a stile. Cross the fence and walk up the fire break to reach the forest road.

❹ Turn left on to the road and continue until a large, green waymarker indicates the entrance to Rosal village. Leave the road and turn right on a track through the trees leading to a gated enclosure. Through the gate is the Rosal village.

• DON'T MISS •

Strathnaver Museum in the former St Columba's Parish Church at Bettyhill, some 12 miles (19km) north of Syre, tells the story of the Sutherland clearances in graphic detail, featuring models and artefacts from the period. While you are at the museum look out for the intricately sculptured Pictish Cross, located in the church graveyard, which dates from about AD 800.

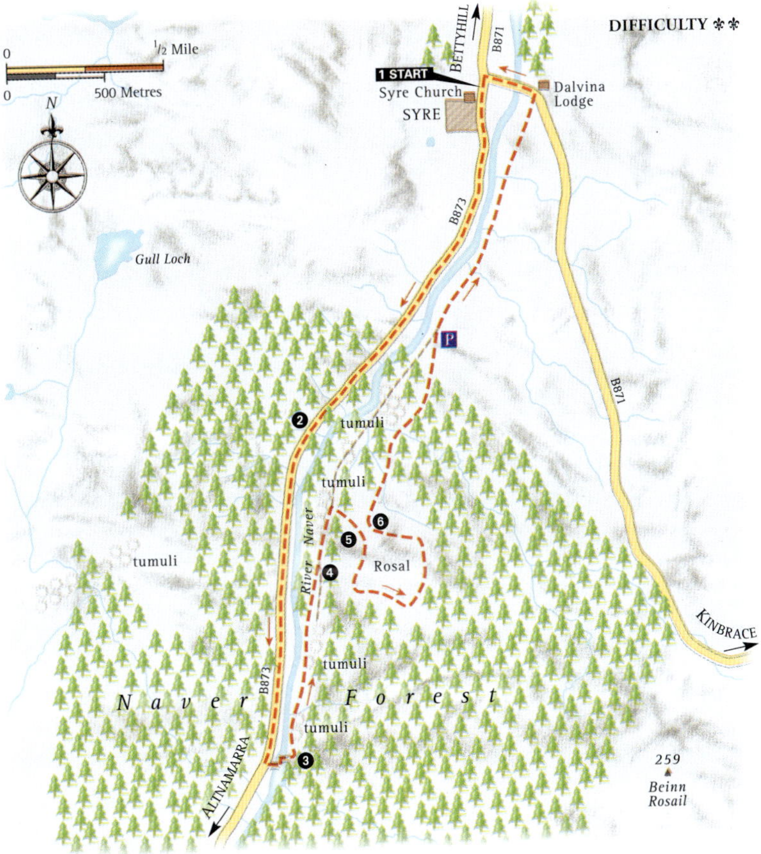

DIFFICULTY ✻✻

Map labels: ½ Mile / 500 Metres / N / 1 START / Syre Church / SYRE / BETTYHILL / B871 / Dalvina Lodge / B873 / Gull Loch / P / tumuli / River Naver / Rosal / tumuli / Naver Forest / ALTNAMARRA / KINBRACE / 259 Beinn Rosail

❺ Walk clockwise round the village following the numbered interpretation boards, which tell the story of the clearances. (At the top cairn turn around and shout in the direction of Beinn Rosail and listen to the echo.) Continue on the trail, then leave through the enclosure gate and retrace the path for 20 yds (18m) to the right.

❻ Follow a very faint track uphill and into the forest, where it becomes a well waymarked trail. When it rejoins the forest road turn right and go through a gate. Continue to the junction with the B871, turn left and return to the start and your car.

ABOUT • MENAI BRIDGE

The Menai Suspension Bridge (1826) was considered a feat of modern engineering. Started in 1819, Thomas Telford's design consisted of seven archways which supported the massive roadway, linking Anglesey to mainland Wales for the first time.

Isle of Anglesey • WALES

DISTANCE • 5 miles (8km)

TOTAL ASCENT • 104ft (32m)

PATHS • some minor roads; paths can become muddy and slippery in wet weather

TERRAIN • minor roads through village and farmland

GRADIENTS • roads mostly flat or slightly uphill; paths can be steep in places

REFRESHMENTS • Liverpool Arms Hotel and The Mostyn Arms public houses; tea rooms on Cadnant Road towards town centre

PARK • Coed Cyrnol car park, behind the Jade Cantonese restaurant in Menai Bridge; ample car parking

OS MAP • Outdoor Leisure 17 Snowdonia – Snowden & Conwy Valley

Crossing the Menai Bridge

❶ Leave the car park down a small flight of steps and turn right on to a tarmac path. Gently descending, this soon forks. Straight ahead is Church Island; to the left a broad promenade now runs parallel with the Straits. Continue along what is now a road through the arches of the Menai Suspension Bridge. Turn right immediately before the Liverpool Arms Hotel and walk on, bearing left into St George's Road. Pass The Mostyn Arms, go through the no entry signs and veer left.

❷ At the T-junction, turn right on Cadnant Road and, after 273yds (250m), cross to pass through a kissing gate. Ascend a waymarked path between the houses, cross the roadway part way up and follow the footpath sign carefully. An uneven path eventually leads to a stone stile. Turn left.

❸ After 22yds (20m) turn right on to a tarmac road, which later becomes a grassy, waymarked track. Go through a gate and continue along the right-hand field edge and through the hand gate. Go straight ahead towards the single tree and through the hand gate in the right-hand corner ahead. Follow the right-hand hedge, going through two more hand gates, then go down steps.

❹ Turn right along the roadside verge and take the next turning on the right (signed Llandegfan and Beaumaris). Follow a surfaced road and in ½ mile (800m) turn right on to a waymarked track.

❺ At the end of the track, just before the house, go through the gate on the left (waymark arrow on fence). After passing through

DIFFICULTY ✹✹

three small paddocks, head for a wooden stile on the left-hand side of the field. In the next field cross another stile half-way down the right-hand field edge. Descend a narrow path towards the left, cross a stream by a rock bridge and turn left through a wooden gate ahead.

❻ Pass Cadnant Mill on the left and, bearing right at the waymark sign, continue through the

farmyard to a T-junction. Bear right and continue for ½ mile (800m). At another T-junction, bear right to join the main road after 328yds (300m). Turn right, cross Cadnant Bridge, immediately turn right and 11yds (10m) along on the left, head along a waymarked path. The path gently rises, passing a large house on the right. Bear left here through a break in the hedge. Continue along

the path then, as the it veers right, turn left on to a narrower path. Go down to Cadnant Road again at the kissing gate and retrace your steps to the car park.

• DON'T MISS •

*Near Menai Bridge is **Church Island**, the 6th-century home and refuge of Prince Tysilio, the son of Brochfael Ysgythrog.*

Queen Victoria's reign saw the British Empire at the peak of its influence and confidence, extending so far around the globe that 'the sun never set' over its territories. This was also the era when Britain emerged as the world's leading industrial power.

VICTORIAN

1837–1901

Age of Optimism

The Machine Age gathered speed in the 19th century; factories and mills became the focus for new communities, formed higgledy-piggledy wherever there was the promise of work. Cheap housing was thrown up and families at the bottom of the industrial heap lived in terrible squalor. In his novel *Sybil*, or 'The Two Nations', future prime minister Benjamin Disraeli described a society divided into 'haves' and 'have-nots'. The misery and poverty of the rapidly expanding industrial cities was also vividly documented by Charles Dickens and Elizabeth Gaskell. Throughout the century, the ballooning urban centres were worlds of extremes. Pompous civic buildings and monuments, neo-Gothic libraries, schools, churches and railway stations typified the self-assurance of the age, while back-to-back houses and belching chimney stacks characterised the working-class areas. A pronounced prudery and outward piety in the middle-class drawing rooms contrasted with the increasingly popular and raucous music halls and a thriving trade in prostitution.

In the face of glaring inequalities the Chartist movement called for a 'people's charter' guaranteeing a number of democratic rights: universal male suffrage; a secret ballot, and salaries for MPs, to make parliament accessible to those without private incomes. The road to reform, however, was to be long, slow and piecemeal.

GREAT EXPECTATIONS

Despite the problems of working and living conditions, poor sanitation (leading to several bouts of cholera) and sometimes violent unrest, Victorian Britain was proud of its achievements and of the progress made in industry and science.

In 1851 the Great Exhibition opened at Crystal Palace, in London's Hyde Park. The brain-child of Victoria's beloved prince consort, Albert, this was a showcase of international crafts, inventions and cultures, dominated by 7,000 British exhibits. It attracted over a million visitors a month, and with the funds generated, Albert oversaw the establishment of the Victoria and Albert Museum.

In 1861 Prince Albert died of typhoid fever and Victoria entered a period of profound and protracted grief, closeting herself away from all public appearance and ceremony. Her prolonged absence from the public stage provoked mockery and complaint from the press and public, especially when her manservant John Brown was deemed to be too close to the Queen – or 'Mrs Brown' – for comfort. Some of the anti-monarchy sentiments of the time took a more extreme form and there was more than one suspected anarchist plot; other threats to the establishment were perceived in the Fenian Movement, calling for Irish independence.

Meanwhile the Liberal government of William Ewart Gladstone ushered in a stream of reforms to cope with the changing face of Britain. A secret ballot was introduced; schooling was extended; and attempts were made to address the 'Irish Question', though attempts to introduce Home Rule in Ireland fell flat.

As the 20th century loomed, new discoveries encouraged the development of a consumer society. The electric telegraph made communications faster and wider. Photography, cinema and gramophones heralded a new kind of mass entertainment. Motor cars and bicycles began to appear on the roads, and at the turn of the century powered flight became a serious possibility.

Victoria celebrated her Gold and Diamond Jubilees – to huge popular acclaim. By the time she died, in 1901, her reign had seen Britain transformed beyond all recognition.

HISTORIC SITES

Palace of Westminster, London: Pugin's neo-Gothic home for the 'Mother of Parliaments'.

Osborne House, Hampshire: the superb home of Queen Victoria and Prince Albert in the Isle of Wight.

Saltaire, West Yorks: purpose-built mill town created by Sir Titus Salt.

Forth Rail Bridge, Lothian: world's first major steel bridge (1890).

Blackpool Tower, Lancs: opened in 1894 at the height of the seaside holiday craze.

ABOUT · CALEDONIAN CANAL

Of all the canals built during this era the Caledonian Canal, designed by Thomas Telford and completed in 1847, is undoubtedly the most impressive. Its 60 miles (97km) length includes an impressive flight of eight locks known as Neptune's Staircase.

Highland · SCOTLAND

DISTANCE · 5 miles (8km)

TOTAL ASCENT · 64ft (19m)

PATHS · firm, dry path

TERRAIN · waterside and woodland

GRADIENTS · level, apart from one short descent

REFRESHMENTS · hotels in Banavie, Corpach and Fort William

PARK · Banavie Station or at Neptune's Staircase and cross canal by lock gate

OS MAP · Outdoor Leisure 38 Ben Nevis & Glen Coe

Telford's Caledonian Canal

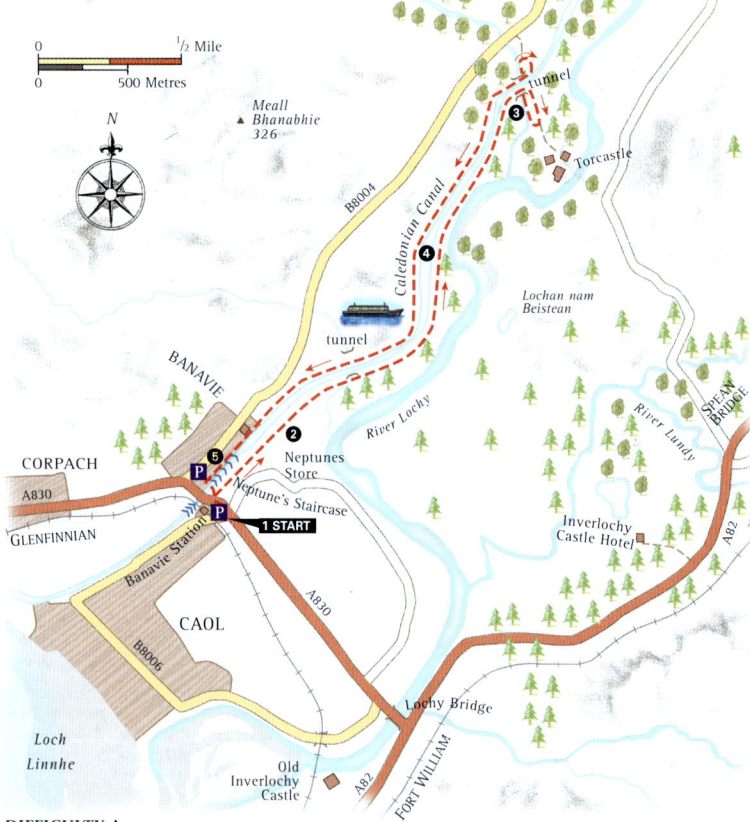

❶ From the car park at Banavie Station, cross the main road (A830) and go through a metal gate on to the canal towpath. On your left is Neptune's Staircase, a flight of eight locks that raises the canal 64ft (19m) in height. Above the locks, yachts lie moored in a sheltered basin.

❷ Follow the towpath, with the canal on your left, for approximately 2½ miles (4km). The ground drops steeply to the right and through gaps in the woodland there are fine views of the Ben Nevis range and of Inverlochy Castle Hotel, a Gothic mansion that is now one of Scotland's most exclusive hotels.

❸ The canal and towpath bridge a stream, with some houses visible below. Continue for 20yds (18m), then turn right down a path between the trees. Beyond the gate at the bottom, turn sharp right to follow the stream through the tunnel under the canal and past a weir. Reaching an

· DON'T MISS ·

*The **old capstans** beside the locks had to be rotated with long poles to operate the gates. This was heavy work, since 126 full turns were required to ascend the staircase. It was not until the 1960s that the system was converted to hydraulic power. Also worth noting are the two **Inverlochy Castles** located across the Lochy and, upstream, the remains of two **Tor Castles**.*

DIFFICULTY ❀

intersection, turn sharp right to return to the canal and right again along the towpath.

❹ On the return walk there are fine views along Loch Linnhe to the Corran Narrows and of the 4,406ft (1,343m) summit of Ben Nevis, Britain's highest mountain. The town of Fort William, on the east shore of the loch, was still a military garrison at the time of the canal's construction.

❺ Pass Neptune's Store, a small post office and shop, offering tourist information, toilets and facilities for yachtsmen (limited winter opening). The bow-windowed cottages overlooking Neptune's Staircase date from the early 1800s. Cross the canal by the lock gates to return to the car park.

ABOUT • MARSDEN	West Yorkshire • N ENGLAND

The rise of the textile industry brought great prosperity to a number of towns during the 19th century, including Marsden. The effect this had on the landscape is evident as you walk from the town and view its rows of terraced houses and mills.

DISTANCE • 6 miles (9.6km)

TOTAL ASCENT • 920ft (280m)

PATHS • tracks, moorland paths and country lanes

TERRAIN • rough moorland, pastures and farmland

GRADIENTS • variable, steep in places

REFRESHMENTS • pubs and cafés in Marsden

PARK • parking places in Argyle Street, also plenty of roadside parking

OS MAP • Outdoor Leisure 21 South Pennines

Marsden: a West Yorkshire wool town

❶ From Argyle Street turn into Station Road. Climb to the station, turn right into Reddisher Road, and left into Spring Head Lane, a steep track rising to Inglenook. Turn right along a vehicle track to a radio mast. Turn left up a narrow, enclosed path, climbing steeply to a horizontal track at a top gate.

DIFFICULTY ✲✲

❷ Turn left and follow the track behind a farmhouse. A short way on, when the track forks, go left, descending. The track shortly turns right. Keep following the main track, which later becomes surfaced for a while, descending steeply. When the track next forks, just past Hey Cottage, bear right.

The route is obvious, enclosed by fences or walls. Go past farm buildings on the left and keep on the track until the next junction (waymarked). Turn right, soon leaving the lane for a walled path that breaks out on to the hillside.

❸ Keep forward on an obvious grassy path to a gate, beyond which it continues as a waymarked route across rough pasture, passing a derelict farmhouse to descend into a stream gully. Cross the stream, turn left, and climb beside a wall, go through a gate on to a

narrow lane. Turn left, continue to a bridge opposite the entrance to Hey Green Hotel. Cross the bridge and take a rising lane to the A62.

❹ Cross the A-road to a step stile, beyond which a rough path rises, right, on to Marsden Moor Estate. At an estate signpost, bear left, climbing across the hillside, below rock outcrops and through low, hummocky terrain.

❺ The route continues, always parallel with overhead power lines, and on to the Pule Hill part of Marsden Moor. Aim for the lower of two prominent ventilation shafts, beyond which an improving path strikes across the moor, finally, as it approaches the Carriage House pub, moving away from the power lines.

❻ When the path reaches a moorland road, turn left until, 80yds (73m) before a cattle grid, where you turn left into Old Mount Road. Almost immediately branch left on to an access track signed Hades Farm.

❼ Follow the farm track for 547yds (500m), past two paths to the right and branch right on to a grassy track beside the wall. Descend to a gate, beyond which the track, overgrown with rushes, continues between dilapidated walls. The distinct track continues towards a farm. Just before the farm, bear left, descending steeply beside a wall to a step stile below.

❽ Cross the stile and bear left across a hill slope, soon walking beside a wall until you meet a step- stile in a the corner of a wall. Cross the stile, turn right and descend to meet the A62 again. Turn right and, near the church, turn left into Towngate. Take the first turning on the right, cross a bridge and turn left into Argyle Street to return to the start point of the walk.

River Colne

A62

HUDDERSFIELD

reservoir

B6107

Hey Cottage

Huck Hill

Hey Green Hotel

reservoir

Marsden Station

church

MARSDEN

Marsden Moor Estate

air shaft

Hades Farm

tunnel

High Gate Farm

Binn Moor

Close Moor

Marsden air shafts

Moor

Pule Hill

The Carriage House PH

A62

OLDHAM

reservoir

reservoirs

reservoirs

N

reservoir

0 — 1 Mile

0 — 1 Kilometre

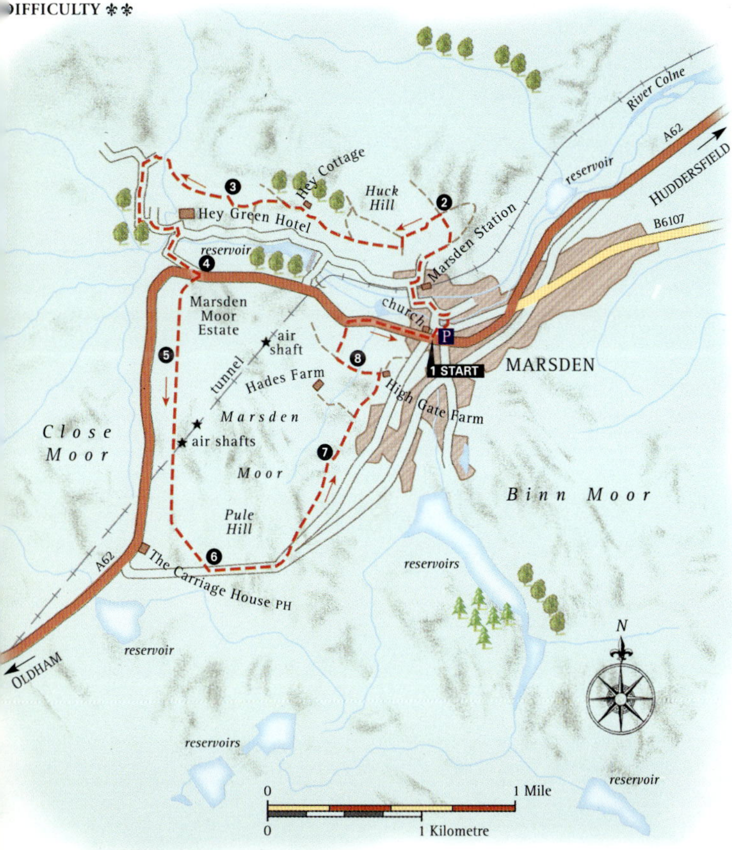

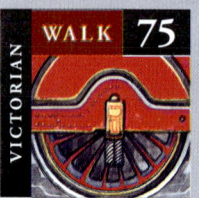

ABOUT • GEEVOR

Cornwall • SW ENGLAND

In this walk you will discover another side of scenic Cornwall – its 2000-year-old history as a tin mining area, which was at its peak during the Victorian era. While you're there visit the Geevor Heritage Centre, the largest preserved mine site in Britain.

DISTANCE • 5 miles (8km)

TOTAL ASCENT • 246ft (75m)

PATHS • undulating coast path, gritty tracks and field paths

TERRAIN • coastal cliffs and farmland

GRADIENTS • some non-strenuous ascents and descents on coast path; inland paths fairly level

REFRESHMENTS • Queen's Arms, Botallack; The North Inn and The Radjel Inn in Pendeen; café at Geevor Tin Mine

PARK • free parking at Pendeen lighthouse, signed off the B3306 at Pendeen (St Just to St Ives road)

OS MAP • Explorer 102 Land's End, Penzance & St Ives

The tin mines of Cornwall

❶ Walk inland up the lane for ¼ mile (400m). Opposite Enys, No 6 of the row of whitewashed cottages, turn right signed Cape Cornwall. Follow the marked path downhill, descend stone steps to cross a stream, then up and over two stiles to a wooden bench at the top of a steep slope (views of the tin workings ahead). Follow coast path signs through the workings, ignoring signs to Geevor.

❷ Continue along the coast path to pass Levant Beam Engine, right. Walk straight through the car park and along a gritty track, following a coast path sign, to meet and walk by a wall, left.

❸ Keep on the coast path for ¾ mile (1.2km), ignoring tracks leading inland, to reach Roscommon Cottage and then the remains of Botallack mine, marked by two big chimney stacks (left and right), and a huge metal headworks gantry, left. Just before the gantry, at a coast path sign, bear right on the narrow path and descend. In 50yds (46m) reach a flat area with views down to the restored engine houses of the Crowns mine. Return to the track.

❹ Continue ahead on the main route and in a few yards pass Botallack Count House Workshop. Continue to Botallack Manor Farm, left. Just beyond the farmhouse, where the lane bends right, turn left (right of way, not signed) along a grassy path to the right of the entrance to farmyard. Continue for a few yards by a stone hedge on the right, then join a track. In 300yds (274m) emerge between stone hedges, bear left and descend gently. A solitary granite

chimney stack lies ahead. Ignoring side tracks, keep on the main track for 400yds (366m) to reach the entrance to a field.

❺ Go through the entrance, turn right, go up stone steps and over a stile. Walk along the top of the next field, which you leave between two walls. Walk round the top edge of the next field (houses and buildings, right); keep on to cross the stone bank (right) and cross the next field, keeping the wall on your right. Cross a wooden stile, a track and a stone stile, to join a narrow path.

❻ Turn left. The path joins a track. Turn right then keep right at a junction to meet Levant Road and turn right. Just past the 30mph sign at Hillside, turn left by

Pentrew and follow the lane straight on past Merivale House, left. Keep straight on through the farm. The lane becomes a track, then a narrow path, which you follow to pass Geevor Tin Mine. The path ends at a T-junction with a huge boulder, left. Go up and over the bank ahead and walk downhill (wire fence, right) to rejoin the coast path at the Levant/Geevor signpost (Point ❷).

❼ Turn right, retrace your steps along the coast path to your car.

DIFFICULTY ✽✽

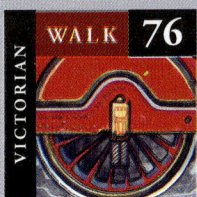

ABOUT • SOMERSBY	Lincolnshire • C ENGLAND

Follow in the footsteps of the poet Alfred Lord Tennyson (1809–92). The walk begins at The White Hart Inn, frequented by Tennyson who is reputed to have enjoyed a drink by the fire, and takes you to his birthplace, a rambling, yew-fronted rectory.

DISTANCE • 5 miles (8km)	**REFRESHMENTS** • White Hart Inn and Cross Keys
TOTAL ASCENT • 65ft (20m)	
PATHS • good	**PARK** • White Hart Inn (ask permission beforehand)
TERRAIN • surface roads, grassy fields, cultivated fields	**OS MAP** • Explorer 273 Lincolnshire Wolds South, Horncastle
GRADIENTS • slight	

Tennyson's home in Somersby

❶ Turn left out of The White Hart Inn and follow the road round to the left through the village. Continue until you reach a fork in the road, take the right fork past the attractive stableyard on the right.

❷ At the next junction, with Wood Farm on the right, turn left and continue past the old school building on the right.

❸ Follow the road as it bends left past the new doctor's surgery and continue to the junction overlooked by a war memorial. Turn right at the memorial and continue towards the Cross Keys pub. Turn left on to the public bridleway just before the pub.

❹ Stroll along this pretty, grassy track through the corridors of brambles before entering more open countryside. When the bridleway meets a public footpath ensure that you follow the bridleway, keeping the open fields to your left and the hedge and earth bank to your right. When the path meets a minor road, turn left and walk along the road alongside a shallow wood.

❺ As you walk along this road note the small carved face in the rocky outcrop set back to the left-hand side of the road. Pass the junction signed Ashby Puerorum and Horncastle and carry on into Somersby village. Look for Grange Cottage on the right with its white fence, and then next door, the birthplace of Tennyson. Opposite is

the church where Tennyson's father was rector.

❻ Walk through the churchyard and around to a gate diagonally opposite the entrance. Turn left along the road until you come to Somersby House Farm. Turn right up the birdleway opposite the farm. Continue to Warden Hill Cottage. Turn left through the outbuildings, following the footpath signposts.

❼ At the edge of Warden Woods turn left down a limestone path with the wood on your right.

As the path rises again at the end of the wood, turn right and follow the path along the bottom edge of the wood. At the T-junction turn left and follow the bridleway up and over the hill.

❽ As you go down the hill note the no right of way over the stile. Follow the track down to the road, turn left then right on to a footpath over a footbridge. Trek across a lovely chain of fields to St Mary's Church in Tetford. Pass through the graveyard to the road, turn left and return to the White Hart Inn.

• DON'T MISS •

Harrington Hall (further along from Bag Enderby) is a 17th-century manor, once the home of Rosa Baring, who would come down from the steps to the terrace garden to walk with Tennyson. His famous line 'Come into the garden, Maud' was probably about Rosa. (The Hall is not open to the public, but the gardens are on occasions.)

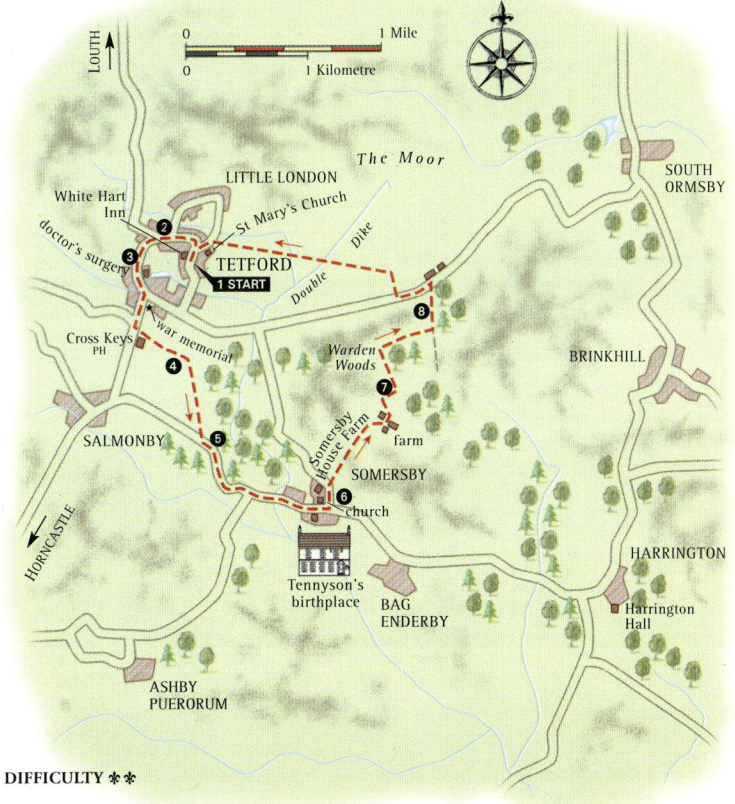

DIFFICULTY ✳ ✳

The Tracks of Industry

Following the course of a disused railway line in the county of Cardiff through the former industrial heartland of Wales

Transforming a Landscape

The mineral-rich valleys that run from the Brecon Beacons to the major urban centres of Cardiff and Swansea have teemed with industrial activity for centuries. This walk traces a route that, until relatively recently, was a major artery for the transportation of goods and people. Since the decline of the coal industry, the South Wales slagheaps have changed from black to grassy green, railways have become country tracks, and – ironically – as mining communities struggle to maintain their existence, the scenery has regained some of its pre-industrial beauty.

The Taff Trail runs, in its entirety, from Brecon to Cardiff; this section of the trail leads along part of the former Barry and Rhymney railway lines, skirting the hillside above the River Taff, the original means of moving cargoes from the Rhondda Valley mines to the southern shipping ports, and from there to all over the world.

Mines and Railways

South Wales was already a target for industrial speculators by the late 18th century. At first, iron was the main resource, but coal was needed to smelt it, and soon furnaces and pits were mushrooming all along the river valleys south of the Brecon mountains. Canals, river barges and horse-drawn trams shifted the produce at first, but

the quicker, cheaper steam engine came hot on the heels of the industrial boom. It was in Merthyr, further up the Taff, that steam-driven transport had an early breakthrough, when Richard Trevithick's locomotive train made its first brief trip on an old tramroad in 1804. This was the first steam-powered journey along iron rails. From then on, the 19th century was destined to be the age of steam. Railways appeared all over Britain, providing fast links between centres of industry and ports, improving communications and sparking off a craze for seaside holidays, as quick jaunts to the coast became a possibility even for people of modest means.

In South Wales the emphasis was on King Coal, as mines churned out millions of tons of the 'black gold', to fuel the engines and furnaces of the world. Around each pit, a mining town appeared, with rows of terraced houses clinging to the hillsides. People poured in to this once rural area; farm labourers abandoned the land, and workers arrived from abroad looking for employment. Mining families lived and worked in appalling conditions, while industrial barons reaped huge profits. The Valleys became hotbeds of radicalism, and the whole shape of Welsh political, cultural and social life changed beyond recognition. Having passed the estates and factories of the Taff Vale towns, the route ends up at Castell Coch, a folly built for the coal magnate Lord Bute in the 1870s.

WALK 77 DOWN THE VALLEY LINE

❶ Start at the Treforest Park and Ride, at the railway station, and near the University of Glamorgan, originally founded as the South Wales and Monmouthshire School of Mines. To reach the old railway bed, cross the footbridge and go down the slope. Cross into Castle Street; at the end of the street, cross Forest Road and the pedestrian bridge over the Taff. Bear left to go under the road bridge and follow the pavement under the motorway bridge. Cross the road with care. Go round to the left and into Cemetery Road.

❷ Turn right and pass the cemetery and crematorium. Cremation was made legal in

1884, after local man Dr William Price had been prosecuted for cremating his baby son Iesu. Follow the Taff Trail sign to the right. The track passes between the houses of Ryhdyfelin, whose name probably derives from *rhyd felen*, 'yellow ford': iron in the clay turned the water here a distinct yellow.

❸ Presently the trail moves into oak woodland and passes the remains of an old colliery on the hill to the left. Above the trees, glimpses of sheep grazing on the mountain recall the pre-steam, pre-industrial era, when travellers admired the natural drama of the 'Glamorgan Alps'. At Nantgarw

the trail twists down into another estate and across the road on the valley floor, before climbing to the top of the opposite ridge.

❹ As the trail approaches the beech woods of Fforest Fawr, it passes Tŷ Rhiw Farm, built before the railways and the coal boom. You can leave the trail here, following the sign left past the farm, to descend to Taff's Well station for the train back to Treforest. But it is worth continuing to Castell Coch, the fairytale 'red castle' designed by William Burges. It's a 1½ miles (2.4km) on foot or by bus from Tongwynlais to Taff's Well station.

Distance: 6 miles (9.6km) to Taff's Well; 1 mile (1.6km) to Castell Coch

Total ascent: 250ft (76m)

Paths: surfaced paths, tracks: can be muddy and waterlogged in poor weather

Terrain: streets, paths, tracks

Gradients: one steep stretch

Refreshments: cafés, pubs in Treforest, café in superstore at Upper Boat (access from trail)

Park: Treforest Park and Ride

OS Map: Explorer 151 Cardiff & Brigend

Difficulty: ✱✱

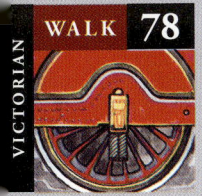
ABOUT • DOWN HOUSE

Down House, Charles Darwin's home for 40 years, has been carefully recreated by English Heritage. This walk explores the countryside he knew, and passes the former estate of High Elms House, where his friend the naturalist, Sir John Lubbock, lived.

Greater London • SE ENGLAND

DISTANCE • 6½ miles (10.4km)

TOTAL ASCENT • 500ft (152m)

PATHS • clearly waymarked and defined tracks; mud; some roads

TERRAIN • woodland and downland

GRADIENTS • one fairly steep woodland descent; otherwise well-graded

REFRESHMENTS • bar, café, toilets at High Elms golf club house; pubs, tea room and shop in Downe; tea room at Down House

PARK • public car park for High Elms Golf Course between Downe and Farnborough; roadside parking in Downe

OS MAP • Explorer 162 Greenwich & Gravesend

Evolution at Down House

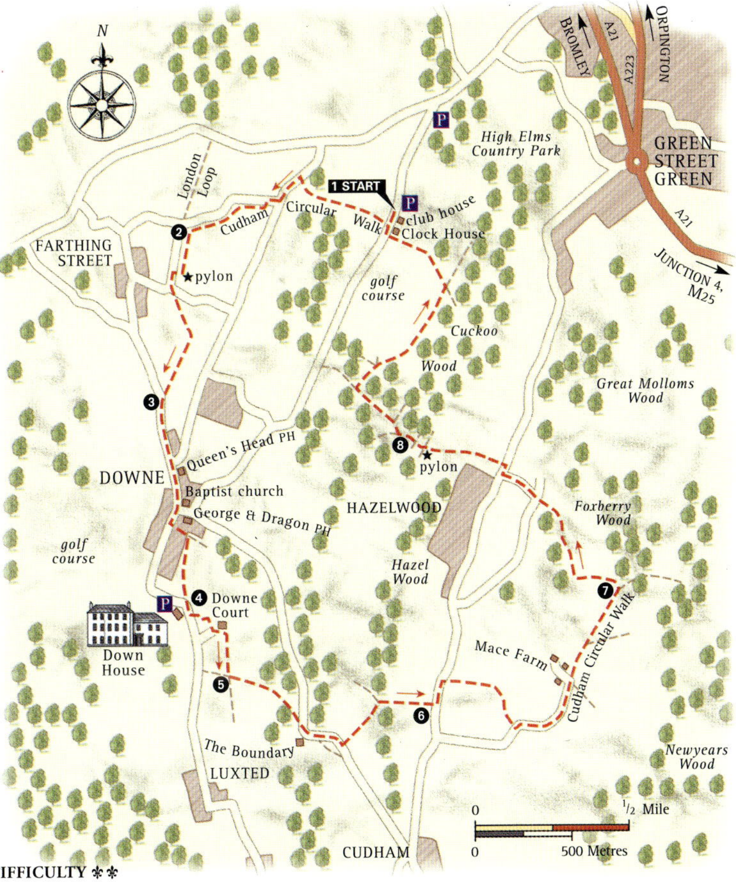

❶ Turn left out of the car park, on to the road. Opposite the Clock House, turn right on a path by a post-box, signed Cudham Circular Walk, follow this to Downe. Turn left on the road, then right on to a track, Bogey Lane. Soon ascend the steps on your left and go along the field edge.

❷ Avoid the London Loop which bears right, and continue to the far field corner by a pylon. Cross a stile and left on a track. Go ahead at the junction of tracks, signed Downe, across the fields (yellow waymarks). Continue to the road.

❸ Turn left on to the road. At Downe village centre, go forward along Luxted Road, past the Baptist church. Turn left before railings (signed Cudham with a red and white English Heritage sign denoting route to Down House), between the houses and along a field edge. In the second field keep right at a junction of paths and go forward into the next field to cross a stile on the right on to the road opposite Down House.

❹ After visiting Down House return to the field by the same stile opposite Down House. Turn right along the field edge, turn left in the field corner to a stile and go forward to take a waymarked path on the right (Leaves Green Circular Walk). Pass Downe Court Farmhouse, go over a concrete drive and left along the field edge.

❺ Go left at the path crossing midway through the field; go along the next field edge, and down through the woods. Turn right on to the road, then left on a signed bridleway by Cudham

DIFFICULTY ✽ ✽

village sign. Ascend steps, avoid a left turning, and go forward by buildings to a road junction.

❻ Go left along the road. After 70yds (64m) turn right on a field path (Cudham Circular Walk, continues to the car park), which bends right at the end of the third field. Go left along a lane. Continue forward at a junction by some houses, on a track signed

Green Street Green. Later, ignore the path to your right.

❼ In woodland, turn left at the junction, to go out of the woods. Go forward at the next junction, along the road. At the main road, turn right and immediately left through a gate, along a field and into Cuckoo Wood near a pylon. Go uphill on the path and forward at two junctions.

❽ Ignore the path into the field but keep right, inside woods, and continue up to the track corner. Keep left uphill. Turn right at Cudham Circular Walk sign, then take the next right fork (near the edge of a golf course), along a broad path. Go left by a barrier and signpost, on to a fenced path which leads down through the golf course to the road. The car park is on the right.

Map

N

BROMLEY
A21
ORPINGTON
A223

GREEN STREET GREEN

A21

JUNCTION 4, M25

P

High Elms Country Park

1 START
P
club house
Clock House

London Loop

Cudham Circular Walk

FARTHING STREET

❷

★ pylon

golf course

Cuckoo Wood

Great Molloms Wood

❸

Queen's Head PH

DOWNE

Baptist church
George & Dragon PH

HAZELWOOD

❽
★ pylon

Foxberry Wood

golf course

Hazel Wood

❼

Cudham Circular Walk

P
❹ Downe Court

Down House

❺

Mace Farm

❻

Newyears Wood

The Boundary

LUXTED

CUDHAM

0   ½ Mile
0   500 Metres

WALK 79

VICTORIAN

ABOUT • LLANDRINDOD WELLS

The promise of health-giving waters at Llandrindod Wells brought Victorians here in their thousands. The walk takes you past the Pump Room and Temple Gardens before heading out of the town to the open countryside and views of the town.

Powys • WALES

DISTANCE • 7 miles (11km)

TOTAL ASCENT • 443ft (135m)

PATHS • good; can be muddy in places

TERRAIN • town streets, woodland, heathland

GRADIENTS • gradual; one short steep descent

REFRESHMENTS • selection of cafés in Llandrindod Wells

PARK • lakeside picnic area, at the top of Princes Avenue

OS MAP • Explorer 200 Llandrindod Wells & Elan Valley, Rhayader

Llandrindod Wells

❶ Follow Princes Avenue towards town, turn left at the end and cross the road on to Spa Road. Follow this, bearing left before and after the railway bridge, to a roundabout. Go through Rock Park Spa gate and descend the main path. Cross the wooden footbridge towards the pump house.

❷ Turn sharp left to the stone bridge and chalybeate spring in the wall. Over the bridge, take the steep path (left, right) up the hill ahead. Continue under the railway arch and keep to the main path, lined with street lights.

❸ At the main road, cross, turning left and immediately right into a side street leading to a path through the park, back up Princes Avenue. In 109yds (100m) beyond the picnic area is Lake Cottage; go 82yds (75m) beyond this and turn left through a signposted gate.

❹ Follow the tarmac path for 55yds (50m); when the route swings left go ahead on the main path through the woods, for about 328yds (300m), to a clearing. On returning to the trees bear left (keep the boundary fence on your right). Cross the stile and go down towards a sign at the bottom of the field. Through the gate here, by the new houses, turn right, then immediately left between gardens, following the waymark arrow.

❺ Turn right on to the street; after 273yds (250m) take waymarked footpath to the right between numbers 9 and 10. Cross the stile and follow the path up through the woods, for 273yds (250m).

❻ Through the gate, follow the path between the gorse bushes to an open field; bear right towards a stile bisecting a conifer plantation.

Cross a stile and immediately take the small path, left, cross another stile to leave the plantation.

❼ Bear right, with waymarker. In 164yds (150m) cross a farm track; recross it 55yds (50m) further on. Continue for 219yds (200m), skirting a small hill. When this green track curves left, cross a stile ahead. Go through the gateway, right, in 11yds (10m), then cross the stile, left, following path with further stiles and gates down to Bailey Einon farm and the minor road.

❽ Turn right, then right again after 219yds (200m). Descend for 273yds (250m), cross stile, left, heading diagonally, and steeply, down the field to a stile at the bottom. Cross this, turn right to tarmac road, then left to a picnic area.

❾ Take the path opposite, ascending through the woods, emerging from conifers after 109yds (100m). At a lane, turn right and continue to a stile on the right opposite a plantation at the brow of the hill.

❿ Cross the stile and follow the path to the trig point. Bear slightly left to a stile and cross two fields. Bear down, right towards gorse bushes, behind which is a signpost and a stile. Cross the stile and head towards the woods, keeping right where the path forks near a pond. Continue for 328yds (300m) to another stile. Cross and turn left, to another stile in 44yds (40m). Cross to rejoin the outward route.

DIFFICULTY ✹ ✹

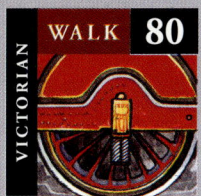

ABOUT • LAKE VYRNWY

Lake Vyrnwy, a reservoir built in the 1880s, was created to give the expanding city of Liverpool a new water supply. It is now a renowned beauty spot and panoramic views of the dam and lake can be enjoyed just before the end of the walk.

Powys • WALES

DISTANCE • 4½ miles (7km)
TOTAL ASCENT • 400ft (122m)
PATHS • good; can be muddy in places
TERRAIN • dam road, lanes, forestry tracks
GRADIENTS • two moderate climbs

REFRESHMENTS • two cafés in Llanwddyn
PARK • village car park, entrance opposite workshops and Tourist Information Centre
OS MAP • Explorer 239 Lake Vyrnwy & Llanfyllin, Tanat Valley

Lake Vyrnwy: giving water to Liverpool

❶ Leave the village car park at the end nearer the village. Follow the path and steps up the side of the woods. On reaching the road follow the footpath past the visitor centre car park on the right. Turn right on to the dam and cross.

❷ At the far end of the dam turn right immediately down the steps. Follow the path to a footbridge, cross and keep along the side of the fence. On reaching the track follow it to the left, through the gate and along the river bank.

❸ Shortly go over a footbridge, cross the stile you see ahead, left. At the top of the path, cross another stile and turn left on to the lane. In 109yds (100m) take the right fork, (not Grwn Oer). In 219yds (200m) continue ahead, following a blue waymarker, and later round a right bend.

❹ When the tarmac lane bears down and left to a farm track, keep straight on, following the unmade track (blue marker). Enter forestry 328yds (300m) beyond. Follow the track, which later descends pleasantly, for 766yds (700m).

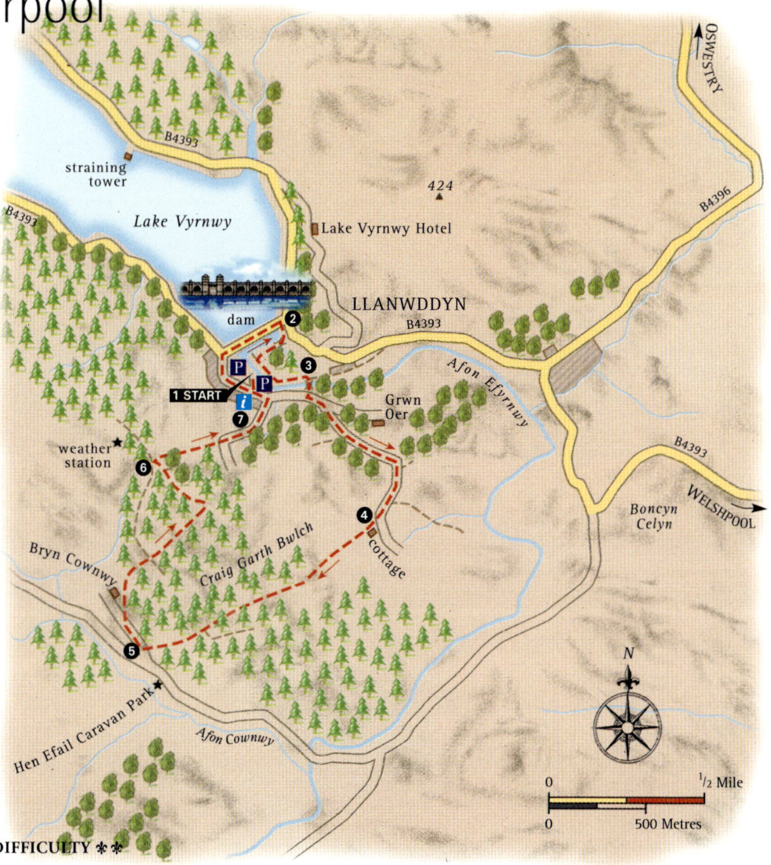

• DON'T MISS •

*There is a lovely scenic drive right round **Lake Vyrnwy**. A Sculpture Trail has been established with natural wooden sculptures, which includes dolphins, otters, a giant dragonfly and the Pecking Order Totem Pole in the areas around the various visitor car parks. Details are available from the visitor centre in the village.*

Map labels:
OSWESTRY
B4393
straining tower
Lake Vyrnwy
424
Lake Vyrnwy Hotel
B4396
dam
LLANWDDYN
B4393
Afon Efyrnwy
1 START
Grwn Oer
weather station
B4393
WELSHPOOL
Boncyn Celyn
Bryn Cownwy
Craig Garth Bwlch
cottage
Hen Efail Caravan Park
Afon Cownwy
N
0 ½ Mile
0 500 Metres

DIFFICULTY ✽✽

At the left hairpin bend, keep ahead, soon descending again.

❺ On meeting a T-junction with a lane, turn right. Just before Bryn Cownwy farmhouse, fork right and follow the forestry track steeply and steadily uphill. At a crossroads of forestry tracks keep straight on.

Keep on the main track, later following it round to the left.

❻ At a junction of tracks as you leave the trees, look for the waymarked gate straight ahead of you. Go through this and follow the waymarked path steeply descending by the side of the

fence to a stile in the far right-hand corner.

❼ Cross, turn right and go through stile and gate in 55yds (50m). Join a lane and follow it back down to the village. Cross the road, head left then right, and follow the access road back to the car park.

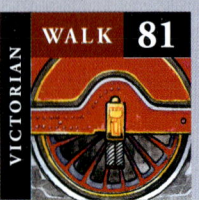

VICTORIAN

WALK 81

ABOUT • SCARBOROUGH

By the end of the 18th century Scarborough was a magnet for people of good fashion – ever since Elizabeth Farrer discovered medicinal waters springing beside the beach. The waters, no longer thought fit to drink, still flow from a niche near the spa.

North Yorkshire • N ENGLAND

DISTANCE • 6¾ miles (10.8km)
TOTAL ASCENT • 590ft (180m)
PATHS • town pavements and beach, tides permitting
TERRAIN • two wide bays set either side of headland
GRADIENTS • one gradual climb form North Bay; ascent to castle entrance quite steep

REFRESHMENTS • plenty of hotels, pubs, restaurants, cafés and tea rooms throughout Scarborough
PARK • Albion Road car park on the South Cliff, off A165 Bridlington road
OS MAP • Explorer 301 Scarborough, Bridlington & Flamborough Head

Medicinal waters at the seaside

❶ From the car park, follow Albion Road towards the sea. Turn right and by Esplanade Gardens take the cliff lift (tramway) down, or the winding path beside it, to the spa buildings. At the seashore, turn left, along the beach or the road.

❷ Walk towards the harbour. Pass the lifeboat station and follow the road past the harbour, bending left through an archway on to Marine Drive (closed in bad weather). Follow Marine Drive for 1½ miles (2.4km) to a roundabout.

❸ Turn left, and left again at the next roundabout, then take the next left. Turn left again, along Queen's Parade. Follow the road along the cliff top. Go left of the Boston and Norbreck hotels, to descend along Mulgrave Place to a crossroads.

❹ Turn left to visit the castle. Return from the castle to the crossroads, and turn left. Anne Brontë's grave is behind the wall to your left. Follow the lane downhill, going left along Paradise, then bending right. Take the second turning right, Longwestgate.

❺ Go left down St Mary's Street. Continue downhill by the Leeds Hotel, bending right down a cobbled path for 22yds (20m) to join a main road. Turn right, uphill. At the traffic lights turn left along St Nicholas Street, bending right by the Royal Hotel. The Grand Hotel is to your left.

❻ Continue along Falconers Road. At the roundabout, take the second exit (the Crescent Hotel is now on your right) and walk round

the Crescent. Turn left by the Chessington Hotel, cross the next road and go straight on. At the top, turn left and then left again at the traffic-lights.

❼ At the next traffic-lights go right towards Tesco. Follow the

road as far as Falsgrave signal box and turn left. At the bottom turn left, then left again after 33yds (30m) down Valley Road. Cross at the roundabout beyond Valley Bridge, then bear left to pass the Rotunda Museum.

❽ Continue up the slope and steps and over Cliff Bridge. At the end bear right up steps beside the Spa Chalet. Follow the road past the Crown Hotel, and go right at the Villa Esplanade along Albion Road to the car park.

• DON'T MISS •

Scarborough's Rotunda Museum is a fascinating collection of local treasures, housed in a domed building. A spiral staircase rises to the main room, with paintings of Yorkshire geology above the 19th-century display cases. The museum was inspired by William Smith (1769–1839) who is known as the father of English geology.

DIFFICULTY ✳✳

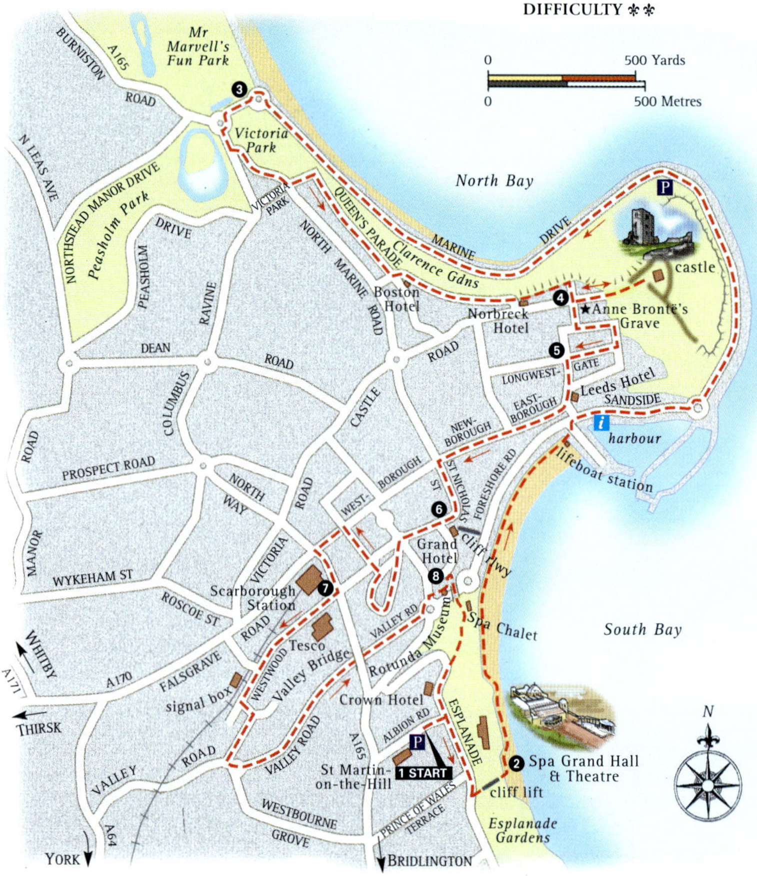

[Map of Scarborough showing the walk route, North Bay, South Bay, castle, Anne Brontë's Grave, harbour, Grand Hotel, Scarborough Station, Tesco, Valley Bridge, Rotunda Museum, Crown Hotel, Spa Grand Hall & Theatre, cliff lift, and START point at the car park on Albion Road]

0 — 500 Yards
0 — 500 Metres

*As the 20th century opened, the world was shrinking.
Aeroplanes, cars, the telephone and the cinema were extending
global communications and seemed to promise increased
understanding and even peace. But within two decades such
hopes had been buried in the trenches of World War I.*

EDWARDIAN

1901–1918

A New Century

Edwardian Britain was the hub of a rich empire, and still a society divided into sharply defined classes: 'upstairs' and 'downstairs' had precious little overlap. Women were starting to make inroads into education and professions, but only in individual, exceptional cases. On the whole, women played a decidedly backstage role in public life, and in the early years of the century there was a growing call for change. Many men and women pressed for further electoral reform – demanding the vote not only for all men, but for some women as well.

Frustrated at their lack of progress, a section of the suffrage movement began to employ headline-grabbing tactics. Known as the Suffragettes, women such as Emmeline Pankhurst chained themselves to railings, broke windows and led public demonstrations to bring attention to their cause; some who were gaoled went on hunger strike, and endured the horrors of force-feeding.

The need for reform was, in fact, acknowledged in a series of policies that sought to tackle industrial Britain's problems of poverty and inequality. While the new Labour Party brought the working-class voice into the political forum, Chancellor of the Exchequer Lloyd George laid the foundations of a welfare state, taxing luxury items such as motor cars to pay for old age pensions. Nevertheless women had to wait until 1918 for even a limited right to vote, as the normal business of government (which also included Home Rule for Ireland) was suspended during four years of devastating warfare.

Meanwhile technology was progressing quickly at the turn of the 20th century, with important advances in medicine, communications and entertainment. In 1903 the Wright brothers made the first successful man-powered flight in North Carolina; the next goal was to travel long distances by air. A prize of £1000 was offered by *The Daily Mail* for the first flight across the English Channel. The winner was Frenchman Loius Blériot who made the 43-minute journey from Calais to Dover Castle on 25 July 1909. Within five years Britain and the rest of the world was at war and the air force brought a new dimension to international conflict.

THE GREAT WAR

In 1914 a Serb terrorist assassinated the Hapsburg Archduke Ferdinand, and plunged the world into chaos. A complex network of alliances and enmities brought nation after nation on to the stage of war, and hundreds of thousands of men suffered in rat-infested, waterlogged trenches as battles raged on to gain a few feet of muddy field on the European front. The effects of relentless, deafening shelling and appalling mustard-gas attacks were characteristics of war on a previously unknown scale, recorded by a generation of young poets such as Siegfried Sassoon and Wilfred Owen. Nevertheless it took a long time for the full magnitude of events to filter back to those at home, who had, on the whole, greeted the outbreak of hostilities with patriotic fervour.

By the time the war ground to a close, a generation of young men had virtually been wiped out. The survivors were promised homes fit for heroes, but too many came back to unemployment and despair. Meanwhile, women had proved their ability to do 'men's work', stepping into the breach in factories and on public transport; and at the same time the common experiences of officers and the lower ranks had at least begun to break down some class barriers. In just four years, lives and attitudes had been shattered. The only generally held certainty was that this had been the war to end all wars.

HISTORIC SITES

Civic Centre, Cardiff, South Glamorgan: outstanding Beaux-Arts architecture.

Glasgow School of Art, Glasgow, Strathclyde: designed by Charles Rennie Mackintosh and displaying his unique style and its art nouveau influences.

Alhambra Theatre, Bradford, West Yorks: restored Edwardian splendour from the age of music hall.

The Cenotaph Memorial, London: memorial to the dead of World War I, designed by Sir Edwin Lutyens.

Dartmouth, Devon: an important naval base was established here in 1905.

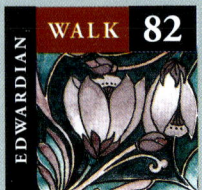
ABOUT • WINDERMERE

This walk follows in the footsteps of Beatrix Potter. It passes Far Sawrey and climbs the rolling hills to Moss Eccles Tarn. Passing through the forests of Claife Heights, you will catch glimpses of Bowness and Windermere through the tree boughs.

Cumbria • N ENGLAND

DISTANCE • 6 miles (9.6km)

TOTAL ASCENT • 850ft (259m)

PATHS • field paths can be muddy in winter

TERRAIN • rolling hills and woodland

GRADIENTS • Steady but gentle climbs. The descent back to the car park can be slippery after rain

REFRESHMENTS • Tower Bank Arms in Near Sawrey

PARK • National Trust car park above Windermere Ferry landing stage

OS MAP • Outdoor Leisure 7 The English Lakes – South Eastern Area

The world of Beatrix Potter

1 From the south of the car park follow the footpath signed to Far Sawrey, Near Sawrey and Hill Top. After a short way it crosses the road, eventually to emerge on the High Cunsey Lane (not named), close to its junction with the B-road.

2 Turn right, then left, up the B-road. At a sharp left-hand corner turn right, along a track marked to Far Sawrey, Near Sawrey and Hill Top. Follow it northwest through woodland and past a few cottages.

3 Rejoin the B-road, turn right, then first left, descending along the lane towards St Peter's Church. Go right through a kissing gate by a whitewashed cottage, then follow the clear cross-field path towards Near Sawrey. The path returns to the road just short of Hill Top Farm.

4 Through the village turn right along the lane opposite a post-box. This becomes a stony track that climbs past Moss Eccles and Wise Een tarns before entering the Claife Heights conifer plantations.

5 Ignore the footpath on the left, and instead stay with the forestry road. Turn right along a path signed to the ferry and Far Sawrey. White waymark posts (look out for these as path may be unclear after major tree felling) highlight the route from here back to the car park. The winding path climbs to the Claife Heights viewpoint, where you can look down the length of Windermere.

6 The continuing path crosses a wide forestry track. Turn right to reach High Blind How (the viewpoint is off the path). Just south of the viewpoint the path rounds some huge rocky outcrops. Beyond the outcrops follow the path to the left back into thick woodland.

7 Turn right at a junction of paths and head south, signed Far Sawrey. The path becomes a wide track on entering an open area of pasture and crag with a wall on the left. Turn left at the T-junction of tracks, following the signed route to Windermere ferry and the lakeshore. At the next signpost turn right through a kissing gate, signed to ferry.

8 After traversing high fields with a view to Bowness the path re-enters the woods and zigzags down steep slopes to the ruins of the old viewing station. Beyond these, descend the stepped path back to the car park.

• DON'T MISS •

Explore the places in **Windermere** *that were home to Beatrix Potter – where Peter Rabbit, Tom Kitten and others came to life on the pages of her books.*

AMBLESIDE

B5285

HAWKSHEAD

Wise Een Tarn

Water Side Wood

Esthwaite

Water

NEAR SAWREY

Tower Bank Arms PH

Hill Top Farm

Out Dubs Tarn

C l a i f e

Three Dubs Tarn

Moss Eccles Tarn

H e i g h t s

Cuckoo Brow Wood

Castle Cottage

FAR SAWREY

Sawrey Hotel

B5285

St Peter's Church

viewpoint

Heald Wood

High Blind How

Belle Isle

ferry

W i n d e r m e r e

WINDERMERE

A592

ULVERSTON

N

0 ———— ½ Mile

0 ———— 500 Metres

P 1 START

Bishop Woods

DIFFICULTY ✳✳

EDWARDIAN

WALK 83

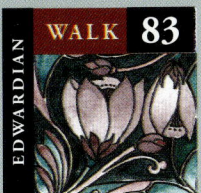

ABOUT • LETCHWORTH

The Garden City of Letchworth pioneered the idea of conscious town planning. Inspired by a pamphlet written by Ebenezer Howard in 1908, Letchworth aimed to resolve the problem of unhealthy slum dwellings and overcrowded terraces.

Hertfordshire • SE ENGLAND

DISTANCE • 6 miles (9.6km)

TOTAL ASCENT • negligible

PATHS • pavements, with a short stretch through a park

TERRAIN • town, parkland

GRADIENTS • some gentle ascents

REFRESHMENTS • plenty of choice in the town

PARK • Station Place West long stay car park next to the station; multi-storey car park behind the cinema

OS MAP • Explorer 193 Luton & Stevenage, Hitchin & Ampthill

Letchworth: new town

❶ In Station Place, with the war memorial on the right, head west out of the square, noting leafy Broadway down to the left, and the Broadway Hotel. Turn right over the railway bridge. Admire the Spirella underwear factory, left.

❷ Turn right into Nevells Road. Pass houses dated 1914 to more individual, small houses, built as experimental low-cost homes in 1950, with different building materials, such as the rock-like tin cladding at No 212. The Settlement, built as a temperance pub, is now a community centre. Retrace your steps and turn right up Cross Street.

❸ Turn left at the end on to Icknield Way, and near the unusual brown timber-clad house at the entrance to The Quadrant, cross the main road and take the tarmac path straight across the park of Norton Common.

❹ Where the path emerges on Willbury Road, cross over and turn right. Pass the crescent of Westholm, on the left, the epitome of Garden City design, with its white rendered and gable houses grouped around a tree-filled green. Eastholm is a corresponding arc on the next corner. Cross Willbury Road again, and descend, right, into Norton Way North. Note the bigger houses, set back from the road with trees and hedges.

❺ At the modern St George's Church, turn left into Common View. The further you walk up here, the more interesting the little terraced groups become, with each distinctive row of four proclaiming its designers. Keep right along here to the end, then retrace your steps to Cromwell Green, a lower-scale contrast to Westholm.

❻ Turn down here between the houses, and right on to Glebe Road, back towards the town centre. The factories are only a row away, but this is still very pleasant. At the junction, go left down Norton Way North and pass under the railway bridge.

❼ Bear left, cross at the bollards, and enter Rushby Mead, a long and delightful breath of country in the town. Stay on this road across two junctions, and at the end, turn right and cross at the crossing.

❽ Continue to the next traffic-lights, turning left into Willian Way, a beautiful avenue of bigger individual houses. Turn right into Barrington Road to pass the extraordinary Cloisters (private), and turn right again into Cloisters Road, past modern, much less individual housing. Cross the main road and the little green (note the thatched kiosk, right) and bear left into Sollershott East. Pass Sollershott Hall, left, and turn right up the main avenue of Broadway.

❾ At Souberie Avenue, turn right and follow this curve to its junction with Meadow Way. Turn left here, and right into the big Broadway square. Pass the museum on your right, turn right, and bear immediately left at the cinema into the main shopping area of East Cheap. Follow this back down to Station Place.

DIFFICULTY ✻

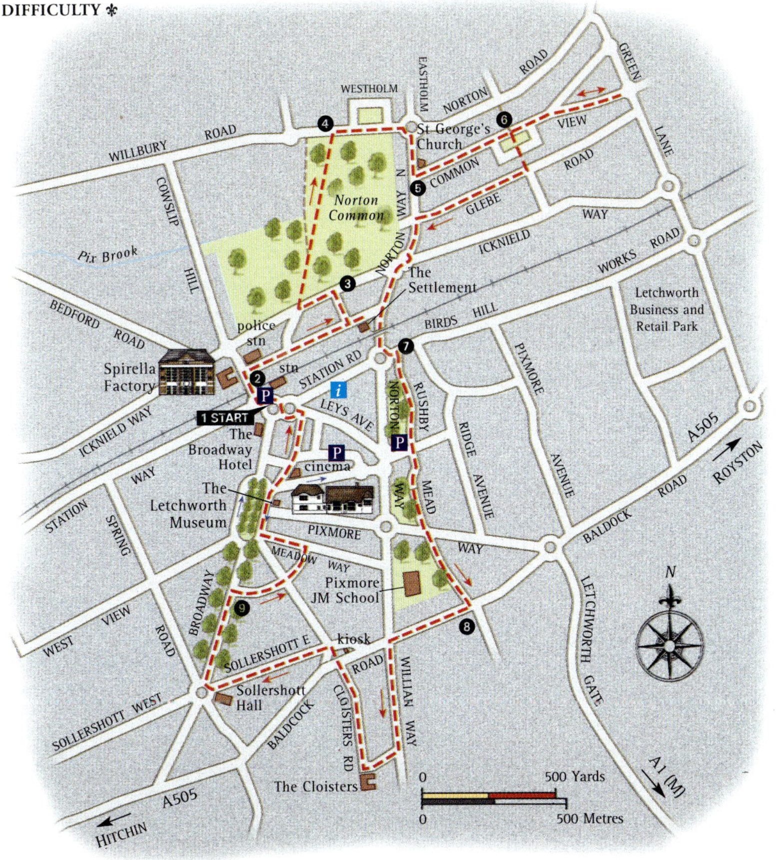

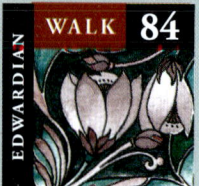

EDWARDIAN

WALK 84

ABOUT • SANDRINGHAM

Sandringham offers the epitome of an Edwardian royal country house. It was designed to be a large, comfortable home, suitable for entertaining large parties. Opened in 1968 as a country park, this part of the estate offers free access for walkers.

Norfolk • SE ENGLAND

DISTANCE • gardens 1½miles (2.4km); country park 3½ miles (5.6km)

TERRAIN • landscaped, formal gardens with wheelchair access throughout; woodland

PATHS • gardens: mainly firm, gravel paths; country park: mostly firm, but sections in woods can be muddy

GRADIENTS • gardens: level, easy walking;

country park: some slopes and steps

REFRESHMENTS • tea room and restaurant at visitor centre; tea room by museum

PARK • car park by the visitor centre

CONTACT • the Estate Office (01553) 772675 for details of opening times

OS MAP • n/a

A very royal estate

❶ From the visitor centre, cross the main road, pass the war memorial on your right, and bear left, via the ticket office, into the gardens. Turn left on a gravel path, and follow it through the woods.

❷ Leave the path to see a wall, with memorials to Sandringham's working dogs. Keep along the main path and through an area of rhododendrons. Go under the arch and turn left to see Norwich Gates.

❸ Retrace your steps and turn left through another rhododendron arch, following the main path. Note the *Wellingtonia gigantica*, right, before you bear left on to the main drive. Follow this round to the yew hedges in front of the house, turning right to the main entrance.

❹ Leaving the house via the ballroom, turn left and right through the hedge, and take the path diagonally right to rejoin the main drive. Keep straight here, and take the small path, left, to visit the museum and tea room (and toilets) in the old stable block.

❺ Walk out of the courtyard, turn left on the drive and bear right at a grass triangle, downhill. Leave the path and turn right along the stream, with York Cottage up to the left. Turn right on the path, and keep left, passing the lake on your right. At the gates, follow the path right for views of the house.

❻ At the intersection of paths, turn right and go up to the house, exploring the terrace. Bear left through the formal North Garden, and at the Old Father Time statue turn left and join the path, passing memorials to the Queen's corgis.

❼ Turn right and pass through the turnstile to the church (or exit via the entrance). Leave the church and go left to the car park.

❽ With the visitor centre behind you, face the adventure playground and take the woodland path to the left, following yellow spots on the trees. At the sign turn right, following the yellow trail, and pass through a squeeze gate. Cross the estate road, follow the path across the grass and go through the wooden arch.

❾ Descend shallow steps, passing a pond and hide on the right, and through another squeeze gate. Continue through the woods and follow the yellow marks left. After about ¼ mile (400m), ignore the path on the left and keep straight on. Follow the yellow arrow up the steep path and steps to the left, to emerge on heathland.

❿ Turn right on the estate road and follow it to meet the main road. Cross over and descend the sandy track through woods.

⓫ At the bottom, follow the yellow arrow left up a straight grassy sward through trees, parallel with the road (right). Continue past the Donkey Pond, follow the yellow spots into the trees at the top, and turn right on to a broad grassy ride. At the triangular junction, cross the road to the left and pick up the yellow arrow, right, into the trees. Follow this path back to the visitor centre.

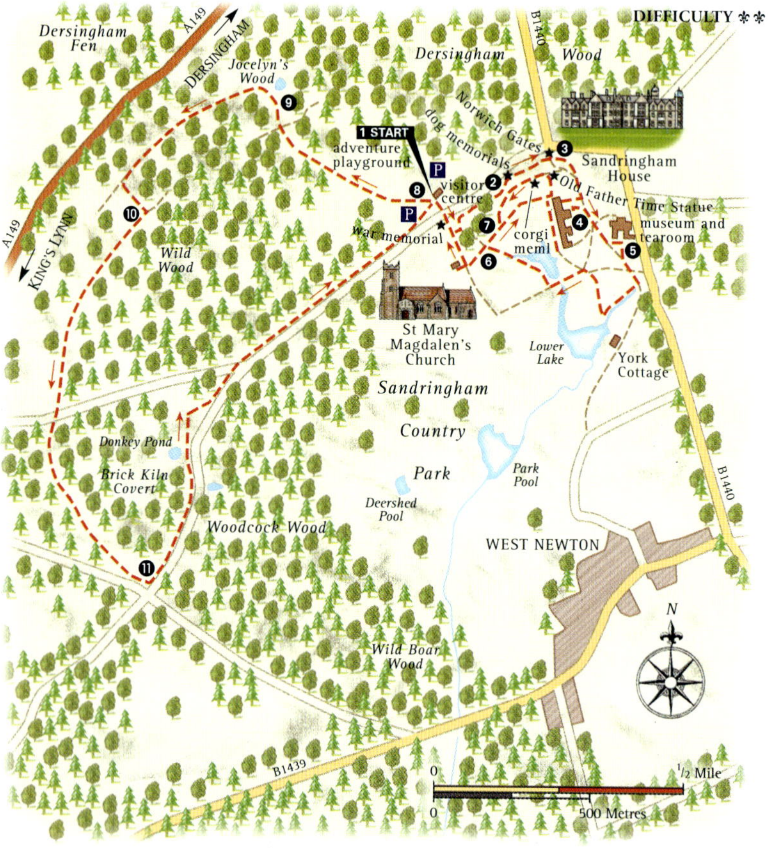

DIFFICULTY ✷✷

Map labels:

Dersingham Fen

Dersingham Wood

A149

DERSINGHAM

Jocelyn's Wood

Norwich Gates

dog memorials

❾

1 START
adventure playground

visitor centre

Sandringham House

Old Father Time Statue

war memorial

corgi meml

museum and tearoom

❽ ❷ ❸ ❹ ❺

❼ ❻

❿

A149

KING'S LYNN

Wild Wood

St Mary Magdalen's Church

Lower Lake

York Cottage

B1440

Sandringham

Country

Park

Park Pool

Donkey Pond

Brick Kiln Covert

Deershed Pool

Woodcock Wood

WEST NEWTON

⓫

Wild Boar Wood

N

B1439

0 ½ Mile

0 500 Metres

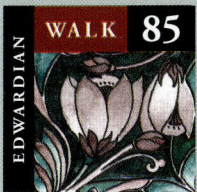
Edward Elgar (1857–1934) is best remembered for his music, inspired by the dramatic backdrop of the Malvern Hills. It was here that he composed some of his greatest pieces and chose it to be the final resting place for himself and his beloved wife, Alice.

DISTANCE • 6 miles (9.6km)	
TOTAL ASCENT • 750ft (228m)	
PATHS • good; slippery in places	
TERRAIN • tracks, field paths, stiles and tarmac roads	
GRADIENTS • some quite steep but not long	

REFRESHMENTS • kiosk (hot and cold drinks) and hotel near the end of route

PARK • Blackhill car park 328yds (300m) past Malvern Hills Hotel on B4232

OS MAP • Explorer 190 Malvern Hills & Bredon Hill, Tewkesbury

Music in the Malverns

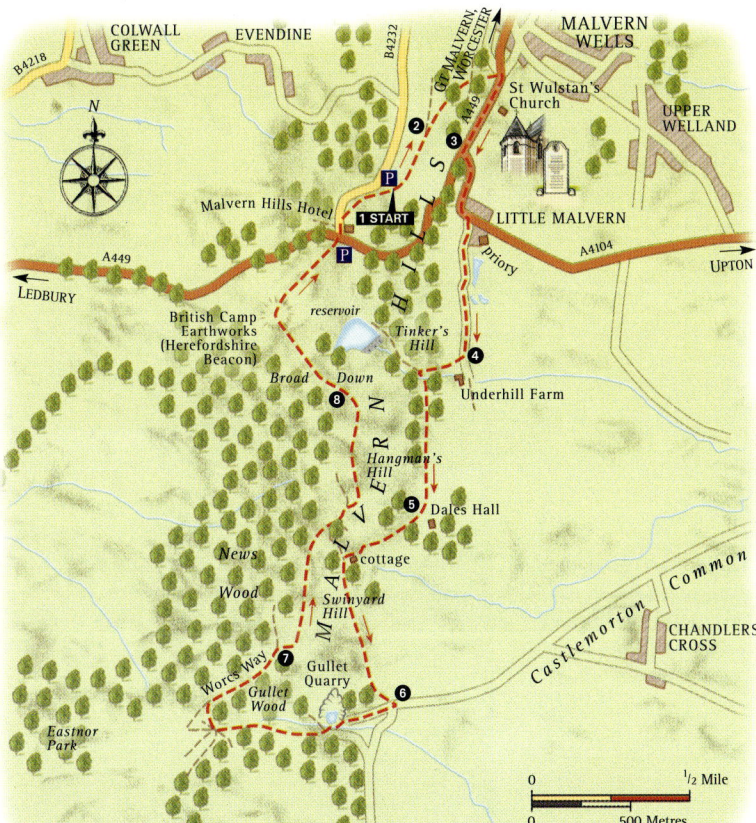

double (not single) wooden poles are almost overhead.

5 Turn two-thirds right, uphill through bracken. Ascend moderately, then later steeply, to eventually pass to the right of a faded-pink cottage. Here a farm track soon joins another. Descend steadily on this stony track to reach a road junction.

6 At the road turn sharply back right along it to soon skirt Gullet Quarry and pool. Go straight ahead up a stony path to where seven tracks meet. Turn right, signed Worcs Way North, and continue for several hundred yards.

7 At a clearing go up, right, to the ridge. Turn left. Look out for a low pointer (not obviously an arrow), marked Hangman's Hill, Broad Down, set in cement and stones at a junction. Take the right path to the indistinct top of Broad Down, continuing left along the ridge.

8 Aim for a partly flagged stone path visible ahead to the left, to reach British Camp Earthworks (Herefordshire Beacon). Continue ahead, descend steps and gravel path, and, bearing right, take any of the clear paths leading down to a large car park opposite the Malvern Hills Hotel (kiosk and toilets nearby). Cross to take the B-road opposite (brief pavement then cross to a path) to return to the Blackhill car park.

DIFFICULTY ✱✱

1 Take a gently rising footpath from the far left-hand corner of Blackhill car park. Walk slightly to the left of the crest to a wooden seat dedicated to Florence Stuart and Harold Woodyatt Harvey.

2 Take the right fork, soon descending steadily through woodland (ignore crossing path) to reach a tarmac road. Turn right, then right again at the main road,

to view St Wulstan's Church and Elgar's grave. Afterwards, continue to the road junction.

3 Follow the road signed Upton A4104. At a sharp bend cross carefully to take a bridleway marked Little Malvern Estate Trust. Pass behind Little Malvern Priory, a former monastery, to admire the topiary in an extensive yew hedge. Reach a large solitary yew tree,

just as farm buildings become visible ahead.

4 Turn right across a stile into a field. Walk diagonally left across the field to a rusty gate, well to the left of a modern grey gate. Continue to follow the path into dense woodland. At a T-junction turn sharply left. Come out of the woodland and continue until telephone wires supported on

Port Sunlight: Model Village

The garden village of Port Sunlight, purpose-built in the late 19th and early 20th centuries

Enlightened Employment

William Hesketh Lever was an enlightened employer, all too rare a creature in the industrial north of England. He believed that the workers at his Port Sunlight soap factory should have decent housing, which was both of good quality and attractive, and with plenty of recreational space around. To provide this he employed 30 architects, who designed a range of houses, each different, lining spacious streets in Port Sunlight.

Lever also provided his employees with their own hospital, two schools, two village halls, a church, an inn, social clubs and – very advanced for the time – both a swimming pool and a gymnasium. Workers also received an allowance of Port Sunlight soap, an allowance which continues to this day for the houses, which are mostly still in private hands.

Port Sunlight today is a Conservation Area, and is unique among such model industrial villages not only for its architecture but because it retains its original boundaries and remains much as it was when first built.

The World of the Workers'

There are several examples of towns or villages in the north of England that were purpose-built to house factory workers. Saltaire in Bradford is one such, but perhaps the finest example is Port Sunlight on the Wirral. Just across the Mersey is the city of Liverpool, where more typical examples of packed back-to-back terraced housing can be found. Lord Lever wanted better for the people who would be working in his soap factory, however. He believed not only that it was his moral duty but also that a happy work force was a productive work force – very modern thinking for the early 20th century.

Today the visitor is not merely seeing a worthy project, but also fine examples of late 19th- and early 20th-century architecture. Gladstone Hall, for example, was built in 1891 and was a men's dining hall, but today serves as the village's Gladstone Theatre. The modern Post Office dates from the same period, and was Port Sunlight's general store.

Hulme Hall was built in 1900–1 as a women's dining room, and is now used for social functions as well as computer and antique fairs. For a while it was home to Lord and Lady Lever's art collection, still one of the village's prime attractions, the Lady Lever Art Gallery, was begun in 1913 and finally opened in 1922 by Princess Beatrice, the daughter of Queen Victoria. No visit should miss this excellent collection of fine art objects, especially noted for its Pre-Raphaelite paintings by Millais, Rossetti and others.

WALK 86
AROUND THE MODEL VILLAGE

❶ Begin at the Heritage Centre on Greendale Road, close to Port Sunlight railway station, which provides residents with rail links to Liverpool and to Chester. After emerging from the Centre, note the Gladstone Theatre opposite. Turn left and left again into Wood Street, which runs alongside the factory where originally all of Port Sunlight's residents worked and many still do today.

❷ At Poet's Corner turn left and left again to double back down Park Road, built in 1892, towards the Heritage Centre; at the junction with Greendale Road is the Post Office. Walk past the Post Office along Greendale Road and turn right into Bolton Road.

❸ Take the second on the left, Church Drive, which naturally leads to Christ Church, the parish church that was built in 1902–4. It is quite a modest church, whose roof blends in with the domestic architecture and which has some fine stained glass windows. Behind the church take Walker Street, turn left down Pool Bank, left into Circular Drive and Primrose Hill, and left on Lower Road to the Lady Lever Art Gallery.

❹ On leaving the gallery walk left down Queen Mary's Drive, which leads to the war memorial. This imposing village focal point was begun in 1916 and not finished until 1921. Touching bronze sculptures depict soldiers guarding women and children, and civilians protecting each other from the horrors of war. Turn right down the Causeway then left into Greendale Road to return you to the Heritage Centre.

Distance: 3 miles (4.8km)

Total ascent: none

Paths: pavements

Terrain: town

Gradients: very slight

Refreshments: Lady Lever Art Gallery

Park: Heritage Centre. Note that traffic is not permitted on some streets in Port Sunlight

OS Map: Explorer 266 Wirral & Chester

Difficulty: ✳

The Heritage Centre is another building that must be seen, providing as it does the background to the whole project, with old photographs and even movie footage, as well as a scale model of Port Sunlight, to help plan a walk around its streets. During the summer there are also guided walking tours on Sundays and Bank Holiday Mondays.

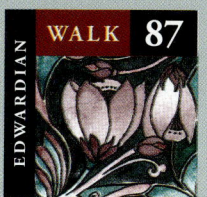

ABOUT • CRAIGLOCKHART HOUSE

World War I, called 'the war to end all wars' suffered more casualties than any other. Thousands more suffered from shell shock, including war poets, Siegfried Sassoon and Wilfred Owen. Being officers they were lucky and sent to Craiglockhart to recover.

City of Edinburgh • SCOTLAND

DISTANCE • 7 miles (11.3km)

TOTAL ASCENT • 275ft (84m)

PATHS • mostly good but can get boggy in wet weather

TERRAIN • pavements and woodland paths

GRADIENTS • moderate to steep

REFRESHMENTS • none on route

PARK • Hermitage Drive

OS MAP • Explorer 350 Edinburgh, Mussellburgh & Queensferry

Craiglockhart House: a World War I hospital

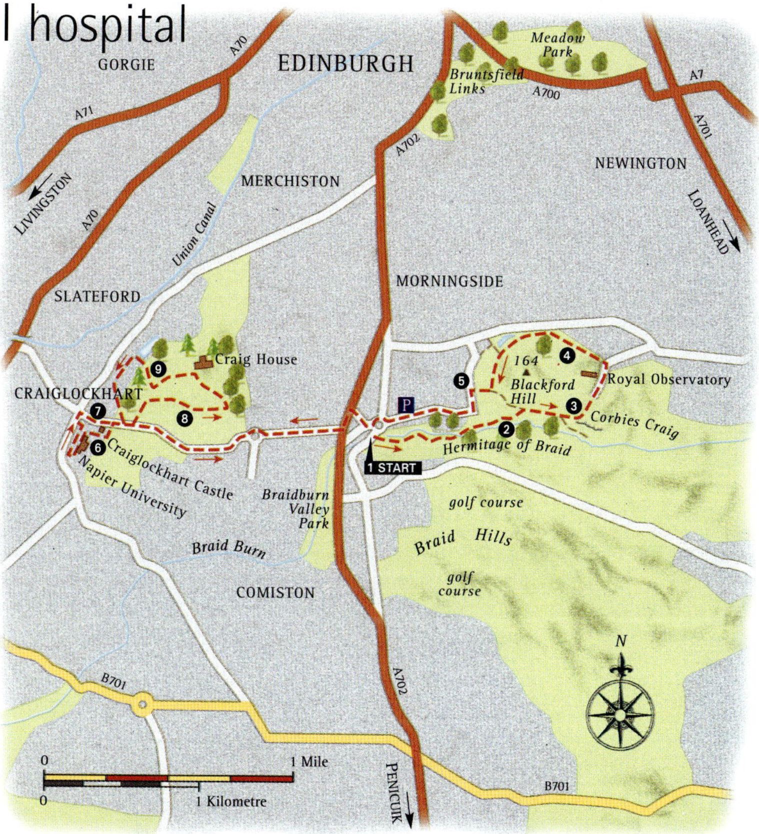

❶ Enter Hermitage of Braid park, turn left through a kissing gate and head along the river path. At the toilets re-join the driveway and at the visitor centre take the left fork and head uphill.

❷ Fork left and keep heading uphill untill you reach a stone wall. Continue along the wall, go through the gap and turn right on to a path. Take a left fork and head up hill keeping Corbies Craig on your right.

❸ At a grassy area turn left and at the top of the hill cross over to the Royal Observatory, keeping the buildings on your left. Follow the footpath to Observatory Road North then turn left at the end of the buildings.

❹ Take the right-hand track, cross another track and fork right and head downhill. Continue on a rutted track, go down steps on to a path, turn left, continue past allotments, then turn right through a metal gate and cross a field.

❺ Exit through a car park and head along Hermitage Drive. Cross Braid Road, turn right into Greenbank Place, turn left at Comiston Road and right into Greenbank Drive. At the roundabout keep right along Glenlockhart Road, then turn left to Napier University.

❻ Follow the road to a large sandstone building and turn right. Turn right again in front of the clock, go down steps and turn right on to a path. Exit through the gate, turn right, then right again at the traffic-lights.

❼ Cross the road and turn left along a path by the white house. Turn right at the end of the wall, go uphill and turn right again through a gap in the wall. Go uphill and pass stone marker 5.

❽ Go through a gate, turn right, then left, following the woodland path behind some buildings. Go right towards the large sandstone building, turn left on to the path.

Continue, turning left through some gorse bushes then right at stone marker 9.

❾ Go downhill and leave the woods through a gate. Follow the path round some houses then turn left on to a path past a pond. Climb the steps, to return to the white house, turn left on to the road and return to the start and the car park.

DIFFICULTY ✽✽

• DON'T MISS •

Roslin Chapel, near Penicuik, was built by the Knights Templar. Like a great French cathedral in miniature, Roslin has a haunting atmosphere and some unique stone carvings, including the death mask of Robert the Bruce.

GORGIE EDINBURGH

Meadow Park

Bruntsfield Links

NEWINGTON

LIVINGSTON

MERCHISTON

Union Canal

SLATEFORD

MORNINGSIDE

Craig House

CRAIGLOCKHART

164 Blackford Hill · Royal Observatory

Corbies Craig

Hermitage of Braid

Craiglockhart Castle

Napier University

Braidburn Valley Park

1 START

golf course

Braid Burn

Braid Hills

COMISTON

golf course

B701

N

0 ——— 1 Mile

0 ——— 1 Kilometre

PENICUIK

B701

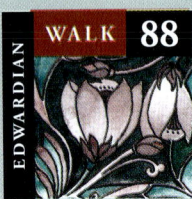

WALK 88

EDWARDIAN

ABOUT • CASTLE DROGO

Castle Drogo, built in 1930, is now owned by the National Trust. Built of local granite, it was the result of a partnership between the architect Sir Edwin Lutyens, one of the foremost architects of the Edwardian era, and millionaire, Julius Drewe.

Devon • SW ENGLAND

DISTANCE • 4½ miles (7.2km)

TOTAL ASCENT • 395ft (120m)

PATHS • good field and woodland tracks; some muddy after wet weather

TERRAIN • steep-sided river gorge, mixed deciduous woodland and open moorland

GRADIENTS • one long, steep climb from Fingle Bridge

REFRESHMENTS • The Angler's Rest at Fingle Bridge; the Sandy Park Inn, Sandy Park

PARK • Roadside parking at Dogmarsh Bridge, just south of Sandy Park on the A382 Whiddon Down to Moretonhampstead road

OS MAP • Outdoor Leisure 28 Dartmoor

Castle Drogo, a famous partnership

DIFFICULTY ✱✱

❶ Walk from your car towards the bridge. Turn left through the kissing gate, following the footpath signed Two Moors Way, to enter the Castle Drogo Estate. Walk along the river, passing through two kissing gates. Go over a footbridge to enter oak woodland then negotiate a stile/small gate.

❷ Turn right to cross the river on a suspension bridge*, ascend steps to cross the big granite wall. Turn left along the track, which leads through a five-bar gate. Continue along this undulating track, soon passing a pumping station on your left, part of the castle's hydro-electric scheme. Continue along the track through Hannicombe Wood to reach Fingle Bridge.

❸ Turn left to cross the old packhorse bridge and take a break at The Angler's Rest. To continue the walk turn right from the pub and up the lane through the parking area.

❹ After 100yds (91m) turn left, following a footpath signed Hunter's path. This narrow wooded path climbs steeply up to reach open moorland above the gorge and joins the Hunter's path (which comes in from the right); keep left and pass through granite gateposts towards the castle, which can be seen ahead.

❺ At the next signpost (Drewsteignton) turn right up wooden steps; do not cross the stile ahead, but almost immediately turn left across Piddledown Common following the signs for Castle Drogo. The next sign directs you along the Gorse Blossom Walk to reach the castle drive.

❻ Turn left; at the car park sign turn right to reach the entrance to the castle and gardens. After your visit, retrace your steps out of the car park and turn left down the drive to continue the walk.

❼ Almost immediately turn right, signed Hunter's Path. Keep straight on downhill, and descend wooden steps, to meet the path along the edge of the gorge. Turn right and

follow the path below the castle, veering right to meet a lane through two wooden gates.

❽ Turn left downhill, signed Fisherman's Path. Cross the cattle grid and follow footpath signs to pass to the left of the thatched Gibhouse and down the wooded path to the river. Turn right over the footbridge and stile, and

retrace your steps across the meadows to your car.

* At the time of going to press the suspension bridge was closed due to flood damage. If it has not reopened, continue on Fisherman's Path close to the north bank, to Fingle Bridge and pick up the directions part way through Point ❸.

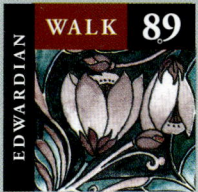

ABOUT • CRICCIETH

Born in the small town of Llanystumdwy, David Lloyd George, the 'Welsh Wizard', was one of the most charismatic politicians of the 20th century. He was elected Prime Minister in 1916 and was responsible for great social and political reforms.

Gwynedd • WALES

DISTANCE • 5 miles (8km)

TOTAL ASCENT • 131ft (40m)

PATHS • some rough tracks; fields may be muddy

TERRAIN • surfaced roads, fields, stony tracks, pebble beach. **Make sure you complete the walk during low tide**

GRADIENTS • gradual

REFRESHMENTS • several pubs and cafés in Criccieth

PARK • Criccieth car park off Y Maes

OS MAP • Explorer 13 (previously 254) Lleyn Peninsula East

In the steps of the 'Welsh Wizard'

1 Start at the Memorial Hall, at the bottom end of Y Maes, the green at the centre of Criccieth. With your back to the hall, turn right, then right again, following the Caernarfon (B4411) sign. Climb the hill away from town.

2 At the Bron Eifion sign just beyond the former Baptist Chapel, now called Pen-y-Maes, turn left. Follow the single-track road past Bryn Awelon and bear right, into the countryside, where the road forks. Continue past the entrance to the Bron Eifion Fishery, right.

3 After visiting Lloyd George's memorial, right, turn back and retrace your steps as far as the entrance to Tŷ Newydd, now on your right. Take this turning, following the public footpath sign.

4 Continue past Tŷ Newydd and follow the public footpath arrow ahead, past a row of cottages. Go through the kissing gate and continue alongside the hedge.

• DON'T MISS •

It's worth breaking your journey to visit the **Lloyd George Museum** and **Highgate**, two minutes' walk away, where the statesman's Victorian childhood home has been recreated, along with a 19th-century schoolroom, his uncle's shoe-making workshop and an immaculate cottage garden. You also pass Tŷ Newydd, the house which Lloyd George bought in 1943 and where he lived until his death in 1945.

DIFFICULTY ✿✿

Climb the stone stile and cross the field towards the road.

5 Cross the road and continue along the public footpath ahead. After crossing the railway bridge the track swings round to the left; fork right to the gate, signed footpath only, and climb the wooden stile.

6 Follow the path round to the right. Go through the wooden picket gate (alongside a wooden five-bar gate) and continue to meet the river. Turn left to follow the river's course to the sea.

7 Continue on the track, which swings left and peters out into pebble beach: take care here and make sure the tide is out. Follow the beach round the headland. Climb to the path above and parallel to the beach, passing a National Trust marker on a boulder where the coast has eroded.

8 At the end of the track turn right towards Criccieth. Where the track bends to the left, take the path along the cliff straight ahead, leading back into the town. Go through the kissing gate and continue ahead following the esplanade.

9 After passing the castle hill, just before the road begins to descend and with the pillar box on the corner, turn left up Tan-y-Grisiau Terrace. Continue to the end and cross the railway line. The Memorial Hall is diagonally ahead, to the right.

EDWARDIAN

WALK 90

ABOUT • STEEP

This hilly walk in Steep introduces the landscape that inspired the poetry of Edward Thomas. The walks visits his two homes and Shoulder of Mutton Hill, his poetic inspiration, and the Sarsen Stone, laid in his memory by Walter de la Mare.

Hampshire • SE ENGLAND

DISTANCE • 5 miles (8km)

TOTAL ASCENT • 545ft (166m)

PATHS • field, woodland paths and tracks

TERRAIN • rolling countryside at western end of the South Downs. Some tracks and paths are suitable for dogs off the lead

GRADIENTS • hilly on the outward leg; steep ascent to Shoulder of Mutton Hill

REFRESHMENTS • the Harrow Inn and the Cricketers Inn at Steep

PARK • roadside parking in the vicinity of All Saints' Church, Steep

OS MAP • Explorer 133 Haslemere & Petersfield

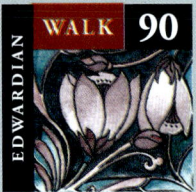

The poet of Steep

❶ With All Saints' Church on your right, follow Church Road for 50yds (46m) to a sharp right-hand bend. Bear left into woodland and swing immediately right. Follow the clear path between trees and down to a galvanised kissing gate. Cross a stream and head towards Steep Farm, to cross two stiles.

❷ Pass the farm and veer right at the end of the buildings. Keep left after a few paces and follow the track down to a stream. As the track curves left, go towards a stile at the foot of a steep bank. Don't cross it; instead turn left and follow the woodland path. Cross a stream and make for a cottage in trees. Cross over the drive and continue on a clearly defined path.

❸ Keep to the left of silos and outbuildings and look for a finger post here. Swing left to a stile and gateway and follow the field edge to the corner. Head for a gap in the trees and take the path uphill, along the woodland edge. Make for a stile in the right-hand boundary and cross the field, parallel to power lines. Look for a stile by a metal gate and join a path which runs up above some woodland. Continue on the enclosed path to the lane.

❹ Turn right and keep left after 400yds (366m) when the lane forks. Bear left after a few paces to a stile and follow the path between lines of trees, up the hillside to a stile in the woodland boundary. Turn left and follow the green lane as it climbs steeply through the trees. Ignore paths left and right, and eventually pass a green sign for Ashford Hangers, followed in 200yds (183m) by a barrier. Further on, the walk coincides with a section of the 21-mile (34km) Hangers Way.

❺ To visit the Poet Stone, follow Hangers Way, left, 100yds (91m) after it joins the main path from the right. After a few paces it goes right, go straight on, steeply descending to the stone. Return to main track, turn left and follow lane until it leads between houses. Look for The Red House, before The Edward Barnsley Workshop, and continue to the road junction.

❻ Bear left, then immediately left again on a sunken bridleway. Descend steeply for 500yds (457m), to a fork. Keep right and rejoin the Hangers Way. Follow it over a stream and between trees. After 600yds (549m), at the road by a barrier, turn left and pass Old Ashford Manor.

❼ Walk along 200yds (183m) to Berryfield Cottage, right, followed by Ashford Chace. Continue for 50yds (46m), and turn right signed Hangers Way. Follow the track and

as it bends right by a private sign, veer left to a woodland path. After a right and left bend, continue for 400yds (366m) then turn right down some steps to a waterfall.

❽ At the road beyond, keep right and continue for 200yds (183m) to a right-hand turning. Bear left here, through a kissing gate. Turn right and skirt the field to a plank bridge and stile in the corner. Cross into woodland, follow the path to a playing field. Cross and emerge opposite All Saints' Church.

N

OAKSHOTT

0 .... ½ Mile

0 .... 500 Metres

Shoulder of **Mutton** *Hill*

Red House

The

★ Poet Stone

❺

❻

❹

silos

❸

STONER HILL

Old Ashford Manor

Berryfield Cottage

waterfall ★ ❽

cottage

STEEP MARSH

A3

GUILDFORD

River Rother

STEEP

Cricketers Inn

START

❷ Steep Farm

All Saints' Church

Bedales School

The Harrow Inn

A3

PORTSMOUTH

A272

SHEET

A272

PETERSFIELD

DIFFICULTY ✱✱

World War I was ended by the Armistice of 1918, but peace did not bring prosperity to everyone. The age of the charleston and the Bright Young Things was also a period of mass unemployment and the hunger march.

DEPRESSION AND WAR

1918–1945

Jazz Age to Atomic Age

Old conventions were thrown aside and taboos broken in the 1920s. Skirts grew shorter and parties wilder; literature became more explicit, as writers such as D H Lawrence dealt with sex and working-class culture. But the Jazz Age was the experience of a privileged minority. For many more people, life in post-war Britain was a struggle to make ends meet. A dispute between coal miners and mine-owners threatening to cut already meagre wages drew in workers from other industries, and in 1926 a General Strike seemed about to bring the country to a standstill. Three years later the New York stock market crashed, and the repercussions were felt across the Western world. Personal fortunes were lost and whole sectors of industry floundered: the Jarrow 'hunger march' to London of 1936 highlighted the plight of ship-builders unable to make a living.

There could be no greater contrast than the world presented in the increasingly popular movies, all-singing and all-dancing since the introduction of sound in 1929. They provided a regular dose of escapism and brought a taste of Hollywood glamour into the most ordinary lives. In the 1920s another form of entertainment had been brought even closer to home, as the radio began to appear in households across the country. Under the sole guardianship of the BBC, established in 1922, it promised to 'inform, educate and entertain'. In 1936 television made its début, but only to a very limited audience.

With the increased use of the car came the spread of suburbs, as families flocked from cities to live in new housing estates that were springing up on their rural edges. Streamlined architecture, using the stylised curves and corners of Art Deco, took its place alongside the ornate finery and terraced brick of the Victorian age. Some of the most notable buildings met the needs of modern electrical industries – consumer goods factories such as the Hoover Building in Perivale, for instance, and massive power stations such as Battersea.

BACK TO THE FRAY

Across Europe, the opposing forces of Fascism and Communism were drawing up their battle-lines during the 1920s and '30s. About 2,000 volunteers joined the Republican forces of Spain against General Franco in 1936, while at home British Fascists looked to former Labour politician Oswald Moseley, figurehead of the so-called blackshirts. But the main concern of the British press was the abdication of Edward VIII, who gave up the throne in 1936 in order to marry American divorcée Wallis Simpson.

As Hitler's Germany set about annexing and occupying territories and persecuting the Jewish population, Britain pursued a policy of appeasement, until the German army invaded Poland in 1939 and made war inevitable. Winston Churchill took the helm as Prime Minister in 1940, the year of Britain's 'darkest hour', as France fell and many British cities suffered devastating 'blitz' bombing. In the following year America entered the war and those who were billeted 'over here' made a deep impression with their easy-going informality.

On 6 June 1944 British, Commonwealth and American forces landed on the Normandy beaches to begin the final thrust that would end in Germany's surrender. The war with Japan dragged on, however, until August 1945, when the first atomic bombs were dropped on Hiroshima and Nagasaki, and the world faced up to the realities of the nuclear age.

HISTORIC SITES

Eltham Palace, Greater London: Art Deco extravaganza.

Tyne Bridge, Newcastle: built in the 1920s as Britain's biggest single-span steel bridge.

Mr Straw's House, Worksop, Notts: time capsule of a middle-class 1930s house.

Delaware Pavilion, Bexhill-on-Sea: modernist architecture.

Cabinet War Rooms, London: Churchill's underground operations centre.

Bletchley Park, Beds: the secret wartime code-breakers' HQ.

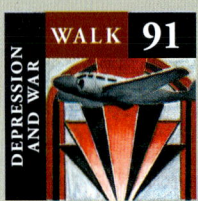

DEPRESSION AND WAR

WALK 91

ABOUT • WIGAN

The Road to Wigan Pier (1936) by George Orwell is a moving testament to the poverty-stricken lives of those living in northern parts of Britain during the 1930s depression. Our walk begins at Wigan Pier which is, ironically, now a centre of enterprise.

Lancashire • N ENGLAND

DISTANCE • 9 miles (14.5km)

TOTAL ASCENT • 390ft (119m)

PATHS • mainly towpaths and surfaced pathways

TERRAIN • canalside pastures and country park woodland

GRADIENTS • gentle

REFRESHMENTS • Wigan Pier; the canalside Commercial Inn and the Kirkless Hall pub; Stables Café, Haigh Hall

PARK • car park at Trencherfield Mill, near the Mill at the Pier

OS MAP • Explorer 276 Bolton, Wigan & Warrington

George Orwell on the road to Wigan

A49
PRESTON
A5106
BOAR'S HEAD
HAIGH
Haigh Hall Country Park
Stables Café & Visitors Centre
Haigh Hall
3
golf course
B5239
ASPULL
Bridge 60
4
B5238
NEW SPRINGS
MARYLEBONE
TOP LOCK
5
Parish Church of St Stephen
Kirkless Hall PH
2
Commercial Inn
B5376
6
B5375
WIGAN
B5238
SCHOLES
Leeds & Liverpool Canal
N
A49
Wigan Pier
Pier Café
A577
NEWTOWN
Pier Gardens
Mill at the Pier
1 START
A577
A571
JUNCTION 25, M6
A49
B5238
INCE-IN-MAKERFIELD
A577
MANCHESTER
A573
0
1 Mile
0
1 Kilometre

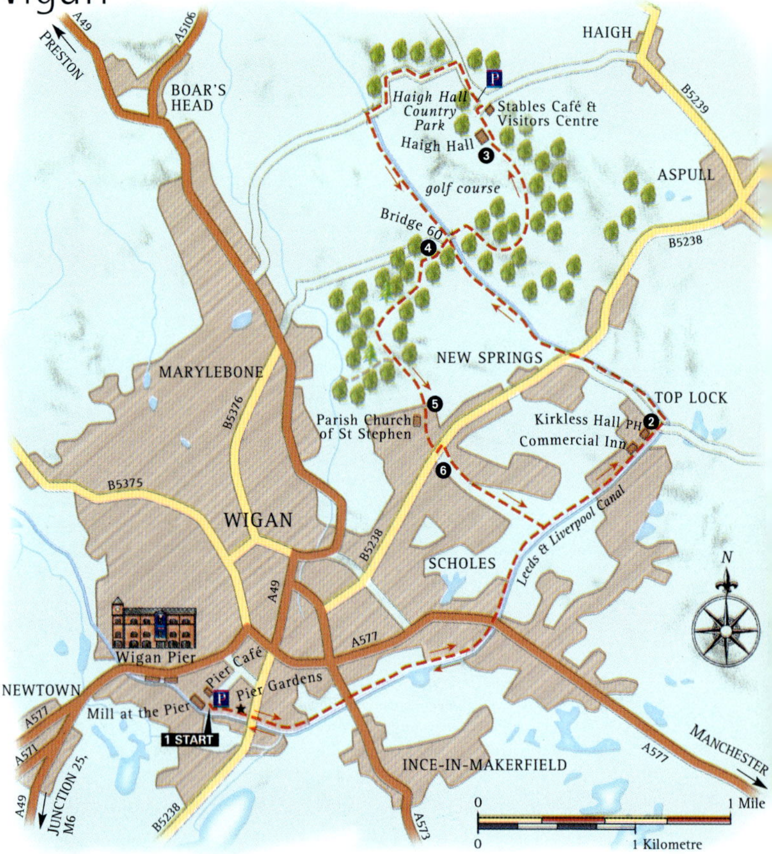

❶ From the car park near the Mill at the Pier, go past the barge *Roland* and through the Pier Gardens to reach the towpath of the Leeds and Liverpool Canal. Turn left and follow the towpath to Top Lock, the last in a long series of locks. On the way cross three busy roads, by pedestrian crossings.

❷ Beyond Top Lock the canal changes direction. Continue on the towpath to reach Bridge 60. Leave the canal and turn right over the bridge. Follow a surfaced driveway to eventually reach Haigh Hall.

❸ Pass to the right of Haigh Hall, and continue ahead until, directly opposite Haigh Golf and Visitor Centre, you turn left into a car park. Walk across the car park to the far right-hand corner, and turn left along a lane. Soon take the first turning on the left, a rough track descending to the Leeds and Liverpool Canal. Cross a bridge and go down to walk along the towpath.

❹ When you reach Bridge 60 again (this time from the opposite direction), climb steps to the right of the bridge, to regain the estate driveway. Turn right, ignore an early turning right, and continue descending gently through mixed woodland until, just as the driveway makes a wide sweep to the right, you branch left on to a rough track alongside a stream.

❺ The track continues to the edge of a built-up area. Go forward to a road junction near the Parish Church of St Stephen. Turn left and walk to the main road a short distance away. Cross the road with care, moving left to a nearby path signed the Leeds and Liverpool Canal. The path initially descends wooden steps, which can be slippery when wet, and joins the trackbed of a disused railway.

❻ Turn right along the trackbed and, always continuing to keep ahead, follow the on-going path to reach the towpath of the canal once more. Here, turn right and retrace your outward route to Wigan Pier and the car park near the Mill, at the Pier.

DIFFICULTY ✻✻

• DON'T MISS •

Haigh Hall stands at the centre of Haigh Hall Country Park. This is the former home of the Earls of Balcarres, an influential family in the history of Wigan and once owners of the massive estate.

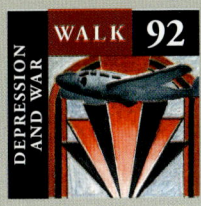
ABOUT • ST IVES

This walk starts at the coast to the west of the town and reveals the aspects of light and landscape that has inspired artists to visit and paint here since the early 1920s. While you're in St Ives visit the Tate Gallery St Ives and the Barbara Hepworth Museum.

Cornwall • S W ENGLAND

DISTANCE • 7 miles (11.3km)

TOTAL ASCENT • 607ft (185m)

PATHS • rocky coast path, lanes, farm tracks and fields

TERRAIN • undulating coast path, narrow town lanes and farmland

GRADIENTS • some fairly steep, short ascents on coast path and in St Ives;

REFRESHMENTS • pubs, restaurants, and cafés in St Ives; coffee shop and restaurant at Tate St Ives; the Tinner's Arms at Zennor

PARK • small car park by the National Trust sign for Rosewall Hill on the B3306 St Ives to St Just road, ½ mile (800m) past the sign to Trevalgan Farm (right)

OS MAP • Explorer 102 Land's End, Penzance & St Ives

Aspects of light at St Ives

❶ Cross the road and follow the path across Little Trevalgan Hill (NT) past a huge boulder and memorial to artist Peter Lanyon. Continue downhill to a field; turn right to the bottom corner, and cross the wall into the lane.

❷ Turn left and in ½ mile (800m) reach Trevega Wartha Farm; 100yds (91m) beyond turn right down a signed bridleway between hedges. Cross a grassy track and follow footpath signs straight on, to walk downhill through a metal gate and over a stream to Trevail Mill. Walk up the drive.

❸ Past the cattle grid turn right, signed River Cove. Follow the path through a wood to meet the coast path. Turn right and continue for 2 miles (3.2km) where it branches. Go left past a sign for Hellesveor Cliff and continue to Clodgy Point.

❹ Continue right along the coast path for ¾ mile (1.2km) to reach a car park above Porthmeor Beach (toilets). At the road keep straight on to pass the Tate St Ives (right).

❺ Follow the road round right, then left at a junction, passing

DIFFICULTY ✿ ✿

Harry's Court and Alfred Wallis' cottage. Continue for 250yds (229m) then turn sharp right down Fish Street to the harbour. Turn right along Wharf Road to reach West Pier and the lifeboat house.

❻ Turn right up Lifeboat Hill; take the second lane right (Back Street) to the entrance to the Barbara Hepworth Museum. Turn left up Ayr Lane and across a junction to a T-junction (Kenwyn Place sign). Turn right, and left at the top of the hill. Keep on this road for

¼ mile (400m) until you reach Burthallan Lane.

❼ Right along Burthallan Lane for ¼ mile (400m), then just past the house named Bryward follow signs for Zennor, left, over a stone stile and along a narrow hedged path, to a stone stile into a field. Keep ahead, then cross the wall right. Reach a grassy area, go right to a hidden stile next to two metal gates. Follow right-hand field edge for ¾ mile (1.2km) through fields and over stiles to Trowan Farm.

❽ Cross a stile into the lane; turn left, then right, through a farmyard. Go left over a stile at the next cottage, and right over another stile. Follow the field path to pass behind Trevalgan Farm. Go over a stile alongside a gate beside the final buildings. Go straight across the field to a stile and continue through small fields and over stiles to a surfaced lane. Turn left and reach the end of Point ❶ in 200yds (183m). Retrace your steps across Little Trevalgan Hill to the car park.

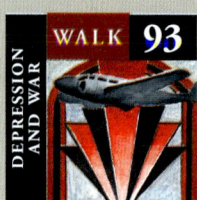

WALK 93

Since the first Roman invasion in 55 BC, Dover has borne the brunt of invading forces. This walk takes you along a historic stretch of the White Cliffs to Dover Castle, which was used as an underground nerve centre during World War II.

DISTANCE • 7 miles (11.3km)

TOTAL ASCENT • 498ft (152m)

PATHS • generally good, some field paths can be muddy

TERRAIN • clifftop, farmland and some pavements through the town

GRADIENTS • gentle climbing along cliff; otherwise fairly level

REFRESHMENTS • café at visitor centre; pub and tea room at St Margaret's Bay; pubs and a tea room in St Margaret's at Cliffe

PARK • NT car park (fee) at Gateway to the White Cliffs visitor centre on Langdon Cliff, follow signs to Dover Castle

OS MAP • Explorer 138 Dover, Folkestone & Hythe

Along the White Cliffs of Dover

DIFFICULTY ✱✱

❶ From the Gateway to the White Cliffs visitor centre walk away from Dover. Take the path at the end of the last parking area and fork right, signed Saxon Shore Way (SSW). Gently ascend to the top of the cliff to a stile. Follow concrete markers and descend beside fence to a track. Cross over with SSW marker and climb out of Langdon Hole (NT), passing the steep steps down to Langdon Bay, to a stile.

❷ Soon turn right with SSW marker and stay on the clifftop path towards South Foreland Lighthouse (NT). At the boundary by properties below the lighthouse, follow the path inland. Pass the gates to the lighthouse and turn right at a junction of paths (SSW). Keep right at a crossing of routes. Follow the track past the windmill to a gate on your right leading on to Lighthouse Down (NT).

❸ Follow the clifftop path to a gate by a house. Rejoin the track, descend to a crossing of tracks and turn right. Pass St Margaret's Museum and Pines Garden and bear right at a junction to reach the road at a sharp bend. Turn right to visit St Margaret's Bay.

❹ Climb the steps on your left by the footpath post. At the top, keep ahead on the pavement for ½ mile (800m) into St Margaret's at Cliffe. Walk through the village and take the road on the left, signed Dover.

❺ Keep to the left-hand verge and soon bear left to a waymarked stile. Walk through a narrow paddock to a stile, then proceed alongside the right-hand fence to a stile. Bear half-right along the defined field path to a stile and maintain direction. Briefly walk by a copse, then follow the path half-right to reach a stile by trees.

❻ Pass to the right of a farm, cross the drive and a stile and walk along the left-hand field edge to a stile. Turn right to the A258. Turn left to the roundabout, cross Jubilee Way and keep to the pavement beside the road for Dover Castle.

❼ In ¼ mile (400m), cross the stile on your left and pass through Broadlees Farm. Descend the track to a gate and turn immediately right through another gate. Walk parallel with the A2 to a stile and ascend steps to a road.

❽ Turn left across the bridge, bear right with the road and shortly take the path right (unmarked). Follow the path left across scrubland, parallel with the A2, and eventually pass in front of cottages to join the SSW. Turn left and climb to the road, turning immediately right back to the visitor centre.

• DON'T MISS •

*The great views of Dover at **South Foreland Lighthouse**, built in 1843 and used for early radio experiments.*

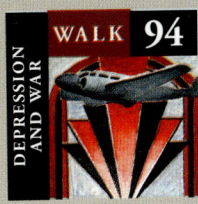
ABOUT • DERWENT DAM

Derwent Dam will forever be linked with 617 Squadron or 'the Dambusters'. In 1943, the squadron used this area as a practice ground prior to their successful air assault on dams in Germany, which fed vital Nazi armament factories.

Derbyshire • C ENGLAND

DISTANCE • 6 miles (9.6km)

TOTAL ASCENT • 564ft (172m)

PATHS • lanes and moorland paths

TERRAIN • rough moorland paths, requiring boots and waterproofs

GRADIENTS • a gradual climb to Pike Low and steep descent down Abbey Bank

REFRESHMENTS • refreshment kiosk at Fairholmes

PARK • Fairholmes Visitor Centre, Upper Derwent Valley

OS MAP • Outdoor Leisure 1 The Peak District – Dark Peak Area

The Dambusters' of Derwent

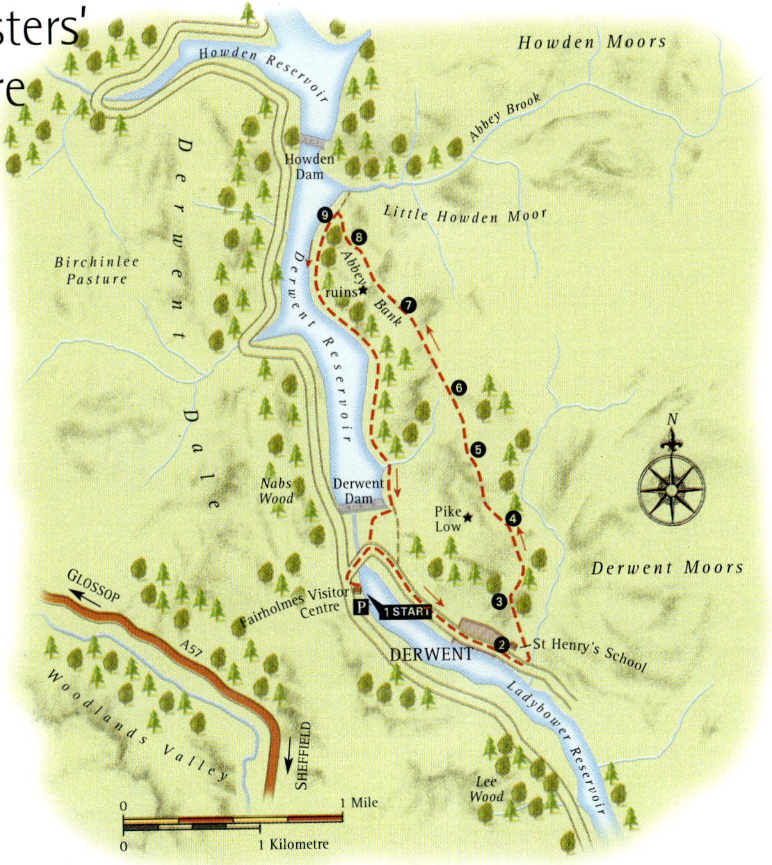

❶ From the Fairholmes Visitor Centre, take the signed path to the road which passes under Derwent Dam. Follow the road to the right, passing through Derwent hamlet.

❷ After about a mile (1.6km) St Henry's schoolhouse can be seen on the left-hand side. Three hundred yards (274m) further on there is a track off to the left with a gate and stile set slightly back off the road. Cross the stile and follow the path as it passes a ruined barn, left, and a private National Trust barn, right.

❸ Continue along the path to the left of the barn, cross the stile and ascend the steep tree-lined hollow way crossing several more stiles before reaching a farmhouse on the left. Here the path divides; follow the left-hand course as it ascends in zigzag fashion out on to Briery Side. Keep to the marked footpath to reach a wall and stile marking 'Open Country'. Here look back and admire the view down across Ladybower reservoir towards Bamford in the distance.

❹ Follow the path as it bears left for 200yds (183m) before turning right on to a broad track with a ruined wall on the right. Follow this for about ½ mile (800m) climbing past Pike Low, a Bronze Age burial mound (no access) at 1329ft (405m) on the left. This is the highest point of the walk.

❺ Continue on this track with the wall on the right. As the route nears a linear group of trees on the right the path bears left and crosses a ruined wall. Follow the path across the open moorland for about 250yds (229m) to another

DIFFICULTY ✽✽✽

ruined wall. Follow route signed Abbey and Howden Dam.

❻ With the ruined wall on the left, walk up the gradual slope and at a gate cross a stile. Here the path gradually descends. Continue to another signpost.

❼ Continue on the path that bears slightly left and downhill with the ruins of Bamford House Farm on

the left. Follow this path (ruined wall on left) down Abbey Bank; Howden Dam comes into view. The path bears left and descends steeply for about 50yds (46m) to a sign marking the way to the now submerged Abbey Grange. Follow this path as it drops steeply towards the reservoir.

❽ Go through the gap in the wall, leaving Abbey Bank behind, and

follow the path through the trees down to the reservoir service road.

❾ Turn left and follow the road for 2 miles (3.2km) along the eastern shore of the reservoir. At the dam turn right over a stile and follow the hedge-lined path down to steps which drop to the foot of the dam wall. At the bottom cut left across the grassed area to the road back to Fairholmes Visitor Centre.

Portmeirion: Fantasy Village

A walk around the bizarre Italianate village on a quiet North Wales headland

Creating Portmeirion

In 1925, Clough Williams-Ellis bought an overgrown finger of land at the base of the Llŷn Peninsula. In its day, this had been occupied by two castles – Deudraeth and Aber Iau – as well as a foundry, a shipyard and some cottages. But it had since been abandoned, and the neglected site provided Clough, already a distinguished architect, with the opportunity to realise a dream.

Williams-Ellis was one of many who became preoccupied with the need to combine functional building with aesthetic beauty. Portmeirion was a chance to put his theories into practice. Here, he would prove that a new development need not ruin its surroundings; he would reconstruct 'fallen buildings' rescued from demolition, and give his own architectural imagination free rein. Between 1925 and 1976 the project evolved, staying true to Clough's motto: 'Cherish the past, adorn the present, construct for the future.'

A 1920s Oddity

Portmeirion is the embodiment of one man's ideas and, in many ways, the embodiment of an age. It was begun in the inter-war years, when Britain was caught between economic difficulty and post-war euphoria. Thousands of soldiers had returned from the trenches in 1918 to find themselves out of work; no new homes had been built during the hostilities, and there was an acute shortage of housing. At the same time, in the face of urban expansion, many began to fear for the survival of the countryside, which seemed all the more precious and vulnerable after four years of global warfare. These concerns all played a part in Williams-Ellis's career. He became involved with the housing movement, taking up a challenge, issued by the editor (his future father-in-law) of *The Spectator*, to design affordable rural accommodation. He was also a tireless campaigner for conservation, helping to found the Council for the Protection of Rural England in 1926 and the Campaign for the Protection of Rural Wales in 1928. The natural landscape was an essential part of his plans for Portmeirion, and for all its eccentricity, the village still sits in perfect harmony with the surrounding wooded hills and coastal scenery.

As well as being an experiment in town development, Portmeirion was a splash of colour in a world made bleak by war. Clough's intention was always to give everyone 'a taste of lavishness, gaiety and cultivated design'. Its strange and wonderful mixture of styles brings together Arts and Crafts, Palladian, baroque and Eastern mystic. A year after its completion in 1965, cameras moved in to film the cult television series *The Prisoner*.

WALK 95

AROUND THE VILLAGE AND ITS ENCHANTED GARDENS

❶ The walk begins with a circuit around the village itself, reached past two pink Palladian tollbooths, where you pay your admission fee (which funds the upkeep of the village and grounds). Follow the path under the arch of the Gatehouse, with its painted ceiling, and then of the Classical Bridge House, and pass Toll House, a weatherboarded building decorated with bells, signs and a painted statue of St Peter. To the left is the Battery, and behind that the Italian-style bell tower, partly built with stones from Deudraeth Castle. On the right is the Pantheon, or Dome; beneath it, a painted loggia houses a gilt Buddha. The path continues to the central Piazza, with its fabulous arrangement of pool, fountain, gloriette, Gothic pavilion and columns bearing Burmese dancers.

❷ Throughout the walk, as it leads round the village and out to the headland gardens, there are unexpected touches – a painted mermaid; intertwined dolphins; a bust of Shakespeare; a stone lion. Walking through this Snowdonia landscape is like stepping into an elaborate Hollywood set.

❸ Having left the village itself past Fountain, the house where Noël Coward wrote *Blithe Spirit* in 1941, and the Portmeirion Hotel, the route leads round the headland, passing the Observatory Tower with its figure of Nelson, on the way to the Lighthouse, at Portmeirion's southernmost point. You soon reach a left-hand track to a viewpoint above White Sands Bay; after enjoying the sea view, return to the main route and continue to the Ghost Garden, named after the whispering of the wind through the eucalyptus leaves. You now turn back towards the village, passing the June-flowering rhododendrons before re-entering the site past Salutation, originally a stable block and now housing a shop selling Portmeirion pottery, designed by Clough's daughter, Susan.

Distance: 3 miles (4.8km)

Total ascent: 150ft (46m)

Paths: surfaced paths, woodland tracks: can be muddy and slippery

Terrain: village streets, cliff path, woods, stone steps

Gradients: some steep climbs in the gardens

Refreshments: Cadwallader's ice-cream parlour; Town Hall self-service restaurant; hotel restaurant

Park: car park near entrance to village

OS Map: Outdoor Leisure 18 Snowdonia – Harlech, Porthmadog & Baal

Difficulty: ✹✹

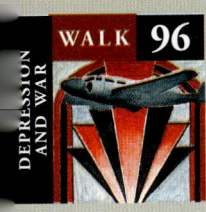
ABOUT • SLAPTON SANDS

Slapton Sands serves as a reminder of the lives that were both lost and saved in World War II. In 1943, the US army trained here for the D-Day landings but during a rehearsal a convoy of vessels was torpedoed by German craft, killing 1,000 soldiers.

Devon • SW ENGLAND

DISTANCE • 5 miles (8km)

TOTAL ASCENT • 328ft (100m)

PATHS • narrow, quiet country lanes and paths; some muddy after wet weather

TERRAIN • shingle beach, rolling farmland and freshwater ley

GRADIENTS • level on beach and round ley; some short steep ascents/descents inland

REFRESHMENTS • the Start Bay Inn at Torcross, also cafés and fish and chips; pubs at Stokenham and Slapton

PARK • memorial car park on Slapton Sands off A379, just below Slapton Bridge

OS MAP • Outdoor Leisure 20 South Devon – Brixham to Newton Ferrers

Victory and tragedy at Slapton Sands

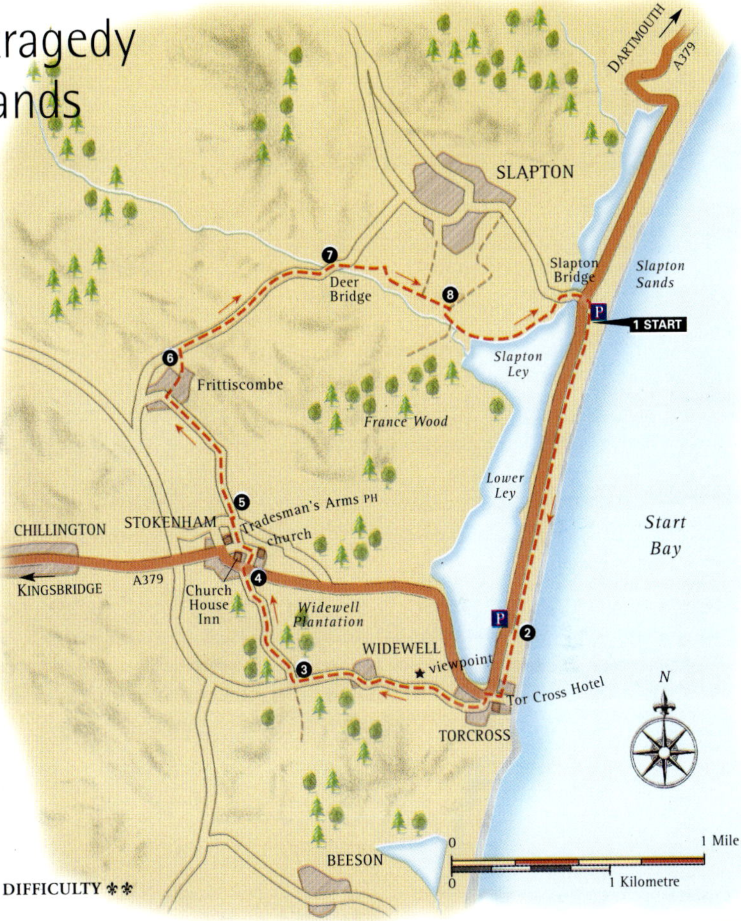

❶ Walk along the back of the beach, keeping the toilets and road on your right, and the sea on your left, to reach the edge of Torcross. The Sherman tank memorial is across the road in the car park.

❷ Follow the concrete walkway between the houses and sea. At the end, turn right before the old Tor Cross Hotel (holiday apartments), then left before the post office up a steep narrow lane (toilets, right). Pass Torcross viewpoint, a butterfly garden. Continue up the lane to pass through the hamlet of Widewell.

❸ After 400yds (366m) turn right down a narrow unsigned lane, opposite a footpath to Beeson and a post-box. Walk steeply downhill past Widewell Plantation to reach the A379 opposite the Church House Inn at Stokenham.

❹ Cross the road and go up the lane between the pub and the Church of St Michael and All Angels. The lane veers left; when you can see the Tradesman's Arms ahead turn right by Sunnyside up a narrow lane to meet Kiln Lane. Turn right.

❺ Almost immediately, turn left up another quiet lane. Leave the houses and descend to ancient Frittiscombe. Pass the farmhouse on your right and an old barn on your left. When the lane veers left and uphill, turn right along the track signed Scrubs Lane to Deer Bridge Lane. Follow this as it veers left uphill to meet the lane.

❻ Turn right and proceed downhill, with views of the ley to your right, to cross Deer Bridge.

DIFFICULTY ✽✽

❼ Turn right along a small wooded path signed Marsh Lane. The route follows the marsh edge to reach a junction of paths; Slapton village is signed to the left. Walk straight ahead along the boardwalk, signed permissive route to nature reserve, passing through an area of willows. Ascend wooden steps to a T-junction and follow another footpath, left, which leads to the village.

❽ Turn right, signed Slapton Sands via nature trail, and follow the narrow, undulating path as it weaves along the ley edge. There are four dog-friendly stiles and occasional wooden steps along this section, but nothing difficult. As the road comes into view note the pillbox below the path, right. The path meets the road via a gate; turn right towards the sea, then right to reach your car.

• DON'T MISS •

*The remains of **Hallsands**, just to the south of Torcross, provides another example of how this part of the coast has suffered over the years. This small fishing village was almost completely destroyed during a huge storm on the night of 16 January 1917.*

Map labels: DARTMOUTH, A379, SLAPTON, Slapton Bridge, Slapton Sands, Deer Bridge, Frittiscombe, France Wood, Slapton Ley, Lower Ley, Start Bay, CHILLINGTON, STOKENHAM, Tradesman's Arms PH, church, KINGSBRIDGE, A379, Church House Inn, Widewell Plantation, WIDEWELL, viewpoint, Tor Cross Hotel, TORCROSS, BEESON, 1 START, 2, Start Bay, N, 0 1 Mile, 0 1 Kilometre

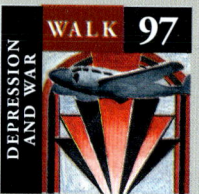
ABOUT • CULZEAN CASTLE

General Eisenhower was presented with the gift of an apartment in Culzean Castle in recognition for his contribution during World War II. An exhibition at Culzean tells about his role as Supreme Commander of the Allied Expeditionary Force.

South Ayrshire • SCOTLAND

DISTANCE • 5½ miles (8.8km)

TOTAL ASCENT • 150ft (46m)

PATHS • very good, although some stretches can be boggy in wet weather

TERRAIN • estate roads, farm tracks, forest paths, beach, old railway line and roads

GRADIENTS • moderate

REFRESHMENTS • restaurant at visitor centre

PARK • visitor centre car park

OS MAP • Explorer 326 Ayr, Troon, Girvan and Maybole

Eisenhower: Supreme Commander

❶ Go diagonally through the visitor centre courtyard and turn left on to a path. Turn right at the junction, then second left, through an arch and into the castle forecourt. Keep left, go through a gate and at the next gate turn left.

❷ Go down some steps, about turn and follow the path to the sign for the Battery, Cliff Walk and Swan Pond. Turn right, go through the trees, through a gate, across a grassed area and down some steps into the Battery.

❸ Turn left, exit at the other end and turn right on to a forest path. Follow this until you reach a path signed Cliff Walk and turn right. Go right at the T-junction by the Swan Pond.

❹ Turn right again at the sign for Barwhin Hill and Port Carrick. In 200yds (183m) turn right and go down some steep steps to Port Carrick beach. Turn left and head back uphill by the next steps. Turn right.

❺ Follow the cliff path until it descends by some wooden steps to Maidenhead Bay. Turn left and walk along the beach until the pavement beside it turns left.

Cross the grassed area diagonally towards a white cottage with a red roof.

❻ Turn left into Kirkoswald Road and then first right into Shanter Road. Continue to follow the road as it turns into a farm road and then turn left at a derelict World War II building and head for Shanter Farm. Turn left and enter the farm steading.

❼ Cross the farm yard diagonally and exit at the other side. Then continue to follow the farm road round the side of a cottage then turn left, go through a gate and follow the line of the fence until you can cross it and continue along the old railway.

❽ Continue through a caravan park, fork left, turn right on to the A719 and follow it for just over a mile (1.6km) to pass Morriston Farm. Just past the sign for Souter Johnnie's Cottage is a farm track.

❾ Turn left along here, right and down some steps at a railway bridge and follow the line of the old railway to the next bridge. Exit right, via the steps, turn right, then left on to the estate road and follow it to the car park.

DIFFICULTY ✱✱

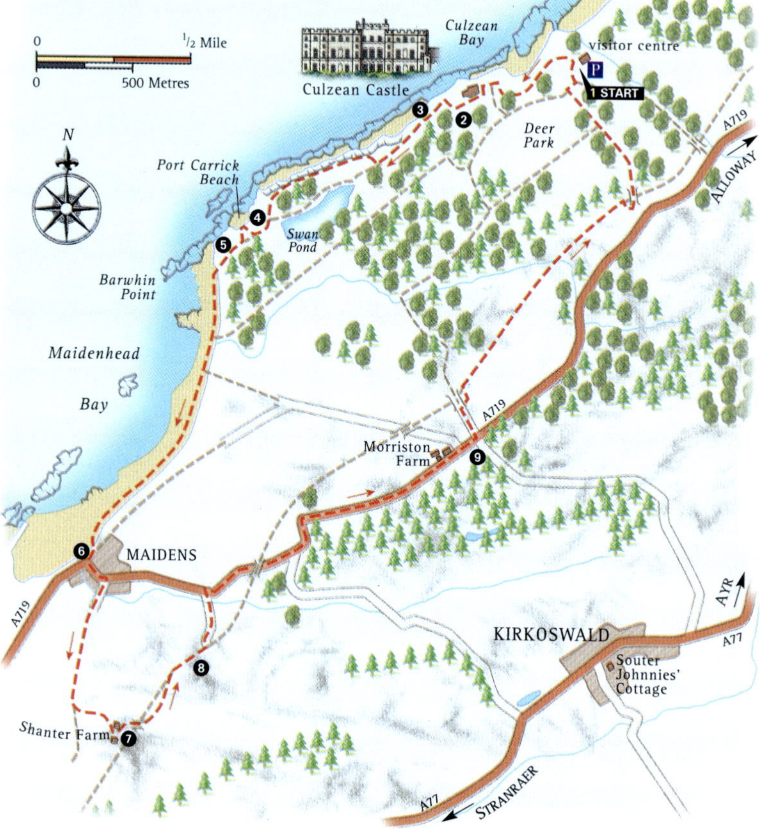

0 — ½ Mile

0 — 500 Metres

N

Culzean Castle

Culzean Bay

visitor centre

P

1 START

A719

ALLOWAY

Deer Park

Port Carrick Beach

Swan Pond

Barwhin Point

Maidenhead Bay

A719

Morriston Farm

9

A719

6 MAIDENS

A719

8

Shanter Farm 7

KIRKOSWALD

Souter Johnnies' Cottage

A77

AYR

STRANRAER

A77

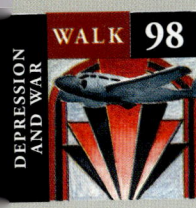
ABOUT • CANNOCK CHASE

POW camps, a military hospital and training camps, Cannock Chase is rich in 20th-century history. Now designated an Area of Outstanding Natural Beauty, it is a place of remembrance to those who lost their lives in World Wars I and II.

Staffordshire • C ENGLAND

DISTANCE • 7¼ miles (11.6km)

TOTAL ASCENT • 492ft (150m)

PATHS • generally good forest paths and tracks

TERRAIN • undulating commercial forest at various stages of maturity, broken by views across areas of natural heathland

REFRESHMENTS • café at Cannock Chase visitor centre

PARK • pay-and-display car park adjacent to visitor centre

OS MAP • OS Explorer 244 Cannock Chase & Chasewater, Stafford

Cannock Chase and the price of war

DIFFICULTY ✽✽

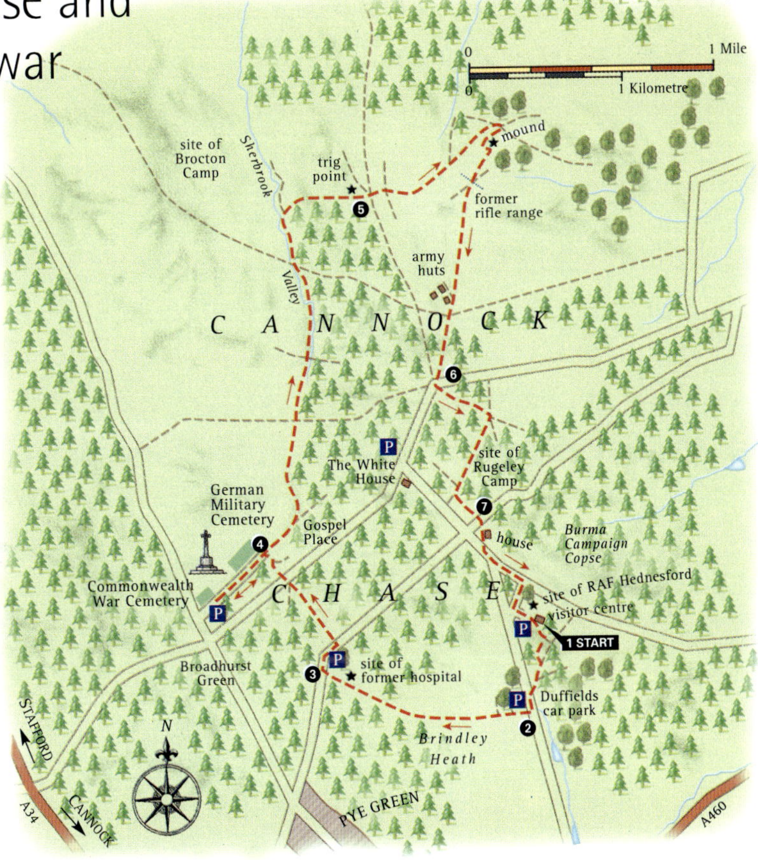

❶ From the visitor centre walk past the toilet block and on along a woodland track. As the trees clear, take the second path on the right and then bear left at a fork. When you reach a tarmac drive, turn right to a main road.

❷ A hundred yards (91m) to the left, a bridleway leaves on the right through Druffields car park. Rising gradually along a shallow valley, the way crosses Brindley Heath towards forest. After ¾ mile (1.2km), you will emerge through another car park onto a road. The site of the former hospital lies amongst the trees on the right.

❸ Go right for 250 yards (230m), then left along another forest bridleway. After half a mile (1km) that, too, ends at a road, but continue along a path directly opposite. Emerging on to a re-planted area at the second junction, bear left to a broad track by the German War Cemetery. Its entrance lies to the left and the Commonwealth Cemetery at Broadhurst Green, 500 yards (460m) beyond.

❹ After dropping through forest to the right, bear left at a junction marked Gospel Place. Beyond there, ignoring crossing tracks, follow the boundary between heath and forest for 1 mile (1.6km) into Sherbrook Valley. Eventually, where the track rises around a right-hand bend to a fork, bear right to climb the valley side, past a trig point to a main junction. Brocton Camp occupied the high ground to the west of the valley.

❺ Continue ahead, descending a quarter of a mile (0.4km) to a fork

above a valley and bear right, rising to a six-way junction a quarter of a mile (0.4km) beyond. Turn sharp right on to a narrower bridleway which, after bending below a high mound, rises beside a former rifle range. Part-way up, bear left along the main track and, after passing a group of huts, keep going to a road. The next section of the walk passes through the former Rugeley Camp.

❻ Go over to a bridleway opposite and follow it 300 yards (275m) to a crossing. Go sharp right along a grass track beside a forest camp site, and after ½ mile (1km), turn left along 'Heart of England Way'.

❼ At a road junction, walk ahead along Marquis Drive towards continue along a wide track to a barrier; the visitor centre is on the right.

• DON'T MISS •

Before beginning the walk, pop into the visitor centre, where there is an interesting display describing the history of the park and some of the plants and wildlife to look out for.

Map labels:

site of Brocton Camp · trig point · mound · former rifle range · army huts · Sherbrook · Valley · CANNOCK · CHASE · German Military Cemetery · The White House · site of Rugeley Camp · Gospel Place · house · Burma Campaign Copse · Commonwealth War Cemetery · site of RAF Hednesford · visitor centre · 1 START · Broadhurst Green · site of former hospital · Duffields car park · Brindley Heath · STAFFORD · CANNOCK · A34 · N · PYE GREEN · A460

0 — 1 Mile
0 — 1 Kilometre

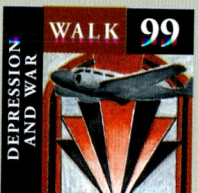
The Boat House Museum at Laugharne was home to Dylan Thomas and where he wrote much of his poetry. Perfect for Dylan fans, this walk will also appeal to birdwatchers, and the 12th-century Laugharne Castle is definitely worth a visit.

DISTANCE • 6 miles (9.6km)	**REFRESHMENTS** • abundant in Laugharne
TOTAL ASCENT • 490ft (149m)	**PARK** • in Laugharne, just past the town square on the left-hand side. This is a tidal area, so check that it won't flood in your absence!
PATHS • good; slippery in places	
TERRAIN • tracks, field paths, stiles, tarmac roads; take care on the short stretch of road just after the caravan park, it can be busy	
	OS MAP • Explorer 177 Carmarthen & Kidwelly
GRADIENTS • mostly gradual	

Home of Dylan Thomas

1 Turn along the shore, away from the castle. Shortly after a modern kissing gate ascend a signed footpath into woodland, emerging on ciffs overlooking the Taf estuary. Take the left, descending fork at information board. After steps, follow a track for 328yds (300m), past Salt House Kennels. Continue to the quarry road (Causeway Cottage).

2 Turn right, up to the A-road. Turn right, following the road for 191yds (175m); take care here. Just after a caravan park, go left. Soon a set-back finger-post points to a stile at the back of a lay-by. Cross stile, go right and cross a field with telegraph poles, parallel to stream.

3 On the other side of the field find a sunken track on the right, just around the left corner of a hedge which juts out. After 109yds (100m) pass a rusty gate. Further along pass a white house to join a dirt track to a tarmac road.

4 Turn right and continue for 109yds (100m). Just after the 30mph sign take the left fork. The Lacques Water Pump is next to the fork on the right-hand side. Where the road bends sharply right and down, go straight ahead along Holloway Road (dead end sign). Beyond a row of cottages take a sunken lane and cross two fields to a minor road.

5 Turn right, over the bridge and soon turn right on to the A-road. Continue for 22yds (20m) then turn left (dead end sign) and right through gates into the churchyard. Pass in front of the church, to cross a footbridge into a second churchyard. Dylan and Caitlin share a simple wooden cross, on the left. Leave through a kissing gate at the top of the churchyard. Turn right to a T-junction.

6 Turn left up a waymarked sunken lane; if wet take care over slabby rocks. Continue for 328yds (300m). When in pasture, near a farm, move right, over stiles by an ash tree. In the field take a vague green track, right. Descend to a small wooded area. The path, later a sunken lane, emerges near a farmhouse.

7 Turn right, away from the house, following waymarkers into a field above a vegetable garden. Cross the field and go over a stile by a large tree. The pasture deteriorates into a field of gorse, thistle and scrub, then rises gently to a good waymarked path through woodland to a hairpin bend on a tarmac road.

8 Cross and follow a small lane. Soon steps on the left descend to Dylan Thomas's house, the Boat House, now a museum. Further along this path (Dylan's Walk), is Dylan's writing shed (a small garage with a blue door). Soon there is a choice of routes.

9 Either take steps down to the shore, and follow a flagged causeway skirting the castle, or continue on Dylan's Walk. Turn left, then follow the road round to King Street. Near by is Brown's, and, opposite, the Pelican (where Dylan's parents lived). Turn left, passing Castle House, where Dylan and Caitlin often stayed, and pass the castle entrance down to the car park.

N

ST CLEARS

A4066

farmhouse

church

LAUGHARNE

The Boat House Museum

Laugharne Castle

River Taf

1 START

Lacques Water Pump

caravan park

Sir John's Hill

Salt House Kennels

quarries

A4066

East Marsh

0 — 1 Mile

0 — 1 Kilometre

DIFFICULTY ✱✱

During the last 50 years of the second millennium, Britain grappled with its identity – as a declining empire, as a European power, and as a multiracial and multinational society.

MODERN BRITAIN

1945 – PRESENT

To the Next Millennium

In the post-war years the last vestiges of empire fell away. Mahatma Gandhi's long campaign of peaceful resistance to British rule in India culminated in independence in 1947, and in the ensuing decades a series of former colonies followed suit.

Britain entered the 1950s a war-weary and austere place, though the Festival of Britain in 1951 made a concerted, and successful, effort to lift public spirits. The economy did pick up and by the late 1950s jobs were plentiful, and immigrants were encouraged, especially from the Commonwealth countries, to swell Britain's work-force.

A new generation, with disposable income and a liberal outlook, exploded into the 1960s and created the permissive age. London and Liverpool were the unofficial capitals of pop, and Mary Quant revolutionised street fashion with mini skirts, high boots and a futuristic look that celebrated the Space Age. Motorways began to criss-cross the country just as railways and canals had before them, and cars became accessible to more and more families – as did luxury goods such as the television, complete with a new commercial channel to promote new products.

Throughout the 1960s Britain had been negotiating to enter the European Common Market, and in 1973 Conservative prime minister Edward Heath finally oversaw its accession. Britons had already had to come to terms with a new currency, replacing pounds, shillings and pence with a simpler decimal system.

But no amount of modernisation could prevent the crisis that hit Britain and the rest of the Western world in the mid-1970s, when Arab-Israeli war provoked a dramatic rise in oil prices. Fuel tanks ran empty; petrol was rationed; and prices rapidly increased. Demands for higher wages to meet the rising cost of living stoked industrial conflict, and strikes and picket lines became an enduring image of the 1970s. The emergence of punk music and fashion seemed to epitomise an angry and disillusioned decade.

CROSSING THE MILLENNIA

The 1980s saw a another shift in the industrial landscape, as computing and service industries flourished and older industries suffered, with the closure of coal mines and steel plants and the decline of ship-building. As whole communities faced the bleak prospect of long-term unemployment, yuppies – young, upwardly mobile professionals – enjoyed the benefits of conspicuous consumption. The Filofax-wielding, mobile-phone-toting city slicker was an icon of late-1980s prosperity.

It also brought the revival of a proposal that had been on the political agenda since the 1880s – an underwater tunnel between Britain and France. The idea was rejected in 1930 and new proposals after World War II were greeted with horror and talk of invasion, smuggling and rabies. However in 1986 a Channel Tunnel agreement was signed between the British and French governments and in 1994 two passenger tunnels and one service tunnel were opened.

In the approach to the 21st century, Britain began to take stock of itself and its place in the world. Devolution of power from Westminster to Scotland and Wales, and continuing the search for a solution to the troubled relationship with Northern Ireland; issues of immigration, multi-ethnicity and an increasingly pluralistic society; and the love-hate association with Europe – all these issues have played a part in shaping the 3rd-millennium nation. Britain now faces the 21st century as fascinated with its future as it is with the past.

HISTORIC SITES

Royal Festival Hall, South Bank, London: legacy of the Festival of Britain.

Milton Keynes: purpose-built 1960s city, tailored to accommodate the car.

Longleat House, Wilts: lots of visitor entertainment and a safari park shows the changing face of the stately home.

Angel of the North: modern testimony to regional pride.

London Eye: a millennial view of the capital.

MODERN BRITAIN

WALK 100

ABOUT • KINDER SCOUT

The Mass Trespass on Kinder Scout in 1932 led to prison sentences for five of the ramblers. However their brave action, combined with many years of peaceful campaigning, eventually led to the opening of the first National Park in the Peak District in 1951.

Derbyshire • C ENGLAND

DISTANCE • 6 miles (9.6km)

TOTAL ASCENT • 1,475ft (450m)

PATHS • lanes, moorland paths and tracks

TERRAIN • high moorland, requiring boots, waterproofs, map and compass. **This route is for experienced hillwalkers only. It should not be attempted in poor weather conditions**

GRADIENTS • stiff climb to the Kinder plateau, followed by a steep, boggy descent

REFRESHMENTS • Royal Hotel, Twenty Trees café in Hayfield

PARK • Bowden Bridge National Park car park (fee), Hayfield; or in the village

OS MAP • Outdoor Leisure 1 The Peak District – Dark Peak area

The first National Park

❶ Start from the National Park car park at Bowden Bridge, turn left and follow the minor road beside the River Kinder. Branch right after ½ mile (800m) by a footpath sign near the waterworks gates. Cross the river, turn almost immediately left, through a gate on to a broad path by the side of the river. Eventually cross the river by a footbridge below the grassy dam of the Kinder Reservoir.

❷ Go through a gate on the right, signed White Brow, and follow the paved path which climbs, with a wall to your right, up the slopes of White Brow.

❸ The path levels and degenerates to a rocky and sometimes boggy footpath. Follow this through a gate and then around Nab Brow, with fine views across the Kinder Reservoir to your right towards the distant cleft of Kinder Downfall – the highest waterfall in the Peak.

❹ The path eventually descends into William Clough by a cascade. Turn left before a footbridge to follow the signed Snake Path up beside the clough (steep valley) into its narrowing confines.

❺ The rough, rocky path rises steeply, frequently crossing the stream or winding high on its banks, passing the point where the trespass took place. Eventually, after climbing a rocky reconstructed staircase of stones, it emerges beneath Ashop Head.

❻ About 20yds (18m) from the top of the stone staircase, a flagged path leads off to the right towards the prominent headland of Ashop Head. Climb the steep, award-winning reconstructed stairway, now on the Pennine Way

(south), which leads to the top of Ashop Head.

❼ Turn right at the top near a large cairn and go over a stile, marked by a sign stating that you are entering an Environmentally Sensitive Area. Follow the edge

path up and below Mill Hill Rocks towards the next prominent headland of Sandy Heys, about ½ mile (800m) of rough walking ahead. This is where the victory meeting was held in 1932.

❽ When you reach the prominent rocks of Sandy Heys, which form the southwestern buttress of Kinder Scout, take the path leading off right (southwest) steeply down the crest of the ridge. Cross rocky

steps and boggy ground, then cross a stream in a dip, and head down towards the foot of William Clough.

❾ On reaching William Clough, cross the footbridge passed on your outward journey and retrace your steps around Nab Brow and White Brow above the reservoir, and down the Kinder Road back to the Bowden Bridge car park and the start of the walk.

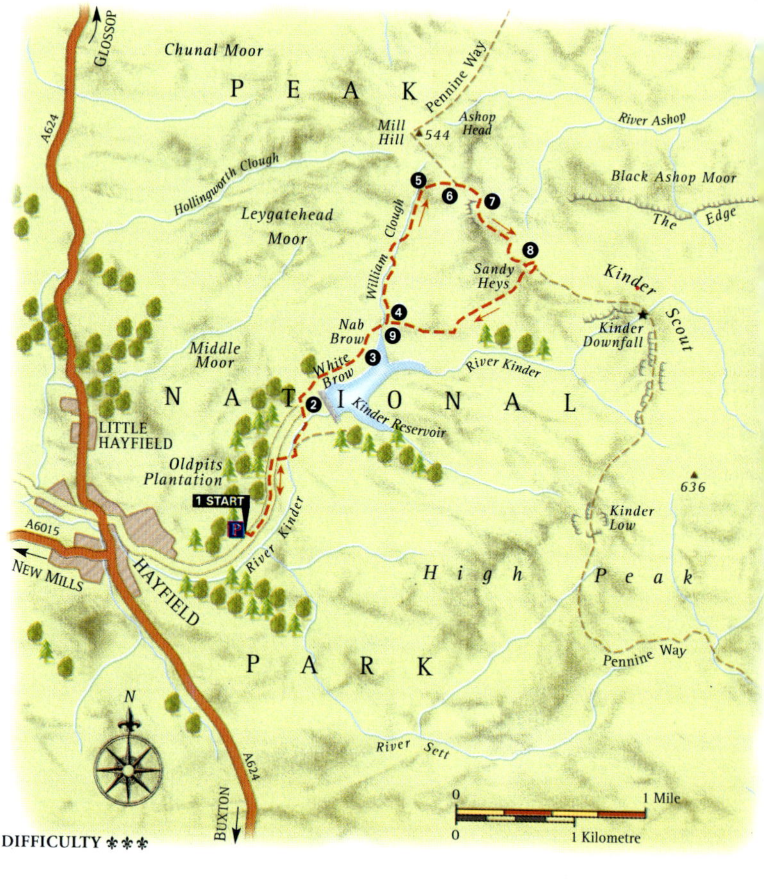

DIFFICULTY ✳✳✳

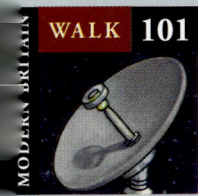

ABOUT • CWM TRYWERYN

Beneath the tranquil waters of Llyn Celyn lies the small village of Capel Celyn. Despite the peaceful protests of villagers to save their town and their rural way of life it was flooded in the 1960s to provide Liverpool with a new water supply.

Gwynedd • WALES

DISTANCE • 6 miles (9.6km)

TOTAL ASCENT • 300ft (91m)

PATHS • mainly clear tracks, paths and lanes; moorland can be marshy at times

TERRAIN • wild, open moorland

GRADIENTS • mainly gradual, one steeper ascent

REFRESHMENTS • none on route; picnic area by Llyn Celyn

PARK • lay-by on A4212, beyond the picnic area on the western edge of the lake

OS MAP • Outdoor Leisure 18 Snowdonia – Harlech, Porthmadog & Bala

The drowned village of Capel Celyn

❶ From the large lay-by turn right on to the road. (If starting from the picnic area, turn left on to the road – this involves a longer walk on the verge of the main road.)

❷ Turn off the road at a small gate with public footpath sign on the right. Follow the path, crossing first the small bridge in the field, then the larger bridge over the Afon Tryweryn. Bear left, and soon see a waymark arrow on the telegraph pole before the hill.

❸ Head up the hill; at the post with the waymark arrow bear right and head towards the gate. Go through and follow the path downhill to the old railway.

❹ Turn left on to the old railway. Where the courtesy/permissive bridleway meets some houses and diverts on to the road, do not return to the railway, but stay on the road for about ¼ mile (400m).

❺ Reach a stile and clear track to the right. Follow this up to Llyn Arenig Fawr, climbing steeply in places. By the dam and the refuge hut, ignore the gate, continuing on the footpath towards the left over the shoulder of the hill.

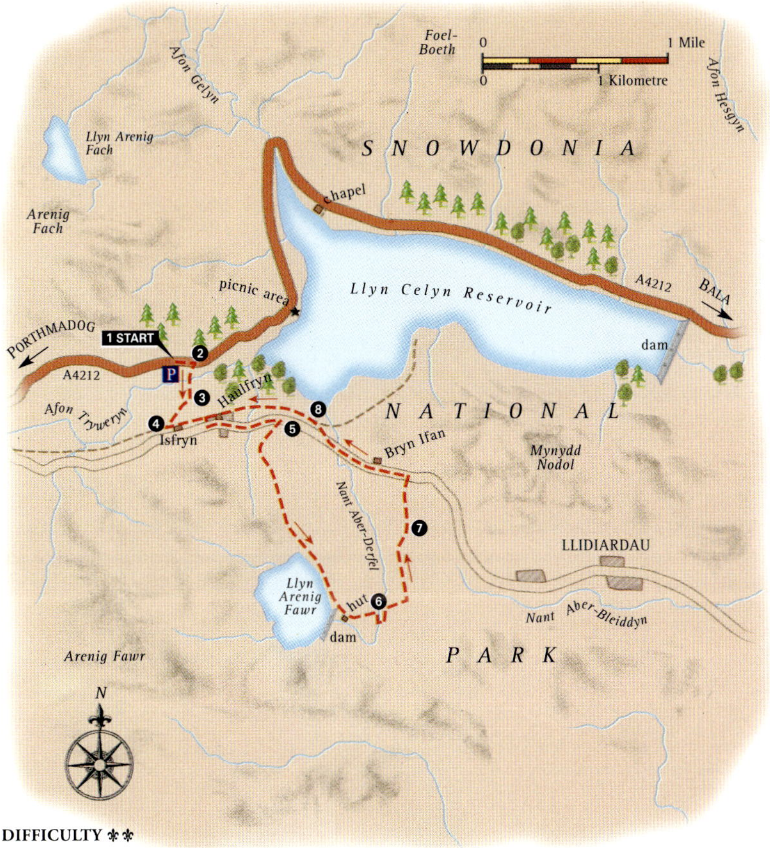

• DON'T MISS •

A lay-by towards the western end of the lake, where a modern chapel stands as a poignant memorial to Capel Celyn; behind it is a cemetery to which the graves were relocated when the original chapel was drowned. Open during the day in summer.

DIFFICULTY ✽✽

❻ In the valley, on reaching the stream, divert to the right to cross the footbridge then return to the path straight on up the hill. At the top of the hill, take the small indistinct path to the left which leads across to the far side of the hill to your left.

❼ Head for the right-hand corner of the stone wall, following the path along the side of this to the road. Turn left on to the road, pass the farmhouse Bryn Ifan and cross a bridge. Take the track to the right (signed) on to the courtesy path along the old railway.

❽ Follow the waymarks, keeping to the course of the old railway. Where the path meets a private garden and diverts on to the road, return to the path through the gate just after the house called Haulfryn, and retrace the route from Point ❹ back to the start.

[Map showing the walk route around Llyn Celyn Reservoir in Snowdonia National Park, with labels including: Foel-Boeth, Afon Gelyn, Llyn Arenig Fach, Arenig Fach, chapel, SNOWDONIA, picnic area, Llyn Celyn Reservoir, A4212, BALA, PORTHMADOG, 1 START, Afon Tryweryn, Haulfryn, Isfryn, Bryn Ifan, NATIONAL, Mynydd Nodol, dam, Nant Aber-Derfel, LLIDIARDAU, Llyn Arenig Fawr, hut, dam, Arenig Fawr, Nant Aber-Bleiddyn, PARK, Afon Hesgyn]

MODERN BRITAIN

WALK 102

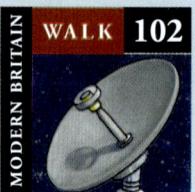

ABOUT • SEVERN BRIDGE

The opening of the Severn Bridge in 1966 was a remarkable event. It was then one of the world's longest spanning bridges and still remains a remarkable landmark. During your walk it is worth pausing at the viewing platform to enjoy the views.

Gloucestershire • SW ENGLAND

DISTANCE • 5½ miles (8.8km)

TOTAL ASCENT • 262ft (80m)

PATHS • field and riverside paths and tracks

TERRAIN • gentle farmland on the eastern shore of the Severn

GRADIENTS • one steep climb near the end of the walk

REFRESHMENTS • Boars Head, Aust; Whi Hart, Littleton-upon-Severn

PARK • roadside parking in Aust

OS MAP • Explorer 167 Thornbury, Dursley Yate

Views of the Severn Estuary

❶ With Aust church behind you, walk through the village and turn left just before the Boars Head into Sandy Lane. Bear right by cottages and modern houses and pass beneath the motorway. Go straight over at the next junction towards Manor Farm offices and keep to the left of the farmhouse.

❷ When the track swings right to a house, continue ahead through a galvanised gate. Head up the right-hand boundary of the field to a waymark by the hedge corner. Veer diagonally right across the field and make for a gate in the bottom corner. Follow the field edge for a few paces to reach a galvanised gate and stile. Turn left here and follow the track to Cote Farm. Just beyond the farm buildings, veer off to the right to a gate and stile.

❸ Pass under power lines and make for a stile in the field corner. Keep ahead, following the field boundary round to the left and right. Head for a gate, cross a stream and then join a clear track which runs all the way to the village of Littleton-upon-Severn. Turn left at Salmon Lodge and follow the road to the White Hart Inn. Head out of the village to a green and turn left at the junction.

❹ Follow the lane through countryside, passing cottages on the left. Oldbury Nuclear Power Station is in the distance, over to the right. Pass a footpath on the left and a bridleway on the right and follow the lane to the entrance to a cottage on the right. Bear left over a stile and join the Severn Way, following the path up the embankment.

❺ Walk along the old sea wall towards the Severn Bridge. When you reach an electricity substation on the left, look for a gate and stile. Cross over and head up the steep hillside to the remains of an old look-out. Keep right and cross two stiles into the grounds of the Severn View service station. Walk along to the Severn Bridge viewin area and follow the path to a sig for Aust.

❻ Go down the steps and across the top of the motorway toll booth. Bear left on the far side an walk down to the next junction. Keep right and pass the Severn River Crossing maintenance unit before reaching the next junction. Turn left and cross the A403, following the road back to Aust and the start of the walk.

• DON'T MISS •

*The **Severn Bridge** was officially opened by Queen Elizabeth II on 8 September 1966. Note the plaque, which records the names of all those involved in the building of the bridge, including Barbara Castle, the then Labour Transport Minister.*

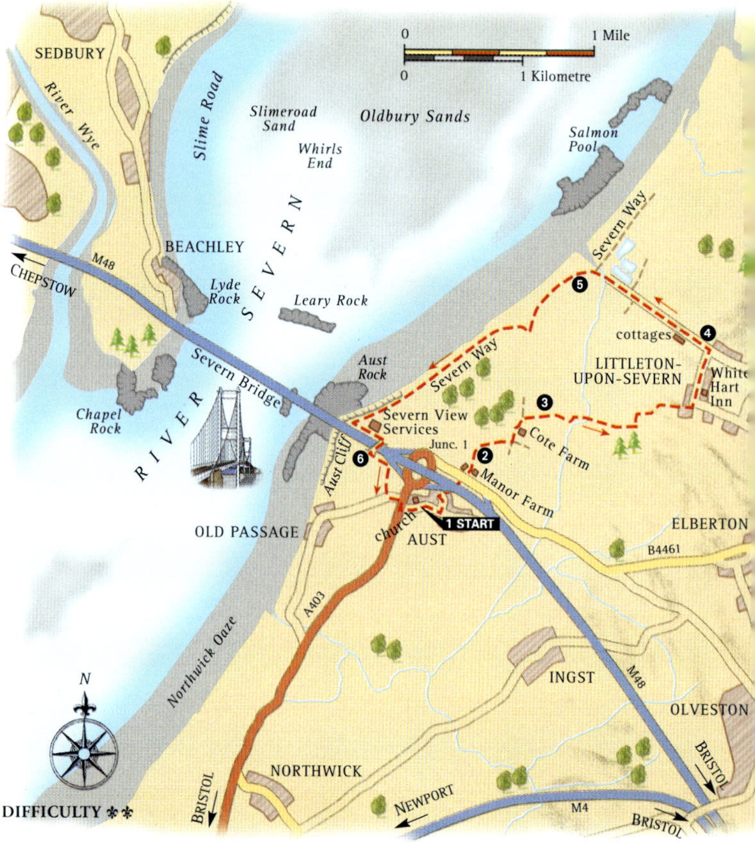
0
1 Mile
0
1 Kilometre
SEDBURY
River Wye
Slime Road
Slimeroad Sand
Whirls End
Oldbury Sands
Salmon Pool
Severn Way
BEACHLEY
M48
CHEPSTOW
Lyde Rock
RIVER SEVERN
Leary Rock
Severn Bridge
Aust Rock
Severn Way
cottages
LITTLETON-UPON-SEVERN
White Hart Inn
Chapel Rock
Severn View Services
Junc. 1
Cote Farm
Aust Cliff
Manor Farm
church
1 START
AUST
OLD PASSAGE
ELBERTON
B4461
A403
Northwick Oaze
INGST
M48
OLVESTON
N
BRISTOL
NORTHWICK
NEWPORT
M4
BRISTOL
BRISTOL

DIFFICULTY ✤✤

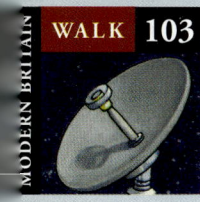

ABOUT • LIVERPOOL

Liverpool is the celebrated home town of the Beatles. This walk through the city takes you to all the famous Beatle landmarks from the Cavern Club on Mathew Street to the Empire Theatre, where the band made its last live appearance in 1965.

Merseyside • N BRITAIN

DISTANCE • 5 miles (8km)
TOTAL ASCENT • 110ft (33m)
PATHS • footpaths
TERRAIN • city streets
GRADIENTS • very gentle

REFRESHMENTS • Tate Gallery Café at Albert Dock; the Philharmonic Pub
PARK • Plenty of free parking at Albert Dock
OS MAP • Explorer 275 Liverpool, St Helens, Widnes & Runcorn

ˍiverpool: city of the 'Fab Four'

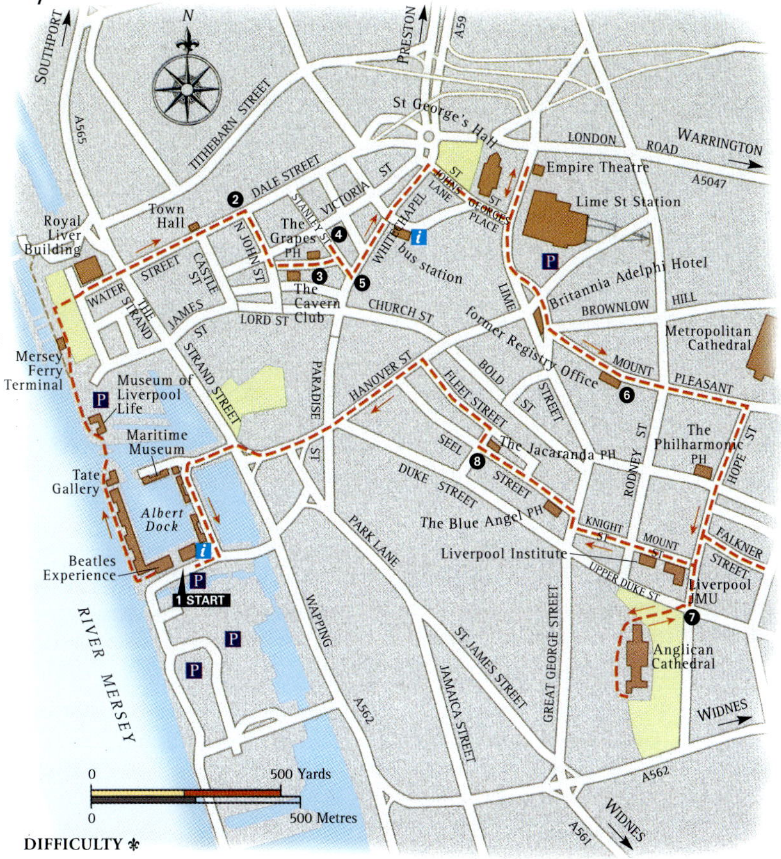

DIFFICULTY ✽

➊ Visit the Beatles Experience on ˌlbert Dock. On leaving, turn right ɔ the waterfront and right again ɔr 700yds (640m) to the Mersey ·erry Terminal. Turn right into Vater Street on the near side of ·he Royal Liver Building – with the ·nmistakable Liver Birds on top.

➋ Pass the Town Hall on your left, ·urn right into North John Street, :ontinue for 200yds (183m) and ·urn left into Mathew Street and ·he Cavern Quarter. On the right is ·he reconstructed Cavern Club, next ·o the Cavern Walks shopping ·levelopment.

➌ In 30yds (27m), on the left, is The Grapes pub, popular with the Beatles; the Beatles Shop is further along. At the end of Mathew Street turn left into Stanley Street to see the Eleanor Rigby statue in 20yds (18m) on the right.

➍ Walk back down Stanley Street, passing the site of Hessy's music shop on the right (currently unoccupied, next to Wade Smith). At the end, look to your right along Whitechapel, where the Ann Summers shop now occupies the NEMS shop, once owned by Brian Epstein's family.

➎ Turn left along Whitechapel, past the bus station, for 500yds (457m), and turn right along St John's Lane, passing St George's Hall, left. Cross to Lime Street Station and turn left to the Empire Theatre. Retrace your steps past the station and continue for 200yds (183m) past the Britannia Adelphi Hotel. Turn left, up the hill, on to Mount Pleasant. Note the former Registry Office on the right, now a cancer resource centre.

➏ Continue and turn right into Hope Street, opposite the Roman Catholic Metropolitan Cathedral, down to the Philharmonic pub. Continue for 100yds (91m) and turn left into Falkner Street to No 36, John and Cynthia's first home together. Return to Hope Street and turn left. At the end, visit the Anglican Cathedral, which has several Beatles connections.

➐ Turn back along Hope Street and left into Mount Street just past Liverpool John Moores University Hope Street Campus. Continue down the hill for 300yds (274m), turn right into Berry Street and left into Seel Street. The Blue Angel is on the left at No 108.

➑ Turn right into Slater Street, the Jacaranda is on the right at No 23. Left into Fleet Street for 500yds (457m) then left into Hanover Street to return to Albert Dock.

• DON'T MISS •

*The **Maritime Museum** at Albert Dock is Liverpool's finest museum. It gives a vivid picture of life in the docks during the 18th century, and the Slavery Gallery does not flinch from showing that part of the city's seafaring history.*

A Scottish Millennium Forest

Renewal of the ancient Caledonian Forest

Scotland's Native Trees

Once the Scots pine was an object of worship and ancient druids lit bonfires of them at the winter solstice to encourage the return of the sun. Glades were hung with lights to represent the divine light of the stars, rituals that became, in time, the modern customs of decorating a Christmas tree or burning a yule log.

Once, most of Scotland, like England was covered in a dense forest. Huge, majestic pine trees, birch and rowans covered the land. The bears, wolves and wild boar that roamed free, using the forest as a source of food and shelter and feeding on a host of smaller creatures, were hunted in turn by the greatest predator of all, *Homo sapiens*.

As well as hunting, early humans gathered nuts, berries and roots, and in time they acquired the skills of husbandry, abandoning their nomadic lifestyle and becoming farmers. They cleared vast areas of the forest to provide land on which to grow crops, and harvested the timber to build their houses and barns, and stockades to contain their domesticated animals. As the pace of development increased, so too did the amount of timber required. Eventually, whole areas were cleared to the extent that today only one per cent of Scotland's original native woodland survives today.

Restoration of the Native Pine Forests

What remains of the native forests represents specimens that descended from the trees that grew here at the end of the last ice age – over eight thousand years ago. Scots pine is renowned for its long life and many of the specimens that grow around Loch Affric are extremely old and knotted. (It is worth noting that the same trees, which you see today, provided shelter for Bonnie Prince Charlie when he fled from Government forces after the Battle of Culloden in 1746.) It is quite possible that many of the trees were mere seedlings back when wolves, bears and lynx still lived here. However, as these natural predators became extinct the forest came under serious threat from increased numbers of red deer, browsing the forests for food.

By the end of World War II, most of the remaining trees were reaching the end of their lives. Continual grazing of deer and sheep meant that none of the young seedlings were surviving to replace them, and the forest faced extinction.

Fortunately, in 1951, the Forestry Commission acquired control of the woodland. In response to the failing forest, they erected fences and started controlling the numbers of deer within the enclosures. They also started a planting programme of young trees raised from seeds gathered in the Glen, in an attempt to kick-start the regeneration process of the forest. Eventually, as the numbers o deer reduced, so the seedlings began to survive and it was no longe necessary to continue planting.

On this walk, you will enter a new enclosure funded by the Millennium Forest for Scotland Project. This is part of a nationwide scheme to increase the area of native woodland that is being managed for conservation.

WALK 104 — AROUND LOCH AFFRIC THROUGH THE MILLENNIUM FOREST PROJECT

❶ From the car park, head back to the road and turn left. At the fork in the forestry road keep left, go over a bridge and then through a gate in the deer fence. Continue on the forest road. Pass a cottage on your right, cross another bridge; go uphill and across a cattle grid. The area on either side of the track is now part of the pinewood regeneration. Follow the road as it winds round the side of Loch Affric. After a couple of miles you will reach the houses at Athnamulloch. Cross the river by the bridge and follow the track uphill.

❷ This path leads to the youth hostel at Altbeith just over three miles away, but keep a sharp lookout for the narrower track that branches to the right in approximately quarter of a mile. Turn right and follow the track uphill. Although it can be muddy at times of high rainfall, the going is generally easy. Pass through another gate in the deer fence and re-enter the regeneration area.

❸ Continue along the track and enjoy the grand view over Loch Affric – but be sure to apply a powerful insect repellent, particularly on this section, to ward off the horse-flies. Exit the regeneration area via another gate and continue on the path past Affric Lodge and back to the fork in the road, and from there return to the car park.

Distance: 8 miles (13km)

Total ascent: 328 feet (100m)

Paths: very good, except in wet weather when some stretches can become boggy

Terrain: forest roads, hill tracks and heather

Gradients: mainly gentle

Refreshments: none available

Park: car park at the end of the road at Loch Beinn a Mheadhoin

OS Map: Landranger 25 Glan Carron & Glen Affric

Difficulty: ✳✳✳

WALK 105

Oil caused havoc in the 1970s as rising prices led to government cuts and threats of petrol rationing but in 1975 oil was stuck in the North Sea. This walk around the old fishing port celebrates the prosperity and tragedy that oil has brought to Aberdeen.

Aberdeen City · SCOTLAND

DISTANCE · 6 miles (9.6km)

TOTAL ASCENT · negligible

PATHS · excellent in all weather

TERRAIN · mainly roads and pavements with a short section of beach (underwater at high tide)

GRADIENTS · fairly level throughout

REFRESHMENTS · Aberdeen Maritime Museum or Harry Ramsden's

PARK · outside Harry Ramsden's on the Esplanade or Queen's Link Leisure Park

OS MAP · Pathfinder 246 Aberdeen

Striking oil in the North Sea

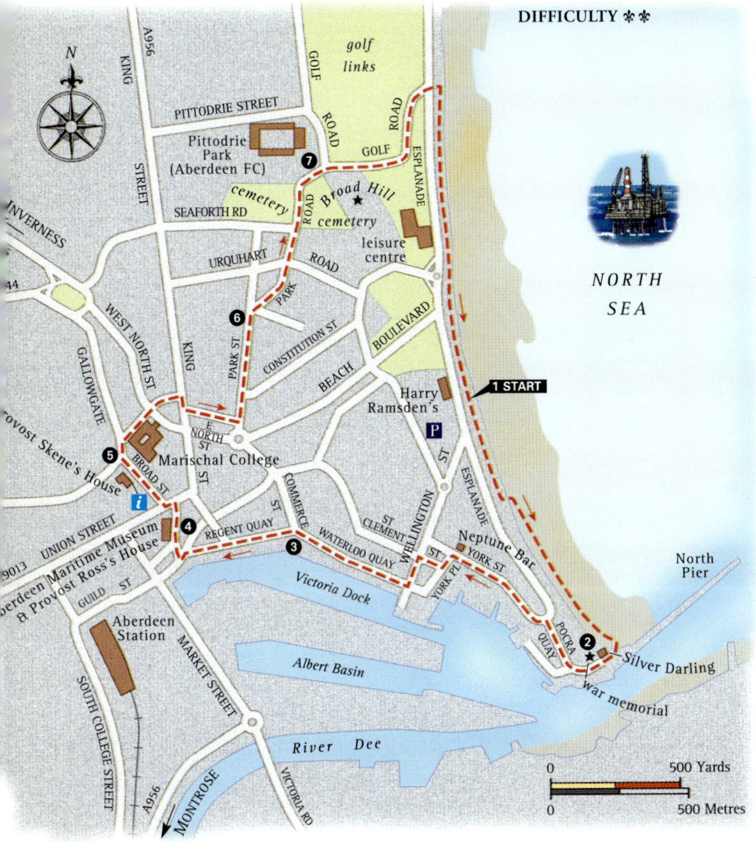

DIFFICULTY ✳✳

golf links

NORTH SEA

North Pier

A996 KING STREET

PITTODRIE STREET

Pittodrie Park (Aberdeen FC) ⑦

GOLF ROAD

ESPLANADE

Broad Hill

cemetery

SEAFORTH RD

cemetery

INVERNESS

URQUHART

leisure centre

ROAD

PARK ROAD

⑥

WEST NORTH ST

KING ST

PARK ST

CONSTITUTION ST

BOULEVARD

BEACH

GALLOWGATE

Provost Skene's House

⑤

NORTH ST

BROAD ST

Marischal College

ℹ

UNION STREET

Aberdeen Maritime Museum & Provost Ross's House

REGENT QUAY

④

COMMERCE ST

WATERLOO QUAY

③

ST CLEMENT ST

WELLINGTON ST

Neptune Bar

YORK ST

YORK PL

1 START

Harry Ramsden's 🅿

Victoria Dock

Aberdeen Station

MARKET STREET

Albert Basin

SOUTH COLLEGE STREET

A9013

GUILD ST

POCRA QUAY

② Silver Darling

war memorial

River Dee

A96

MONTROSE

VICTORIA RD

0   500 Yards

0   500 Metres

---

and John Ross's House, Provost of Aberdeen between 1710–1711.

❹ From here head along Exchequer Row, turn left into Union Street, continue and turn right into Broad Street, where you will find Provost Skene's House and the Tourist Information Office on the left, behind the offices.

❺ Continue past Marischal College (which houses the Marischal Museum), turn right into Littlejohn Street, cross North Street. At the end of Meal Market Street turn right into King Street and then left into Frederick Street. At the junction with Park Street turn left and keep walking until the road crosses the railway.

❻ Shortly after this is a roundabout. Head along Park Road, almost straight ahead. Follow it through the cemetery and towards Pittodrie Park, home of Aberdeen Football Club, and its junction with Golf Road.

❼ Turn right into Golf Road and walk through the golf links. Detour to the top of Broad Hill, the mound behind the cemetery, for magnificent views to the north and out to sea. The road turns sharply left towards its junction with the Esplanade. Cross the Esplanade and turn right on to the promenade which you can follow back to the start of the walk.

· DON'T MISS ·

Provost Skene's House is the oldest private dwelling in Aberdeen, dating from 1545. It was the home of Provost George Skene from 1676 to 1685, and is preserved, almost unchanged, as a representation of a comfortable 17th-century burgher's residence.

---

❶ Head southwards on the promenade beside the shore with the sea on your right. Go down the slipway on to the beach and continue for a short distance. Step over the rocks to reach the wooden steps on the right and leave the beach into a children's play area.

❷ Walk past the Silver Darling restaurant and into the harbour area. Continue past the war memorial, keeping the blue storage tanks on your left, and along Pocra Quay. Turn left into York Street and at the Neptune bar, turn left into York Place. Then, take the first right, the first left

and first right again to emerge on Waterloo Quay.

❸ Where Waterloo Quay becomes Commerce Street, turn left into Regent Quay and at the T-junction cross the road at the pedestrian lights. Turn left, then first right to reach Aberdeen Maritime Museum

MODERN BRITAIN

WALK 106

ABOUT • MACHYNLLETH

This walk around Machnylleth celebrates the town's long history: from the foundation of the first Welsh Parliament by Owain Glyndŵr in 1404 to the Celtica Centre founded in 1995 which offers a superb exhibition of Welsh culture and language.

Powys • WALES

DISTANCE • 5 miles (8km)

TOTAL ASCENT • 675ft (206m)

PATHS • pavements, tracks and paths

TERRAIN • town, river meadows, moorland

GRADIENTS • one fairly steep climb; one moderate descent

REFRESHMENTS • various pubs and cafés Machynlleth

PARK • main car park, off Heol Maengwyn, Machynlleth

OS MAP • Outdoor Leisure 23 Snowdonia – Cadair Idris & Bala Lake

Machynlleth's long history

1 From the clock tower at the end of the main street, Heol Maengwyn, take the road to the north for 328yds (300m), towards the station. Pass the station and Dyfi Eco Park, and just before the Dyfi Bridge, take the surfaced footpath to the right along the river bank.

2 Keep ahead, leaving the surfaced path where it goes over the new footbridge, and carry on along the river bank, crossing a low barbed wire fence. Follow the river through the meadows for 547yds (500m), crossing a stile.

3 As the route nears the railway and the river swings left, climb the stile to the right and cross the railway with care. Bear left up the hill. On leaving the trees, bear right across the field towards a stile uphill from the gate; cross and turn right on to the track.

4 Where the houses start, join the road and continue straight on for 656yds (600m), past Maes-y-Garth; at the T-junction by the cemetery, turn right. After the side turning, (Maes Dyfi, on the left, before the 'no entry' signs), turn left down the one-way street. At the end turn left on to the main

street then right, up the road signed Llyn Clywedog/Llanidloes.

5 Past Treowain Enterprise Park, opposite where the houses finish, take the signed footpath to the right. Follow the waymarkers, and after 219yds (200m) follow the wall for 328yds (300m), then bear

right at the corner of the wall before zigzagging up a fairly steep hill. At the top of the hill, bear right to the corner of the forest.

6 On reaching the trees, take the path to the right, away from the trees, passing between boulders 22yds (20m) ahead. In 328yds (300m), go through a gate and follow the track downhill for 109yds (100m). Go through the gate at a T-junction with a track, continue downhill, past the shale track on the left, through the woods, and past the farm Brynglas.

7 In 437yds (400m) at the road, turn right. After 219yds (200m) turn right on to the path signed Glyndŵr's Way, cross the drive to the cottages and follow the path to the road. At the bottom, turn right into the grounds of the Celtica Centre.

8 Cross the car park; go round to the front of the Plas (mansion) and entrance to the Celtica Centre. Follow the drive round to the left in front of the leisure centre, turning right at the roundabout to return to the clock tower.

DIFFICULTY ✳✳

• DON'T MISS •

From the hills above Machynlleth you will see one of the windmills belonging to the Centre for Alternative Technology (CAT), about 2 miles (3.2km) to the north of the town. This innovative centre, researches and practices sustainable forms of energy.

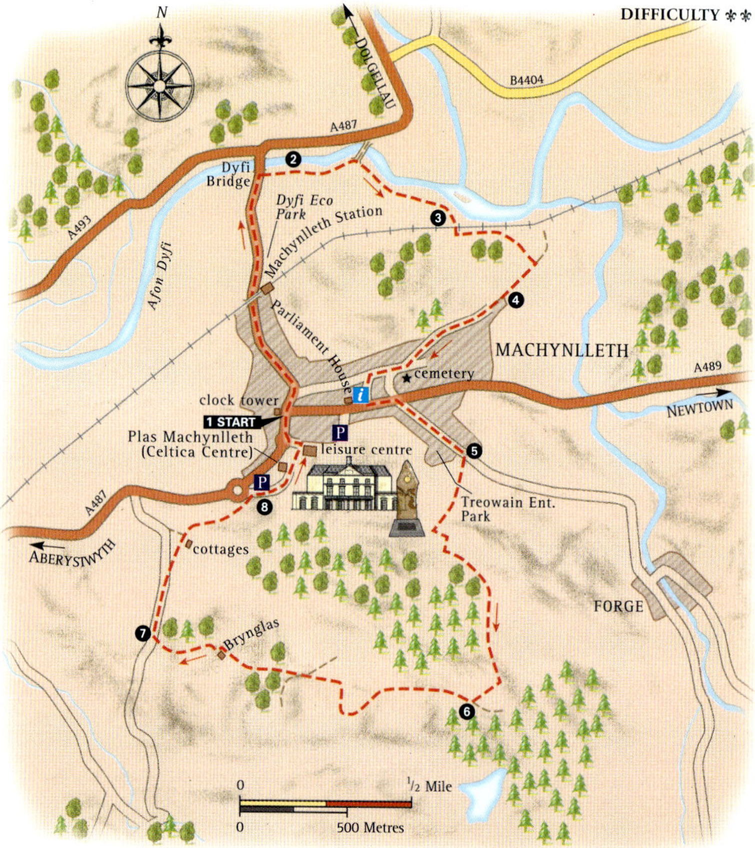

N

DOLGELLAU

B4404

A487

Dyfi
Bridge

Dyfi Eco
Park

Machynlleth Station

A493

Afon Dyfi

Parliament House

MACHYNLLETH

A489

NEWTOWN

cemetery

clock tower

1 START

Plas Machynlleth
(Celtica Centre)

P

P

leisure centre

Treowain Ent.
Park

ABERYSTWYTH

A487

cottages

FORGE

Brynglas

0 ½ Mile

0 500 Metres

WALK 107

ABOUT • THE CUCKOO TRAIL

The Cuckoo Trail, opened in 1990, runs along the track of a former railway and is part of the 9,000-mile (15,000km) Sustrans Cycle Network due to be completed in 2005, which aims to promote a traffic-free 'sustainable transport' network.

East Sussex • SE ENGLAND

DISTANCE • 6 miles (9.6km)

TOTAL ASCENT • 300ft (91m)

PATHS • clearly waymarked tracks and field paths, mostly along Cuckoo Trail and Wealdway; lanes; some muddy sections

TERRAIN • disused railway track, quiet lanes, gently rolling farmland. Many stiles

GRADIENTS • gentle

REFRESHMENTS • pub, café, chip shop and food shops at Horam; Gun Inn, Gun Hill; picnic benches along trail

PARK • Cuckoo Trail car park at Horam: turn off A267 at village centre by Horam Inn on to B2203; first turn on right, Hillside Drive, signed car park and toilets

OS MAP • Explorer 123 South Downs Way – Newhaven to Eastbourne

Along the Cuckoo Trail

❶ Turn right out of the car park, then immediately left at a Cuckoo Trail sign, into a housing estate, bearing right as signed. Ignore the next right, signed Cuckoo Trail with horse-rider symbol, but keep ahead on the Cuckoo Trail (a former railway track), signed Hailsham/Polegate.

❷ After passing under a brick bridge and 130yds (119m) after a wedge-shaped bench on your left, turn right down steps to a stile and follow yellow arrows, first turning left along a field. The route continues along the left edge of three larger fields, then down through woodland and crosses over a footbridge.

❸ Emerge from woodland, continue forward to the top left corner of field, over a stile, then along the left edge of the next two fields (cross by stile). Cross another stile on the left. Turn right along the driveway, cross the A267 and take Swansbrook Lane opposite. Continue for 547yds (500m) to Forge Cottage on your right.

❹ In ¼ mile (400m) past the cottage take the right-hand path of two signed paths on your left (the left-hand path follows a driveway to Old Barn Cottage). Follow the left edges of three fields. At a farm track, turn left (or to detour to the Gun Inn, turn right, right at a T-junction, then left over a stile after 100yds (91m), and follow the field edge to the pub; return the same way).

❺ Keep right at the first junction (left goes to West Street Farm) and follow WW (Wealdway) waymarkers, almost immediately

DIFFICULTY ✸✸

turning left as signed just after the entrance to Rock Harbour Farm. Follow the left edge of the field and continue forward across the middle of the next two fields.

❻ Beyond the third field go through a small wooded area, then turn right along field edges (avoiding a path branching to the left). Near the end of the second field take a stile on your right then

turn left inside the edge of the wood, then go over a footbridge.

❼ Leave the wood and go up into the field, soon joining the left edge, then cross a stile to the right of houses. Continue in the next field, cross a driveway 15yds (14m) right of a cattle grid, and down to a stile. Turn left on the road (leaving the Wealdway), which bends right to the A267.

❽ Cross the A267 and cross the stile opposite, go down a bank and follow the left edges of two fields. Beyond the second field take a stile on your left and cross two fields diagonally to take a stile into trees – avoid a gate to the left of this.

❾ Turn left along the Cuckoo Trail for 2½ miles (4km) to Horam and the start of the walk.

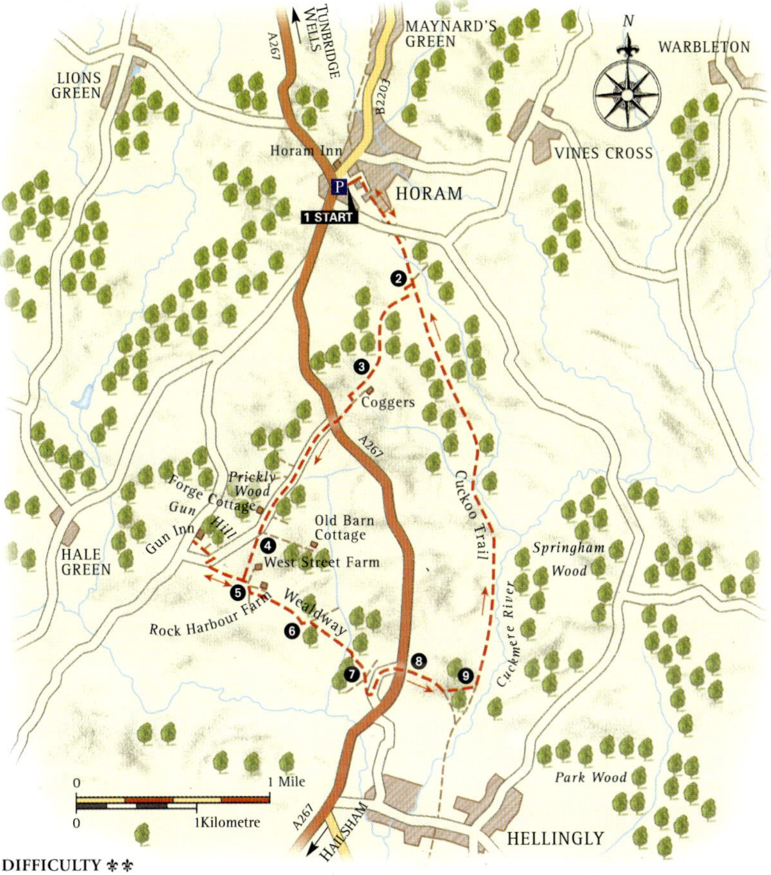

MODERN BRITAIN

WALK 108

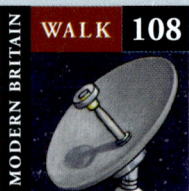

ABOUT · THE EDEN PROJECT

The Eden Project, completed in 2001, is a spectacular theatre which tells the story of human dependence on plants. The huge biomes are able to produce a range of world climates and house a wide variety of plants from arid desert cactii to mature rainforest trees.

Cornwall · SW ENGLAND

DISTANCE · 3 miles (4.8km)

TOTAL ASCENT · 361ft (110m)

PATHS · country lanes and well-maintained bridlepaths (some muddy after wet weather)

TERRAIN · undulating farmland, wooded valleys and old china clay workings

GRADIENTS · one short steep ascent near the start; a long downhill run at the end

REFRESHMENTS · café and restaurant at the Eden Project; The Britannia Arms on the A390 opposite Tregehan Gardens; Cornish Arms at St Blazey Gate

PARK · by the roadside near the Methodist Church in Tregehan village, signposted off the A390 St Blazey Gate to St Austell

OS MAP · Explorer 107 St Austell & Liskeard

Eden: eighth wonder of the world

❶ Walk up the lane from your car, leaving the church on the left and the metal-railed stream on the right. Keep on uphill through a wooded area, with evidence of old mine workings.

❷ After ½ mile (800m), where the lane bends sharp left, turn right up the track signed bridlepath/footpath/cycle route 3 to pass Restineas Cottage, left.

❸ About 200yds (182m) further on you pass a signed path, right, that enters the project. Just beyond this, turn left along a new signed bridlepath created by the building of Eden, which has removed the original path that ran a little to the south. The path runs steeply uphill then veers left to reach a small wooden gate. (For a picnic spot with good views of the coast to the south, turn right just before the gate, walk through the grassy area, then turn right through the shelter belt to reach a second field.) To

continue on the main route walk through the gate; the path runs into a large level area, part of the old china clay workings.

❹ Turn right, unsigned, and continue for 766yds (700m); the broad path runs slightly uphill, then downhill along a field edge, before ascending again to reach one of the entrance roads into Eden. Turn right and within 400yds (364m) you will be able to see the biomes.

❺ If you don't want to visit the Eden Project at this point of this walk cross the road and follow the bridlepath, which runs along a green lane to reach the road at Quarry Park.

❻ Turn right down the busy road to pass another way into the Eden Project on the right; you can see the site through the hedge here.

❼ At the next staggered crossroads turn right down a quiet country lane, signed Tregrehan and St Austell. This lane runs steeply downhill to meet a crossroads in Tregrehan; turn right here and walk past the children's playground and the church to the start of the walk.

· DON'T MISS ·

*If you want a clearer picture of what working life was like in a Cornish china clay quarry, visit the **Wheal Martyn China Clay Heritage Centre** (open Easter–end October), 3 miles (5km) to the northwest at Carthew. This, the nearest working quarry to Bodelva, will give you a good insight into the industrial history of this unique area. There are woodland walks as well as a visitor centre with exhibitions, gift shop and café.*

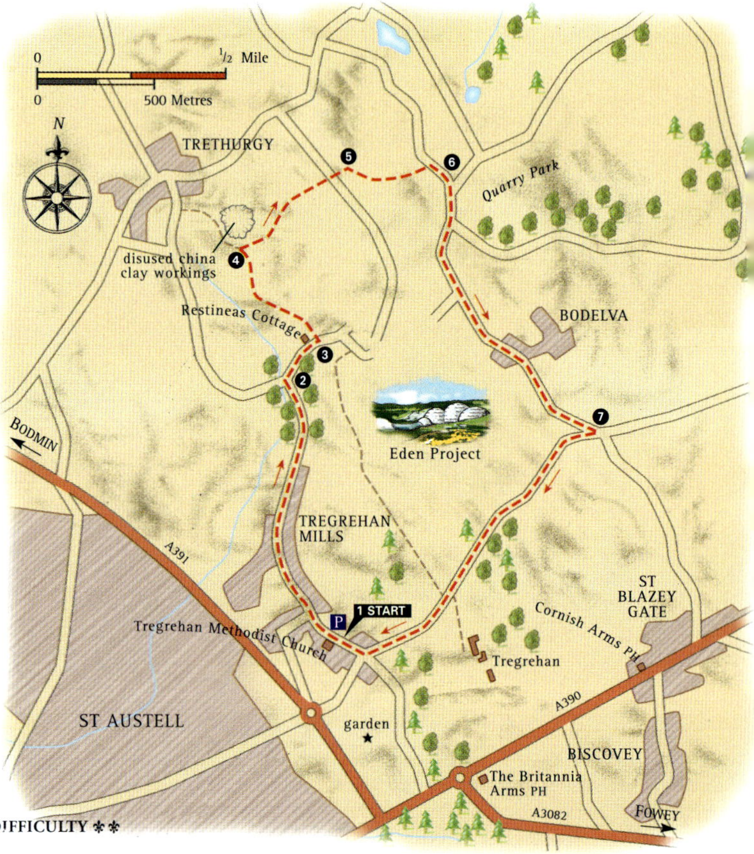

DIFFICULTY ✳✳

TRETHURGY

disused china clay workings

Restineas Cottage

Quarry Park

BODELVA

Eden Project

TREGREHAN MILLS

BODMIN

A391

Tregrehan Methodist Church

P 1 START

ST AUSTELL

garden

Cornish Arms PH

Tregrehan

ST BLAZEY GATE

A390

BISCOVEY

The Britannia Arms PH

A3082

FOWEY